BLOOD IVORY

BLOOD IVORY

THE MASSACRE OF THE AFRICAN ELEPHANT

ROBIN BROWN

FOREWORD BY
CARL G. JONES MBE

THE HISTORY PRESS

First published in the United Kingdom in 2008 by The History Press
Cirencester Road · Chalford · Stroud · Gloucestershire · GL6 8PE

British Library Cataloguing in Publication Data
A catalogue record for this book is available from the British Library.

ISBN 978 07509 4157 0

For Ailish

Typeset in Sabon.
Typesetting and origination by
The History Press.
Printed and bound in England.

Contents

List of Illustrations

Foreword

Blood Ivory: the Massacre of the African Elephant is an exposé of the conflict, politics, personal egos and corruption involved with the conservation of the African elephant. It is a topic, however, which needs exploring because it examines issues central to the conservation of the wildlife of Africa. Such is the passion that these issues arouse, many of those close to the world of elephant conservation would not want to be drawn into the arguments associated with Robin's exposé even though they may share many of his views.

The book has had a gestation period of over two decades as Robin has observed and experienced the complexities of elephant conservation and the broader challenges of problems since he has a life-long involvement with Africa and as a film-maker he has made films on many of the issues and has met most of the main conservationists and biologists involved.

I remember discussing the merits and shortcomings of different approaches to conservation when Robin first visited me at work in Mauritius. He came to the island to make a series of films on my conservation management work with the highly endangered creatures of that fragile ecosystem: the Mauritian kestrel, pink pigeons and other birds, fruit bats, endemic reptiles and the restoration of small islands, which I am working with still. He, like me, was convinced that the practical management of wildlife was one of the most potent approaches to conservation, and in conflict situations, eclipses the hands-off approach of the protectionists.

Robin, with his nose for sniffing out controversy, was even then convinced that there was an elephant conspiracy of elephantine proportions. Robin's exposé suggests levels of complicity that are surprising.

What is clear is that endangered species arouse great passion, and when you add a charismatic mega-vertebrate producing such a valuable commodity as ivory, then the atmosphere is going to get very hot.

Blood Ivory challenges current thinking. It takes on international conservation organisations (International Conservation Movements as he calls them), questions the bureaucracy of the Convention on International Trade in Endangered Species (CITES) that control the ivory trade, and endorses the ideas of management that have been embraced and developed by biologists and game managers in southern Africa. Here elephant populations have been culled and their ivory and meat used. This is bold thinking, but of course when confronted by the desperate plight of the African elephant in some countries and the conflicts with people in others, we need to challenge some of the conventional thinking. The book is, however, a lot more than just an exposé of corruption and skulduggery in the ivory trade; it is a history of the exploitation of the African elephant and charts out changing attitudes to and perceptions of elephant conservation. It is revealing to read this history to see just how our attitudes have changed. Robin records his own experiences of the Africa in which he grew up, meeting its elephant biologists and game managers. This is the part of the book I enjoyed most.

We have learnt a great deal about how, and how not to, manage elephants and *Blood Ivory* charts these many lessons. But it is a knowledge that needs to be incorporated with a better understanding of how to manage conservation projects, understand the issues involved in elephant–human conflict and accommodate that needs of the people that have to live with the animals. There are rapid changes occurring in the way we view animals and in the way we manage them.

The problems of conflicting ideologies, clashing egos, and complex politics are common components that are seen again and again in all endangered species projects and they get in the way of the conservation work. There are, for example, parallels between the human problems seen in elephant conservation and those seen in the conservation of the giant panda, that have been raised in the book *The Last Panda* by George Schaller, and in the conservation conflicts described in *The California Condor* by Noel and Helen Snyder.

What is clear is that most conservation biologists are poorly equipped to address the politics of endangered species management. A university training in conservation biology does not necessarily prepare students for the realities of real-life conservation and consequently the goals that many conservation biologists set themselves are not achieved. We are not approaching conservation in the most efficient way.

Robin examined this underachievement, and in the late 1980s he made a film showing how many of the large flagship projects of international conservation organisations failed to deliver. Projects involving tigers, pandas, whales and elephants all fell short of their goals. With the benefit of hindsight conservationists of the 1970s and '80s were naïve and were trying to achieve too much, too quickly. Time after time, projects were established in developing countries by highly trained western scientists with adequate resources then, after an obligatory three- or five-year conservation departments. Project after project floundered, starved of money, expertise and vision, although their practitioners often convinced themselves that they had been successful. Spin is not the recent invention of politicians; conservationists have been practising it for decades.

Species can be saved and we can restore some habitats and ecosystems but there are no quick fixes. Saving species takes decades and restoring habitats takes longer. Conservationists are increasingly realising that to achieve population recoveries in endangered species we need resources for developing local capacity support and practical management programmes, often for decades.

Who delivers conservation? Increasingly we are realising that international conservation organisations cannot do this at grass-roots level. This is the role of national organisations, especially the smaller specialist organisations and non-government organisations. These are in general more flexible and more effective in achieving species conservation that government departments. Large organisations by nature of their bureaucracies, have to have detailed and rigid work plans and protocols while smaller organisations can be far more flexible and be driven by clear goals.

However, the real drivers of conservation are inspirational leaders; these are the people that make the difference. They have the drive, charisma and bloody-mindedness to achieve results against the odds, are doggedly stubborn and dedicate their lives to their cause. We see these people cropping up time and again in this book and in the African elephant story; Iain Douglas-Hamilton, David and Daphne Sheldrick, Richard Leakey, George Adamson and a host of others. These are not corporate types, not committee conservationists, but determined individuals driven by a vision.

The art of good species restoration is to be able to split the responsibilities between the organisations and people that have the requisite skills. The management of National Parks and large-scale habitat restoration needs to be done by governments and the larger resource-rich organisations, and the detailed species restoration and research should be done by the more flexible and specialist smaller organisations.

I have been lucky enough to work for the Durrell Wildlife Conservation Trust, an organisation committed to restoring endangered species and their habitats. Gerald Durrell, the founder and visionary, realised that saving species meant investing resources and talent in projects for decades and the Trust now has successful species and habitat restoration projects in several countries.

Humans revel in the concept of wild nature; we cherish the idea of pristine habitats. We have long believed that we can restore species and habitats, and once restored they will look after themselves. That is misguided; 'solved' conservation problem are a rarity. Man has left his footprint everywhere, few pristine habitats now exist and the conservation failures of the 1970s and '80s have demonstrated unequivocally the need for long-term management if we want to keep tigers, panda, elephants or the other countless species and their habitats.

During recent decades we have increasingly managed our natural resources. We control some species and encourage others. Our nature reserves and national parks are all managed and there is every indication that the level of management will continue to increase. Wilderness areas that do not need management will require protection, but these areas are few and rapidly declining.

Concomitant with the growth of conservation have been improvements in animal welfare. This has developed as we understand animal needs, and has resulted in a growth in the animal rights movement. It is inevitable that there will be conflict between animal rights and conservation. Conservationists will always put the rights of the species above the rights of the individual, while animal rights activists support the rights of the individual. At its extreme we have seen people lobby to allow the California condor to become extinct 'with dignity' rather than be subjected to an intensive management programme that would save the species. Luckily the exponents of management won, and the condor population is now being restored not only in California but also in the Grand Canyon of Arizona.

We have also seen activists from the Channel Islands Animal Protection Association laying out the antidote to a poison being used to thwart attempts to remove introduced rats off the Channel Islands, California. The rats were killing native wildlife. The activists were unsuccessful and the rats were fortunately eradicated, which resulted in the subsequent recovery of the native wildlife.

The conflict between animal rights and conservation is brought sharply into focus when we look at the plight of elephants. This is no surprise since elephants are large, long-lived social creatures with great intelligence, the depths of which have yet to be fully understood. Our relations with this wonderful animal have not always been sensitive and their exploitation hits a nerve of extreme sensibility in many. Robin discusses the relationship that humans have had with elephants and although they have been trained and worked as beasts of burden for hundreds of years, they have never been fully domesticated in the usual sense of the word. Elephants have never been bred in large numbers in captivity and in Asia working females may breed with working males but they have usually been allowed to mate with wild males. Consequently there has never been the rigorous selection for docility that one sees in many domestic animals. Trained elephants may seem calm and tractable, and most are, but some of these highly intelligent animals become seriously mentally disturbed in captivity and may be dangerous.

The history of elephants in captivity has had many sad episodes of crude and improper care. Robin notes how Marco Polo recorded how war elephants belonging to Zanzibar chiefs were given wine to make them more spirited. It seems that Marco Polo's observation was subsequently taken literally since an elephant given to King James I by his Spanish counterpart in 1623, and kept at the Tower of London, was throughout his short life given nothing to drink but a gallon of wine a day!

Being an elephant keeper or a mahout is a very dangerous job (the most dangerous job in the world according to some!) since many elephants have killed their keepers. Two of these that subsequently met gruesome ends were the Indian elephants Chunee and Topsy.

Chunee, a male, was brought to Regency London in 1809 or 1810. He was originally exhibited at the Covent Garden Theatre, but later joined a menagerie at Exeter Exchange on the Strand in London. When he reached adulthood he became violent, attributed to an 'annual paroxysm' (perhaps his musth) aggravated by a rotten tusk which gave him bad toothache. On 26 February 1826, while on his usual Sunday walk along the Strand, Chunee rank amok, killing one of his keepers. He was clearly disturbed and became increasingly enraged and difficult over the following days, and was considered too dangerous to keep. The following Wednesday, 1 March, his keeper tried to feed him poison, but Chunee, not surprisingly, refused to eat it. Soldiers were summoned to shoot the elephant with their muskets. Kneeling down to the command of his trusted keeper, Chunee was hit by 152 musket balls; he trumpeted in pain but refused to die. He was finished off by a keeper with a sword.

When I first read this account I was filled with the images of Chunee's appalling death. This vision was, however, eclipsed by the images of the death of Topsy, an elephant with the Circus in the USA. Topsy was executed after she killed three men in three years – the last a drunk trainer who had fed her a lit cigarette. The execution was filmed and the resulting *The electrocution of an elephant* is very disturbing to watch. Although I saw the short film many years ago I am still filled with horror whenever I think of it.

In an attempt to kill Topsy they fed her carrots laced with cyanide which she wolfed down without effect. A plan to hang the elephant publicly was opposed by the Society for the Prevention of Cruelty to Animals. Eventually, the inventor Thomas A. Edison (who with his company had previously designed and built the electric chair), agreed to electrocute the massive Indian elephant.

On 4 January 1903, a crowd estimated at 1,500 gathered at Coney Island, to witness what the *New York Times* termed 'a rather inglorious affair'. At about 1.30 p.m., a handful of park employees led Topsy, the 6-ton, 10-foot-high creature to the execution site. There, an employee of the Edison Company helped attach a hawser and a series of electrodes to the elephant, which was clad in copper-lined sandals. At 2.45 p.m. the current was activated. Some 6,000 volts of an alternating current shot through the elephant. 'The big beast died without a trumpet or a groan', the *Commercial Advertiser* noted. 'All this took a matter of 10 seconds' (actually thought to have been 22 seconds). The *New York Times* added 'There had been no sound and hardly a conscious movement of the body.' Nevertheless, to see the grainy film of the animal being killed is truly shocking.

Thankfully our attitudes to elephants have changed and in the last twenty years we have seen standards getting better. However, if we are to continue to keep elephants in captivity then we still have a great deal to learn about how to keep them healthy, happy and behaving normally. In the 1970s and early '80s when I first started working in conservation there was a belief among many that the future for many species lay in establishing self-sustaining captive populations. We now know that this is unrealistic, and is not practical with such large demanding animals. The ideal would be to be able to leave elephants in the wild to look after themselves, but this is not always practical since elephants are increasingly coming into conflict with people. The way forward is to maintain managed populations of free-ranging animals, but we still have to develop techniques and mind-sets to be able to implement effective long-term management from which both elephants and people benefit.

In an increasingly man-modified world the management of our wildlife is going to be more and more important if we wish to keep it. The real challenges lie in how we keep and manage elephants in the wild.

Historically, before firearms, the populations would have probably been limited by food availability, and during times of food shortage by a depressed rate of reproduction. At the time the elephants had vast areas over which to roam and when they had exhausted the food supply in one area they would move to another. They would return to the formerly over-grazed and browsed areas when they had recovered. This natural cycling of vegetation and elephants may not now be possible for most if not all elephant populations as they are now in fragmented populations, in often disrupted habitats, and there are few or no new areas for them to move into should they exhaust their food supply.

The original southern African model of culling surplus animals for ivory, trophies or meat works in controlling the elephants and making them economically valuable, but is distasteful to many and needs tight controls. Trophy and sport hunting are lucrative ways of making wildlife pay. Hunting has its problems, but it is a relatively straightforward way of channelling money from wealthy western countries to poorer developing ones. I can accept the sustainable hunting of antelope or other ungulates for trophies and rationally I can accept there may be a need for hunting elephants, but emotionally it seems brutal. All these difficult concepts are carefully explored in *Blood Ivory*.

In a recent article in *New Scientist* by Mike Norton-Griffiths, provocatively entitled 'Whose wildlife is it anyway?', he argues for the management of Kenyan wildlife along the lines developed in southern Africa and to move away from current protectionist approaches. Since 1977, the year that sport hunting, wildlife ranching and other consumptive uses were banned; Kenya has lost between 60 and 70 per cent of its large wild animals.

Norton-Griffiths argues that since the opportunities to make money from wildlife have been withdrawn it is no longer profitable to maintain wild animal populations. He argues that to reverse the downward trend the legislation needs to be reversed to allow 'activities such as ranching, the sale of live wild animals, the culling of locally abundant populations, the marketing of trophies, and the most valuable of all – sport hunting'.

However, attempts by Kenyan parliamentarians to update and review current wildlife practices were subverted by the activities of two US animal welfare organisations, the Humane Society and the International Fund for Animal Welfare.

Hunting aside, there are many techniques for the management of elephants and there is plenty of room to develop these further and with far more sophistication than is possible at the moment. The great beauty of management is that it can be highly creative and in the future we will manage populations in ways that at the moment we can only dream of. I dream of genetically modified elephants being used to replace the extinct mammoth. How wonderful it would be to travel the treeless steppe-tundra of northern Europe and Siberia, and to come across analogue mammoths moving along in herds, fulfilling the ecological role of their extinct relatives in maintaining a mammoth-mediated vegetation community. Or how about introducing elephants, camels, wild horses and big cats to re-wild North America?

This is not as wild an idea as it may first seem and it has been seriously proposed in the premier scientific journal *Nature*. The authors wish to 'restore some of the evolutionary and ecological potential that was lost 13,000 years ago . . .'. They add: 'Managed elephant populations could similarly benefit ranchers through grassland maintenance and ecotourism. Five species of proboscideans (mammoths, mastadons and gomphotheres) once roamed North America in the Late Pleistocene; today many of the remaining African and Asian elephants are in grave danger. Elephants inhibit woodland regeneration and promote grasslands, as Pleistocene proboscidians probably once did. With appropriate resources, captive US stock and some of the 16,000 domesticated elephants in Asia could be introduced to North America, where they might suppress the woody plants that threaten western grasslands. Fencing, which can be effective in reducing human-elephant conflict in Africa, would be the main economic cost.'

These may be flights of fancy but the elephant story has moved a long way in the last three and a half thousand years and it promises to move still further in the future. We need to understand the past so that we can plan the future. Let us embrace management and plan for the day when we can reintroduce elephants in their former ranges and perhaps even replace mammoths. These really are visions to look forward to!

Dr Carl G. Jones MBE
International Conservation Fellow
Durrell Wildlife Conservation Trust

Preface

Blood Ivory is a *personal* history. When I came to write it, I discovered that I had personally experienced all the events I was about to describe. I had met, filmed, documented or been a close friend of all the people I have used as references. This means that the rise and fall of the African elephant has all but happened in the fifty years of my adult lifetime, and I have been party to virtually every tortuous twist and turn along the way.

What I hope to achieve with this account, some of which is admittedly quite hard on those friends, is to identify what works in elephant conservation, what doesn't, and why. Several of my conclusions are controversial, but this is essentially a hopeful story if new, proven practices for elephant management are employed throughout Africa. There is now no good reason why the largest land mammal on our planet should become extinct, and this was certainly not the case twenty years ago. It is equally a matter of fact that in more than two-thirds of the countries of Africa that could or should be regarded as prime elephant habitat, the animal's conservation is still a disaster.

Robin Brown
Hyde, Gloucestershire, 2007

ONE

White Gold

Fifteen hundred years before the birth of Christ the pharaoh of Egypt, Queen Hatshepsut, sent a fleet of five ships to find the legendary Land of Punt. Three years later the ships returned bearing a 'marvellous' cargo – the tusks of 700 elephants. Although nobody could have dreamt it then, this was the muted death knell of the African elephant.

The success of the journey was of extreme importance to Hatshepsut, who had declared herself queen of Egypt, ergo a living god. Dangerous journeys into the unknown that were rewarded with fabulous treasure demonstrated godlike prowess, and Hatshepsut, the first women ever to declare herself a divine queen, needed the kudos. From this time on no Middle Eastern sovereign, from the Phoenician king Hyram to the fabulous Solomon and the Ptolemies, could manage without ivory. Tutankhamun rested in death on a pillow of ivory. Solomon's great throne was of ivory overlaid with gold. Ahab the Phoenician lived in a palace that became known as 'the house of ivory'. Harkuf, the governor of Egyptian territory around what is now modern Aswan in the Sudan, ruled a province called Elephantine.

By 500 BC elephants were approaching extinction in Syria and by 270 BC the quest for ivory was proceeding rapidly down the Red Sea to special elephant hunting camps, like that of Ptolemais Theron (the Port of Hunters), served by their own dedicated port, Berenice Troglodytica.

By the time the Roman Empire came to an end in Africa, North African herds were well on their way to extinction. Pliny wrote 2,000 years ago: 'An ample supply of ivory is now rarely obtained except from India, the demands of luxury having exhausted all of them in our part of the world [Africa].' So there is nothing new in the sad story of destruction. It is a slaughter as old as man himself.

Recent discoveries by Russian scientists prove that some 15,000 years ago the earliest true men survived the last ice ages on the meat, skins, tusks and bones of ancient elephantines, the mammoths, and there is still an active trade in mammoth ivory from subfossil deposits. Palaeolithic anthropologists working at sites of human habitation in France, Germany and Russia have found human-made tools alongside the remains of many elephantines. At least 100,000 years ago the leviathans were being either hunted or scavenged and brought to the Terra Amata habitations in southern France.

Modern horses, camels and elephants emerged as species 40,000 years ago and began attracting the attention of humankind, who were all hunters at that time. All three creatures were prime targets for domestication because they could be ridden and worked. The elephant was particularly prized not just as mode of transport but as weapon of war. Egyptian hieroglyphs of 5,000 years ago reflect a different symbol for wild and tame elephants.

The first evidence of the over-exploitation of elephants by human hunters or collectors emerged 1,500 years ago. Several races of Asian and African elephants became extinct. *Elephas maximus rubridens* existed in China as far north as Anyang, in northern Honan Province. Writings from the fourteenth century BC state that elephants were still to be found in Kwangsi Province in northern China. However, the small North African elephant was not so lucky and was extinct by the second century BC. There are disputes among biologists about whether the remaining African elephants, *Loxodonta africana africana*, should be subdivided into 'Plains' and 'Forest' *(Loxodonta africana cyclotis)* species. Regardless of the scientific argument, these animals are all we have left.

In Asia, concentrated in India and spreading through to Burma, the smaller Indian elephant, *Elephas maximus indicus*, won a special place in the heart of early man. The species' survival, unlike that of the African elephant, is in no real doubt because its usefulness has so long been acknowledged. It also has a sacred place in Indian mythology and religion. However, signs of nervousness about shrinking elephant numbers have emerged even in India in recent years as elephant usefulness declines in the face of modern technology. Today India is one of the most strident advocates of the international ban on the trade in elephant ivory.

The African elephant, a much bigger beast, has larger ears, is taller at the shoulder, has more wrinkled skin, and both male and female bear tusks. The Indian elephant is tallest at the arch of the back, bears noticeable tusks in the male only (the female having tusks so small that they appear absent), and has one lobe instead of two on its trunk. The Indian elephant has two humps on its forehead; the African elephant's forehead is flatter. A quick way to tell the two species apart is that the ears of the African elephant appear to be remarkably like the map of Africa, and those of the Indian elephant quite like the outline of India.

The African elephant, often weighing in at 7,000kg (15,400lb), is our largest living land mammal. Indian elephants weigh some 5,000kg (11,000lb). In spite of their mass, elephants move with exceptional grace and delicacy. A thick cushion of resilient tissue grows on the base of the foot around hoof-like toes, absorbing the shock of the weight and enabling the animal to 'walk tall'. Elephants normally walk at about 6.4kph (4mph) and can charge at up to 40kph (25mph). They cannot jump over ditches, but they readily take to rivers and lakes and swim effortlessly for long distances.

They live in small family groups led by old cows, in habitats ranging from thick jungle to savannah. Where food is plentiful the groups join together to form larger herds. Most bulls live in bachelor herds apart from the cows. Elephants migrate seasonally, according to the availability of food and water. They spend many hours eating and may consume more than 225kg (500lb) of grasses and other vegetation in a day. Gestation averages twenty-two months. Mature male elephants annually enter a condition known as musth, which is marked by secretions from the musth glands behind the eye, an increase in aggression, and association with females that usually leads to mating.

There can be little doubt in my view that Indian elephants have survived better than their African cousins because they have been willing, or easily induced, to work for men (and possibly because they have much less ivory than African elephants). It is not generally known that African elephants were also trained to work (by mahouts from India) in the heavy transport and forestry industries of the Belgian Congo. An entire government department was for almost two decades devoted to the affairs of working elephant but it died out with the end of colonialism. Since then the only commercial interest in the African elephant has been the value of their tusks. The largest female tusk ever recorded weighed over 32kg (70lb) but anything over half that would be regarded as exceptional. Males, on the other hand, commonly produce over 18kg (40lb) of ivory on each side, with the record for a single tusk standing at almost 104kg (229lb). The most active (visible) market in ivory today operates out of the Sudan, mostly serving a Chinese 'art' industry. The most up-to-date price I can get for ivory values it at between $75 and $105 a kilogram compared to the going price before the CITES ivory ban in 1989 of $16 to $44 a kilogram.

The life span of an elephant rarely exceeds seventy years and is spent almost entirely on the move. The animal's intake of water is high – an elephant siphons about 20 gallons of water at a time using a delicately muscled trunk. Elephants drink by sucking water up into the trunk and then squirting it into the mouth. They eat by detaching grasses, leaves and fruit with the tip of the trunk and place this vegetation in their mouths by means of a small, lip-like protuberance on the tip of the trunk – African elephants have two of these extremities and Indian elephants have one.

The most famous use elephants have ever been put to is as machines of war, quite literally as the first armoured, death-dealing tank. By the time of Pliny their use was so common that they had their own name, *Lucae boves*, or Lucane Oxen. Alexander the Great, at the head of a Greek army, had a nasty shock when he went against the Persians at the battle of Gaugamela in 331 BC – fifteen armoured elephants mounting platforms housing several archers. These elephants were almost certainly Indian. Alexander's army at the battle of Hydaspes in modern Punjab in 326 BC confronted a force of some 200 elephants lined up at 25-metre intervals and designed primarily to stop cavalry. The Macedonian light infantry attacked the elephants with javelins but without success. Alexander then re-formed his troops into squares with locked shields, confronting the elephant squadrons with a mass of spears, and finally drove them back. He captured about 100 of the animals and later built up his own elephant detachment to more than 200. At the end of the fourth century BC, one of Alexander's captains, Nikator, attempted an unsuccessful invasion of the Indian sub-continent. The peace terms included the hand of Nikator's daughter in marriage in return for 500 war elephants. Thereafter almost all the armies of Europe had elephants among their ordnance.

Alexander's successors, the Mauryan kings who controlled much of Asia, treated their elephants almost as a human regiment. In an early treatise of the Mauryan period ascribed to King Ashoka, the duties of the king's elephant-keeper are described and his responsibilities listed, for veterinarians, trainers, riders, foot-chainers, stall-guards and other attendants. The elephants lived in sanctuaries in a semi-wild state with guards to protect them and maintain breeding records. These elephants were then re-enlisted as needed for military or other purposes.

Plutarch describes how elephants employed in the Mediterranean were obtained from India (some records suggest that the elephant was used in battle as early as 1100 BC), but there are indications that the African elephant was also called into service. Alexander the Great may well have imported elephants up the Nile from central Africa. On the famous Black Obelisk, dated around 860 BC, Shalmaneser, King of Assyria, is seen receiving tribute with an elephant, presumably from Egypt.

Battle elephants were exceptionally valuable and used in a very formalised way. Their brute strength was often employed against fortifications, although Alexander and his successors used elephants almost exclusively against cavalry. At the battle of Gaza in 312 BC between Ptolemy of Egypt and Demetrius of Syria some fifty troops armed with javelins, slings, and bows and arrows were positioned between each elephant. The elephants, and the archers on their backs, broke through the cavalry and the infantry cleaned up.

The Achilles heel of the elephant was in fact its sensitive feet and history records that at the siege of Megalopolis in 318 BC heavy wooden frames studded with iron spikes were laid in the path of the animals. Other reports mention spiked devices linked by chains.

In 280 BC Alexander's kinsman Pyrrhus invaded Italy and introduced the Romans to these living tanks. Pliny the Elder writes about Pyrrhus' elephants at some length at the beginning of Book 8 of his *Natural History*, including his belief that their tusks were their teeth. When Alexander died the balance of power he left behind was

largely dictated by military elephants. When the Selucids of Syria
who had access to Indian elephants moved against the Ptolemies of
Egypt where elephants were scarce, the Selucids initially prevailed
thanks to their animals.

Ptolemy Philadelphos decided to reinforce his elephant army with
animals from central Africa. He developed a series of ports for this
purpose on the Red Sea and down the East African coast, including
Philotera and Berenice. Holding-bays for elephants were installed
and the Egyptian port of Myos Hormos was enlarged to become an
elephant entrepôt. The trade in elephants for war may indeed have
opened up East Africa (certainly East African ports) not just to the
movement of elephant livestock but later to the buying and selling of
elephant ivory and gold, and eventually to the lucrative slave trade,
which was directly linked to ivory exports. The first African slaves
were chain-ganged porters sold at the coast after they had carried
ivory from the interior.

Polybius, in his description of the battle of Raphia fought between
the Ptolemies and the Selucids in 217 BC, the year after Hannibal
famously took his elephants across the Alps, mentions that the
African elephant was smaller than the Indian. This North African
sub-species stood about 2.5 metres at the shoulder, compared to the
African plains elephant of 3.5 to 4 metres. It is now extinct.

The Numidians certainly used in battle African elephants captured
in the forests of the Atlas mountains. These mini-tanks were not
mounted with a tower like the elephants of Kublai Khan's time, but
in addition to the mahout they carried a crew of two or three men
armed with bows and arrows and javelins.

The smaller African forest elephants were also commonly ridden
like horses. Both the Egyptians and the Carthaginians are on record
as capturing and successfully training elephants from the Sudan and
Tunisia. The crew of a Carthaginian war elephant typically
comprised four men in a tower – an officer, a bowman and an
infantryman or two armed with the *sacrissa*, a 5-metre, iron-tipped
lance.

In his account of the battle of Raphia, Polybius gives a graphic
description of elephants fighting each other. They met head to head
and, echoing the mating and dominance play of their natural
environment, interlocked tusks. Each pushed with all its strength,

trying to compel the other to give ground. Finally, the stronger would force the weaker to one side and then gore him along the exposed flank.

Armoured towers on elephants seem first to have been used by Pyrrhus when he invaded Italy. The early biblical and pre-biblical records, including the Apocrypha and the books of Maccabees, describe elephants at war mounting wooden towers filled with fighting men. Pyrrhus, who was the king of Epirus (now northern Albania), later took an army of 25,000 men and 26 elephants against the Romans at Heraclea in 280 BC, and wrote that his elephants won the day with a crucial charge. Indeed, for some hundreds of years nothing seemed capable of withstanding an assault by well-trained elephants. Marco Polo, in the employ of Kublai Khan, does describe a rare successful resistance by a later Tartar army that lured an Indian elephant squadron into a forest, split the animals up and then cut them down with a hail of arrows and lances. Subsequently, however, the Great Khan assembled as many fighting elephants as he could lay his hands on.

In 218 BC the fighting elephant reached the height of its fame when Hannibal crossed the Alps at the head of an army that included thirty-seven of the animals. This is certainly the best-known tale of the elephant's bravery and fortitude but in many ways the most ignominious. In fact the elephants should not have been there in the first place, the terrain and the climate proved too tough for the lumbering beasts and a large number perished on the journey, some of starvation. But Hannibal was a military genius and he knew that even a handful of elephants charging down an alp was an intimidating spectacle; it certainly gave him the advantage of surprise. However, when the Roman general Publius Cornelius Scipio invaded Carthage and defeated Hannibal at the battle of Zama in 202 BC, the elephants were famously judged to have been more of a hindrance than a help. (There is a dispute about whether Hannibal's elephants were African, Indian or a mixture of both. His most famous elephant, a very large animal at the head of the battle squadron, was certainly known as 'Sarus', which means 'the Syrian'.)

Gossipy old Pliny gives one of his more detailed species descriptions when dealing with the elephant. Philemon Holland's

1601 translation of the eighth book of the *Natural History* describes
the war of 'Aniball' with the 'Romanes'. Pliny accurately relates the
war of King Pyrrhus, claiming that this was the first time elephants
were seen in Italy (and, we may confidently assume, Europe). Then,
he says, in the year 502, 142 elephants were brought to Rome
'conveyed upon plankes and flat bottomes', surrounded by 'pipes set
thicke one by another. They were caused to fight in the great Cirque
or shew place, and were killed there with shots of dartes and
javelins. L. Piso says they were brought out only in the shew place
or cirque aforesaid, and for to make them more contemptible, were
chased round about by certaine fellowes hired thereto.'

Pliny records how Hannibal made Roman prisoners he had taken
fight single-handed to the death against his elephants, promising
freedom as a prize. One such (to the great 'hearts greefe' of the
Carthaginians) managed to kill an elephant with a sword. Hannibal
set him free but, fearful that this would damage the reputation of his
elephants, had the man pursued by horsemen and his throat cut!

Pliny also reports that bulls were pitted against elephants in the
arena, and in the second consulship of Pompeius, at the dedication
of the temple of Venus, twenty elephants fought against gladiators
armed with arrows and lances. 'Among all the others', Pliny says,
'one elephant did wonders. When his legs and feet were shot full of
arrows, he crept upon his knees and fought even when the entire
company of gladiators fell upon the beast. Even then the elephant
caught his attackers by their shields and buckles and flung them
aloft in the air. This made a wonderful spectacle and gave great
pleasure to the audience.'

In spite of his acceptance of the brutalities of the Roman arena,
Pliny also shared the common human instinct for admiration of
elephants. We think that they 'never forget', that they go to
'graveyards' to die, that they mourn over collections of elephant
bones and so on. Pliny writes admiringly of an arena elephant that
had apparently gone berserk and was put down with one shot. 'The
dart was driven', the author says, 'but entered under the eye deep
into the ventricles of the brain. Whereupon all the other elephants
attempted to break loose, causing panic amongst the crowd, even
though they were well outside the lists which were protected by iron
gates and bars.'

Pliny also anticipates that elephants used in warfare were extremely vulnerable once the opposition had learned how to handle them. 'Their long snouts or trunks which the Latins call Proboscis, may be easily cut off.' Armies developed new and effective ways of dealing with elephant attacks and very mobile armies, such as that of the Tartars, out-thought and out-paced the lumbering leviathans. Also, and we are now considering an era of 1,000 to 1,500 years ago, elephants were already becoming increasingly difficult to find. In the so-called ancient world the supply of Indian elephants started to dry up as the Indians found ever more commercial uses for their animals.

When Kublai Khan began to build the greatest empire the world has ever seen (ironically, an empire the western world knew almost nothing about until Marco Polo returned to Italy and wrote about it), the Moguls commandeered all the elephants of the peoples they conquered for themselves. Large elephant squadrons were still a spectacular status symbol for the potentates overthrown by the Khan and were regularly displayed to demonstrate a ruler's worth. Marco Polo, writing in 1298 about his time at Kublai Khan's court, describes how at a festival called the White Feast held on 1 February to celebrate the start of a new year, the Great Khan's elephants were paraded: 'five thousand of them exhibited in procession covered with housings of cloth, fancifully and richly worked with gold and silk in figures of birds and beast. Each of the elephants supported on its shoulders two coffers filled with plate and other apparatus for the use of the court.'

Marco also records the presence of valuable elephants in 'Ziamba' (Cochin-China) and how the king there paid his annual tribute to Kublai Khan in elephants and lignum aloes. In Basman (Java), where Marco also records for the first time the existence of Asian rhino, elephants were regarded as a national treasure, and in Madagascar he found on sale 'a vast number of elephants' teeth', while in Zanzibar 'they are also to be found in great numbers'. The latter must have referred to tusks, because, so far as I know, Zanzibar had no indigenous elephants. This is therefore one of the earliest records of Zanzibar being East Africa's most important ivory entrepôt (a title it would have confirmed hundreds of years later). Later Marco Polo rather confuses the issue by stating that Zanzibar chiefs occasionally went to war with each other fighting from the backs of elephants on which they placed 'castles' capable of containing between fifteen and twenty men armed with swords, lances and stones. (If this is true, these must have been very large African elephants.) 'Prior to going into combat,' Marco adds, 'they give draughts of wine to their elephants, supposing that renders them more spirited and more furious in the assault.' The truth of Marco Polo's reporting has long been questioned (his stories were judged so incredible that he was known as 'Marco Millione', the teller of a million tall tales), but I have always been impressed by his attention to detail, and this anecdote about Zanzibar chiefs feeding wine to their fighting elephants has an intriguing ring of truth about it.

So while elephants were being widely exploited in classical times, ivory was used much as we use plastic today. Pliny was starting to worry about the future of the elephant if the rich continued to demand so much of the luxury material, but meanwhile the mighty herds of large African elephants remained all but intact. Many, like the hordes roaming in the Congo river basin and the lands of the African great lakes, had yet to be discovered by the ivory traders. Coastal Africa and countries like Ethiopia, which were readily accessible to Phoenician ships and Arab and Indian dhows, were still meeting the demand. However, far sooner than anyone could have suspected, this glorious epoch in the history of the African elephant would end – quite literally with a bang and the stench of black gunpowder.

TWO

Lay Down Your Heart

From about the time of Christ, African elephants ceased to be valued war machines and were sought instead for what they had always been, the earth's most generous bounty of protein, fat, hide, sinew and, above all, ivory.

Homo habilis, the man-ape, formed cohesive societies between two and four million years ago on the ancient African plains. (Richard Leakey, whom we will be meeting later in this book in his role of wildlife warrior and a champion of elephants, is the son of paleontologists Mary and Louis Leakey and he found some of the earliest of the hominid fossils.) There were also plenty of elephantine creatures with ivory tusks of legendary size browsing the ancient plains of Africa. Later hominids, the Neanderthal and Cro-magnon of 150,000 to 30,000 years ago, were skilled hunters using stone-tipped spears and they rated these mammoths as the prize prey.

Ancient native hunters, however, do not really feature large in our story, although there are Greek accounts from the first century AD of Africans selling ivory and slaves to Arab traders in return for wine and iron implements. These people essentially operated with other predators to keep the elephant herds healthy by culling the old, sick and lame. Their activities never threatened elephant species.

The big bang that began the extermination of the African elephant actually happened in Asia with the Chinese invention of gunpowder. Gunpowder, a mixture of potassium nitrate, charcoal and sulphur, was invented by the Chinese around the second century BC and was first employed in rockets as fireworks in religious ceremonies. By the time of the Song dynasty (AD 1100) these fireworks had evolved into 'fire arrows' that carried inflammable materials to the enemy. Scientists claim to have found the earliest illustrations of a cannon at around this period, 150 years before it appeared in the West. The military use of gunpowder, which included the earliest anti-personnel landmines, is believed to have kept the Mongol hordes out of Song territory for several decades. Reports of the battle of Kai-Meng have the Chinese repelling the Mongols with a barrage of 'arrows of flying fire'. Admittedly these were simple rockets, but their effect was psychologically as well as physically damaging. When the Mongols eventually prevailed, Chinese armaments experts taught them how to use explosives and they carried the technology with them when they conquered much of the Middle East and Eastern Europe as far west as the Dnieper. The story of the development of explosive weapons then moved away from the East. Westerners quickly became expert with cannon and began casting them in bronze, so that by the sixteenth and seventeenth centuries the Chinese Ming dynasty had to employ western Jesuit priests to cast bronze cannon for them.

The first 'hand gone', or prototype rifle, emerged in the fifteenth century in the form of a small cannon mounted on a stand that had to be braced against the chest for firing. It was unsteady, ignited through a touch hole that had to be lit with a match, fired its lead projectile only about 30 metres, and must have had a kick like a mule. Pity the poor muskateer who had to fire one of these at a charging armoured knight bearing down on him from behind a long lance. One must concede, however, that gunpowder has indubitably been one of man's most far-reaching inventions. Records from the various Kalashnikov factories in Eastern Europe appear to support the incredible statistic that there are more of these lethal firearms (many of which have been used to slaughter elephants) than there are human inhabitants of the planet.

Fortunately for the world's wildlife in earlier centuries, only minor changes were made to firearms until the early 1700s. Matchlocks proved a considerable advance on the match-lit long gun, as, by automatically lowering a lit wick into a flashpan of gunpowder, it freed up a hand formerly needed to light the gunpowder. But the wicks still had to be lit, which made early musketeers vulnerable to surprise attack, and it was difficult to keep the wicks alight in wet conditions. Like the early Chinese rockets, these guns were mostly valued for their psychological impact, and longbows remained the preferred weapon of war until Francis I organised his musketeers, or *arquebusiers*, into units, which allowed for much more effective and controlled firepower.

By 1540 matchlock design had been improved with a cover over the flashpan that automatically retracted when the trigger was pressed. This weapon, in the hands of French and English frontiersmen, was used in the conquest of the New World, by which time it had also been introduced by the Portuguese to Eastern countries, mainly India and Japan, where it was used right up to the nineteenth century.

The turning point for the hand-held gun came at the end of the fifteenth century when the Austrian inventor Zoller managed to create grooves inside the barrel of a musket, which caused the bullet to travel straight, at least in theory. Musketballs actually bounce from side to side as they travel down a smooth-bored barrel, reducing their muzzle velocity, range and penetrative potential. A German inventor, Koster of Nuremberg, is believed to have proposed a spiral form of rifling in 1520. Thus 'riflemen' and 'rifles', two terms we accept without question today, describe a fairly sophisticated development in hand-held guns.

Rifling was, however, a difficult engineering task and rifles were not used by the military until the following century. In 1680 eight rifled carbines were issued to each troop of the Life Guards. It was not until 1800 that a whole regiment, the old 95th Regiment, later the Rifle Brigade, received them. These weapons were still a long way from the high-powered rifles used in the last part of the nineteenth century to decimate southern Africa's elephant populations. However, they were beginning to be deployed on the African plains in the years around 1800, mostly in the hands of rich English army officers on leave who had realised that the heaviest and most efficient guns were required to bring down the newly discovered monstrous beasts of the region.

It was not until 1851 that the 'Minie' rifle replaced a belted ball, which had to be rammed into the grooves (or rifling) by using a wooden mallet, with an elongated bullet. Even these bullets had to be wrapped in paper greased with beeswax and tallow. And this was certainly not a 'mini' rifle in the usual sense – the bore was .703in! Two years later saw the emergence of what might be termed the first modern rifle, the famous Enfield, weighing a pound less and with a bore of .577in.

It was at about this time that a shift began in the use of handguns on Africa's wildlife. For at least two centuries before the invention of rifled weapons, handguns had been employed in Africa against wild animals, but they had been used for quite limited commercial gain (a tusk or two if you were lucky) and the provision of food. Hunting with guns as sport came about only in the eighteenth century and gained in popularity only when poor hunters were able to get their hands on the new, powerful, more accurate rifles.

To afford an early rifle you needed to be rich, so it was inevitable that the first 'sportsmen' in Africa were European aristocrats. As time went by, and the sport was popularised and acquired a social status – 'bagging' an African lion becoming almost an extension of 'the Season' – rich Americans joined the club, as did some Arab, Asian and Indian potentates. There was only one other way you could go hunting in Africa and that was as a young, tough adventurer with just about enough money to buy a half-decent rifle. These early prototypes of the later legendary great white hunters paid for their safaris with game 'trophies', particularly elephant ivory.

Such European pioneers were following in some very ancient footsteps indeed. There are ivory artefacts, suggesting a long-established trade in the material, dating back to 3,500 years before the birth of Christ. These include gaming pieces, combs, jewellery, furniture legs and ivory-inlaid wood, usually ebony. A thousand years earlier, ivory was being shaped into harpoon heads. This trade was supplied by elephants and ivory dealers from the much wetter Levant – Syria, Libya and the Sudan. The trade followed the Nile (the easiest transport route) and worked its way through the Sudan and into what we now know as Uganda and the surrounding territories of Central Africa, such as the Congo Basin.

But when you were an Arab ivory trader this far from home, how did you get your trophies back or to a convenient port? You arranged for the local black people to carry them for you. If they were reluctant to engage in such heavy toil, you enslaved them. When finally you arrived at your port, what did you do with these people? You sold them to someone else. It was normally not necessary for the traders to enslave these ivory porters themselves, or indeed even to hunt down elephants with inefficient muzzle-loaders. In the African hinterland there were plenty of local chiefs who would swap both ivory and porters for glass beads and rolls of denim. A lot of soul-searching aimed at western guilt for the African slave trade has been going on in recent years when in reality the slave trade was initiated by Africans for Africans. We tend to forget that Arabs are mostly (North) Africans. Europeans and Americans became involved when the trade in the abandoned ivory porters became more valuable than the ivory they had carried to the coast. Even then Europeans were almost always engaged in the purchase and transport of people already enslaved by other Africans.

Bagamoyo and Ujiji, the great Arab centres of the slave trade, were much more substantial places than the fever-infested hinterland villages – 'the white men's graves' – that every English history book once described. In his recent account of the journeys of David Livingstone and Henry Morton Stanley (*Into Africa*), Martin Dugard reveals that Bagamoyo on the coast had buildings made of stone, white-washed houses with hand-carved Zanzibar doors, a mosque and a Catholic church run by the French fathers of the Holy Ghost mission. Ujiji boasted a population of more than 1,000 Africans and Arabs occupying well-built houses, in one of which lived the destitute Livingstone on the charity of the Arab slave-dealers. (An even more intriguing suggestion is that he had a half-caste teenage son with him.)

In the later days of slavery, when the purchase and collection of slaves in the African hinterland became dangerous for Arabs (simply because they had snatched so many), mixed-race indigenes, operating like Somali warlords do today, took over. Nor is it true that all slaves worked for nothing. Many North African slaves, especially those emasculated to eunuchs, became very rich and influential. Others lived out their lives in domestic conditions considerably superior to those at home.

African slaves were simply treated as a commodity (Africa's most valuable commodity in those days), just as elephants and their ivory were a commodity. Long before slaves were sold to wandering Arab traders, Africans were routinely enslaved as a result of the common practice of inter-tribal raiding. My late friend Wilfred Thesiger believed wholeheartedly in this process, convinced it contributed to the health of tribes like the desert Turkhana through the processes of natural selection. Tribes like the Doe of Tanzania actually ate any slaves stuck in Bagamoyo if there was a glut at the coastal markets.

The reason I have digressed into slavery at some length is that you cannot understand the elephant trade unless you understand the slave trade; the two were inexorably linked. In a sense the elephant-ivory trade invented the slave trade. Arab ivory dealers were obliged eventually to forage so far from home that they needed huge numbers of bearers to get their goods back to the coast. The simplest way to meet this labour requirement was to buy bearers from local African warlords.

Some tribes held other whole tribes in thrall. The Matabele, among whom I lived, held the majority population of the country that is now Zimbabwe, the Shona, in a state of slavery for a century. They raided whenever it took their fancy, always taking slaves, particularly young girls. Their chief, Lobengula, had a famous Griqua slave as his most-favoured concubine (and half the country set aside as his private elephant hunting reserve).

When David Livingstone failed to make a single Christian convert at his mission in Kuruman, Botswana, he went north and received so rapturous a welcome on the Zambesi from a tribe called the Batonka that he decided to set up a mission there and brought in his wife, Mary. Mary and the other Christian missionaries died because the river was a malaria hotspot. Tim Jeal in his definitive book on Livingstone has revealed that the Batonka really took Livingstone under their wing because he brought in guns as well as the gospel, guns that the Batonka rightly judged would keep the raiding Matabele at bay. Protected by Livingstone's firepower, the Batonka could maintain their reputation as the region's leading slave and ivory gatherers.

Eventually virtually every European nation was involved in this lucrative ivory-cum-slave trade. The Danes once had forts in Ghana, or, as it was then known, the Ivory Coast. Spain is thought to have started to take slaves from Africa as early as 1479, Holland from 1625, Sweden from 1647 and Denmark from 1697, and of course there had been Portuguese colonies since the 1540s.

In 1487 King João of Portugal sent two secret agents, Pedro da Covilha and Alfonso de Payva, ostensibly to look for the mysterious Prester John, who claimed to be a Christian king lost in the heart of Africa. In fact the two sought the secrets of Arab trade routes in Africa and Asia, particularly the location of the gold mines of King Solomon, the spice routes to Asia, and the whereabouts of the biblical Land of Punt, in the hope that they could find sources of ivory as huge as the hoard with which I opened this book.

Da Covilha got as far as India and came home by dhow, stopping at the ancient port of Sofala in present-day Mozambique, where he found rich evidence of ivory and gold from the hinterland. On the strength of this information and hints he was able to give on the shape of the rest of the African coast, fellow-countryman Vasco da Gama set sail later in 1497. Within ten years of da Gama's landfall on the Cape of Good Hope, Portugal ruled the waves and the coast from Sofala to the Straits of Hormuz. For 400 years it claimed East and much of Central Africa as its sphere of influence. The Portuguese bought gold from the Mwene Mutapa kingdom, whose people were probably descended from the founders of King Solomon's gold mines, and slaves and ivory from warlords whom the Portuguese called *sertanejos*, Africans mostly of mixed race.

Edward Alpers in his *Ivory and Slaves in East Central Africa* describes how the Portuguese operated a lucrative circuit involving African commodities, Indian manufactured goods and Portuguese marine transport. They sailed first to Africa, where they stocked up on gold and ivory, then on to India, where these commodities were traded for cotton cloth and iron goods to be sold to Africans, and spices for Europe. The Indian goods were unloaded in Africa in return for more gold, ivory and slaves, and the Portuguese ships then sailed for home quite literally loaded to the gunwales with all the riches the world had to offer. The Portuguese held on to this monopoly for almost 200 years until Indians and Arabs forced them out of all but Mozambique. By then the gold had almost dried up as the Monomotapa, the kingdom that covered what is modern Zimbabwe, faded into oblivion, and the slave trade expanded to fill the gap. A massive new demand for slaves was generated by the French sugar industry in Mauritius and Reunion.

The *sertanejos* supported inter-tribal raiding by supplying local people with guns and taking slaves in payment, but these wars were so hotly pursued they began to threaten the transport caravans. Heavily armed Arab and Swahili (the coastal *sertanejos*) caravans financed with Indian capital took over the traffic. These were the people with whom Livingstone sought safe conduct as he travelled in search of the source of the Nile.

Places like Bagamoyo and Ujiji became settled slaving centres and there were collection outposts like Nyangwe on the Lualuba where relations between native people and Arabs were always tense and quickly flared into violence. A massacre was witnessed by Livingstone in July 1871. He was trying to hire a canoe to get back to Ujiji and had wandered into the town market. Three Arabs came into the market with rifles and, after an altercation over a chicken, they started firing. The market was jammed with 1,500 people who panicked, many diving into the river. The Arabs fired, as if conducting target practice, on men, women and children, 'wounding them with their balls so that they leaped and scrambled into the river shrieking'. Shot after shot continued to be fired on the helpless and perishing. 'Some of the long line of heads disappeared quietly, whilst other poor creatures threw their arms high, as if appealing to the great Father above, and sank. . . . It gave me the impression of being in Hell.'

Hell was not confined to East Africa. In West Africa, from about the tenth century onwards, the Hausa city state and the Kanem–Bornu empire had traded ivory, gold and slaves with Islam, which was introduced to the region between the eleventh and fourteenth centuries. Firearms bought from the Ottoman Turks were an important part of the trade. Asante (or Ashanti), otherwise the Empire of the Akan people, ruled on the Gold Coast, controlled the gold country and until the early 1800s traded very briskly in slaves and ivory, originally in return for firearms. The Kingdom of Dahomey, or Fon, in Benin, was also based on slaving, and the region was known as 'the Slave Coast'. (Next door was the Ivory Coast.)

Uganda, deep in the heart of Africa, was the territory that most typified the interactivity of the suppliers to the slave trade (African warlords), its middlemen (Arab traders), its financiers (Indians, and later Europeans and Americans) and the shippers, who were mainly Europeans and Americans supplying the plantations of the New World and the West Indies. Islam still controlled much of the action, and a steady flow of slaves and ivory also continued to go to the Middle East.

Nomadic Kunta Arabs began to preach Sufi Islam throughout the western Sudan as early as the fifteenth century. Pastoralists like the Fulani moved out of Senegal and gained converts to Islam throughout the sixteenth century. In 1591 the Songhai empire in the western Sudan fell, attracting the armies of al-Mansur of Morocco. During the break-up of the Songhai empire an intense period of slaving occurred in West Africa at the hands of Arab Islamic missionaries.

But until the middle of the nineteenth century the Great Lakes region of Central Africa remained the epicentre of the ivory and the slave trade. It had its own internal trade system, two dominant tribes (the Buganda and the Bunyoro), and its own inland seas. It became the scene of the first of many ivory wars fought in Africa.

Ivory had been a staple trade for Uganda, via the East African ports, since the time of Christ, but growing demand and the arrival of better guns, particularly rifles, created what amounted to a moving ivory frontier as elephants grew ever more scarce in the territory adjoining the coast. The large well-armed Arab caravans financed by Indian moneylenders slowly worked their way up to the Great Lakes region. They brought with them tantalising new trade goods such as imported cloth, guns and gunpowder. The Buganda's kabaka (or king) was introduced to Islam at about this time by the Arab explorer/ivory trader Ahmad bin Ibrahim, but the kabaka was more interested in guns and, in the longer term, in a cloth called mericani (heavy denim), which was woven in Massachusetts and the harbinger of a quickening American commercial interest in Africa. Mericani cloth was judged much finer than European or Indian cloth, and increasing numbers of tusks were collected to pay for it, tusks that inevitably provoked a commensurate demand for cheap labour to carry them to the coast.

Uganda's other large tribe, the Bunyoro, sought to keep up with the Buganda in what amounted to an arms-race-cum-trade-war. The Bunyoro also found themselves threatened from the north by

Egyptian-sponsored agents who sought ivory and slaves but had a political motive too. Khedive Ismail of Egypt wanted to extend his empire to the Upper Nile, and a motley band of traders in ivory, slaves and other African spoil (gold, big-cat skins, ebony) sought to influence the Bunyoro. The British explorer Samuel Baker was sent to raise the Egyptian flag over Bunyoro but was sent packing. When British colonialism finally prevailed some years later, the Bunyoro lost half of their territory to the more compliant Bugandans. The king of Buganda, anglicised by visitors such as John Hanning Speke, Sir Richard Burton and Stanley, became the first of several generations of Ugandan monarchs to rule under British colonial influence, many of them educated at British public schools.

Further north, the Acholi tribe responded more favourably to the Egyptian demand for ivory. They were already legendary elephant hunters and when they swapped their spoils for better guns the flow of ivory increased dramatically. In 1888 a Muslim state was briefly proclaimed but was soon put down by Protestant and Catholic converts.

While this rolling ivory war was in progress, the Arabs, particularly Omani Arabs who had based themselves on Zanzibar Island for several centuries, consolidated their position as masters of the ivory and slave trade. They even bred a distinctive race of people (and southern Africa's most widespread language) called *swahilis*. The descendants of Shirazis Arabs and coastal Africans (*sawahil* is Arab for coast), the Swahilis became a dedicated trader clan and remain so in Kenya and Tanzania to this day. Their slave and ivory caravans started out from Bagamoyo and travelled up to 1,000 miles inland to the Great Lakes, buying slaves from local warlords on the way. Bagamoyo means 'lay down your heart' and it has long been thought that the place got its name because it was where Africans from the hinterland finally faced the fact that they would never be going home. Most of these people were sold into slavery proper when, having been shipped to the island by dhow, they were sold on at the infamous Zanzibar slave market.

Slavery (and ivory) statistics are another confusing and controversial issue of our time. The best I can discover is that 'Black Holocaust' protagonists suggest that between the years 1450 and 1850 some twenty-eight million people were sold out of Africa.

Muslim traders are blamed for exporting 17 million via east coast ports, and some twelve million went across the 'Middle Passage', primarily to North America and the West Indies. Eighty per cent of these people were shipped during the eighteenth century.

Taking the most conservative of the slave statistics (for no one kept a record of elephant tusks in those days) and a guestimate of one tusk for every ten slaves (which is very conservative), some three million elephants were slaughtered during these years – years when rifles were primitive in the extreme and, as we shall discover in the next chapter, elephants were hard to kill.

Slaving statistics may be vague and sometimes dubious, but there is no doubt that slaves in transit were treated abominably – as a commodity arguably no more valuable than the elephant tusks they carried. The mortality rate on the ships was between 10 and 20 per cent. A smaller but significant number died from maltreatment and disease before they reached the coast, and there were frequent battles known as slave wars between rival warlords. Some of the losses were made up by the new owners when slaves were forced, like cattle, to breed.

'Supplying slaves to European and Arab traders along the coast became the continent's biggest source of revenue,' said the historian Niall Ferguson in his *Oxford History of the British Empire*. Paradoxically, he adds, the Victorians also set out to 'civilise and redeem. An ethos exemplified by David Livingstone.' The British also switched off the slave trade some 200 years after it had begun. The abolitionist movement began in Britain in the 1790s largely as a result of reports from explorer-missionaries like Livingstone and the descriptions of conditions on the slave ships and in the plantations written by activists such as William Wilberforce, Thomas Clarkson, Elizabeth Heyrick, Mary Lloyd and others.

The movement gained rapid support after the Anti-Slavery Society was formed in 1823, and just ten years later slavery was abolished by an Act of the British Parliament in a carefully worded carrot-and-stick piece of legislation. In reality the common law of England had never recognised anyone as a slave and the Slavery Abolition Act had to be cleverly drafted, as was reflected by phrases in the preamble:

- 'the abolition of slavery throughout the British colonies'
- 'for promoting the industry of the manumitted slaves'
- 'for compensating the persons hitherto entitled to the services of such slaves'

To this last was allocated a vast sum – £20 million. Few seemed to have any conscience about claiming compensation; the Bishop of Exeter, for example, received £12,500 for his 665 slaves.

There were a number of exceptions to the Act's implementation. Its application to the colony of the Cape of Good Hope (from whence the objections had been vehement) was delayed for four months. The colony of Mauritius (where the sugar crop had yet to be brought in) was given an extra six months. The Honourable East India Company, Ceylon, and the Island of St Helena were exempted (the Honourable East India Company theoretically administered large parts of India as an agent for the Mogul Emperor in Delhi). But the abolitionists took exception to these exceptions and soon had them repealed. In 1860 the Indian Penal Code was changed to make the enslavement of human beings a criminal offence.

British naval squadrons were stationed at Freetown, Sierra Leone, to stop slave ships. A huge number of slaves were then sent back to Freetown, where they walked through a 'Freedom Arch' labelled 'Freed from Slavery by British Valour and Philanthropy'.

The abolition of slavery should have been good news for elephants, but paradoxically this was not to be the case. Indeed, the opposite was true. African potentates and their Asian middlemen looked to ivory to make up the shortfalls in their incomes and now shipped tusks by more conventional means, particularly river transport. New technologies such as the railway train, the steamship and the internal combustion engine were waiting to take up the loads the slaves had put down.

The 'Dark Continent' also began to attract a new breed of European. Wealthy minor aristocrats sought to emulate the fame and glory of Livingstone and Stanley – Mungo Park, John Hanning Speke, James Augustus Grant, Sir Richard Burton and Sir Samuel White Baker came to Africa not to convert the heathens but out of a powerful curiosity and in search of game bags.

For protection against the dangerous natives and the big game they came armed with the best guns money could buy. Some, like Frederick Courteney Selous, carrying rifles the size of small cannon called elephant guns, had been commissioned by august institutions like the British Museum of Natural History to bring back specimens – preferably the largest they could find.

At the furthermost tip of the continent, in 1652 the Dutch, in need of a watering stop for their East Indiamen, had established a colony at the Cape of Good Hope. Well (if simply) armed 'boers' (farmers) began to spread out into the southern hinterland. The Boers shipped their elephant tusks back to the coast in sturdy covered wagons drawn by huge numbers of oxen often driven by slaves. When the Boers established their outpost, there was no one in the old Cape Province to enslave other than a few 'Hottentots' and 'Bushmen'. Called, contemptuously, *Strandlopers* (beach walkers) because they liked to beachcomb for shellfish along the beautiful dunes under Table Mountain, the San People, as they are known today, disliked farm work, were famous thieves and were generally regarded by the Boers as more trouble than they were worth. But this in a sense is one of the few African slave success stories. Today the descendants of South Africa's first slaves and coloured indentured workers have political control of the Cape.

A third small group relevant to our story, the Griquas, came into existence at this time. The Griquas were a racial mix of Africans from the tribes in Botswana and young white Boers. Griqua girls were famous for their beauty. In fact, the infamous apartheid laws were first introduced because there was so much miscegenation between young Boer farmers and Griqua maidens that the Afrikaaners, as they had become known, feared for their racial purity.

Griqua men were excellent horsemen and famously brave gun-bearers, and they helped the Boers hunt elephant. But the Dutch settlers so hated the British after their occupation of the Cape that they made two 'Great Treks' into the empty hinterland bush, where initially they had to live off what the land could offer. As a result, the South African Boer became nothing less than the finest rifleman the world has ever seen.

This reputation was quickly endorsed in the early days of the Boer War, fought between two tiny Boer republics and the armies of the British Empire. Boer 'kommandos' (the modern term commando has its root here) initially gave Britain the worst bloody nose in its long colonial history by moving through the bush like hunters, living off the land, and, although they mostly used old muzzle-loading guns, being deadly shots. The Boers called the British dressed in their red uniforms *Rooinecks* (rednecks); they would drop them like sitting ducks and vanish into the landscape. It was in the light of these attacks and as a result of the Boer War that the British abandoned their red coats and took to khaki uniforms.

A wave of attrition began to engulf the Southern African elephant at the hands of the deadly Boer hunters, and for the first time elephants began to disappear from large sections of the African landscape. The Boers were infiltrated in the late nineteenth century by a new breed of European sports hunter who, by the turn of the next century, would render elephants all but extinct as far north as the Limpopo river, a third of the way up the continent of Africa. These people were called 'great white hunters'.

THREE

The Big Bang

The beginning of the end of the South African elephant began not so much with a bang as with a 'roer'. The *roer* was a huge, primitive, muzzle-loading rifle that fired a lead ball weighing as much as a quarter of a pound. The Boers employed the weapon against elephants with cold, passionless purpose. The Englishmen who followed in their footsteps with lighter, more powerful, more accurate rifles were regarded as frivolous, effete 'sportsmen' by the Boers and, as such, with contempt.

Most of the Boer hunters have come and gone into the shadows of African history, leaving few records. To the newly arriving English sportsmen and the gun-happy adventurers who lived off game spoils, especially elephant products, the old Afrikaaner elephant hunters such as Jan Viljoen and Petrus Jacobs – probably the most expert elephant hunters ever – were legends. Their fabulously lethal reputations were enhanced by the fact that, like the animals they hunted, they tried to avoid contact with other people, especially *Rooinecks*, who, in their view, wasted good bullets trying to acquire trophies.

The seventeenth-century hunters lived off their kills and also had to feed their workforce, many of them slaves; otherwise they earned a living from the bush through the sale of ivory. Their African servants consumed an extraordinary amount of game: between 12lb and 15lb of meat a day went down the average throat; and meat was all they usually ate.

A famous English hunter, Cotton Oswell, once fed the entire Bakaa tribe of some 600 souls off his rifles. 'You can only get the meat intake down', he wrote, 'if you mix game meat with beans.' David Livingstone, when there was only wild meat to be had, ate 8lb of it a day. In one day of slaughter, Oswell shot 60,000lb of elephant and hippo meat for the Bakaa as a farewell present.

The Boers needed to be crack shots because a *roer* had almost no muzzle velocity. Several dozen lead balls were often required to despatch large game such as elephant or rhino. Much of the hunting was done on horseback with a 20lb gun (and a similar weight of lead and powder) strung around the galloping, plunging bodies of man and horse. Guns were reloaded at the gallop in the saddle, even though bullets had to be rammed home with a ramrod.

Samuel Baker, who hunted in the mid-1800s, carried a 17lb Harris Holland rifle that fired a .577 bullet. He called it his baby. Once the ramrod got stuck while he was under attack from natives, but he fired the gun anyway and impaled the native with the rod.

Cotton Oswell hunted with a 10-calibre double-barrelled smooth-bore made for him in London by J. Purdey and Sons, but he also used a heavy single-barrelled rifle firing 2oz balls. Smooth-bore guns were his favourites because they could be loaded more easily in the saddle. This was a preference shared by many hunters. These primitive guns, even those with rifling, required the hunter to wrap the ball in a scrap of linen, trim off the corners, load the barrel with a torn powder cartridge, and then ram it all down firmly with a wooden rod. Rifled barrels required a good deal more pressure to set the ball or bullet properly and this was difficult to achieve if you were galloping through the bush.

The Boer hunters were utterly scornful of the wasteful English gentry who fired at anything and wasted valuable bullets. The English in turn regarded the Boers as soulless, cruel hunters and abhorred as unsporting the Boer practice of firing for the front legs of the large elephants. Elephants have shorter front legs in order to carry their massive weight and their leg bones are solid, without marrow. When they walk, both legs on one side move together. If you splinter a front leg with a bullet, the elephant is effectively paralysed. Boer hunters would leave the big bulls in this condition while they chased after the rest of the herd, bringing down all the animals they could. Then they would return to finish off the immobilised bulls.

In a very prescient forecast Cotton Oswell observed that the Boers behaved with such cruelty to all species, including Africans (there was a rumour that early hunting licences in the Boer republics had included the taking of 'two Bushmen'), this could only result in the deepening of 'the evil influence and oppression they have at times exercised upon the black race'. That apprehension of course came in the form of apartheid. Another prescient pessimist was the elephant hunter Cornwallis Harris, who wrote of the Boers: 'They are judges and avengers of their own cause. But their path is beset by perils. Thus far their course has been marked with blood. Must it be traced to its termination, either in their own destruction, or in that of thousands of the native population of Southern Africa?'

William Charles Baldwin, a tiny, 5ft 2in Englishman, arrived in Africa in 1852 to hunt anything he could find. Unlike most of his English peers he was not rich. He was, however, determined. At one point he was reduced by malaria to 5st 10lb, but he still toted a 14lb elephant gun. Living a hand-to-mouth existence, he took help wherever he could get it and was treated well by both Boers and Zulus. He learned to survive on Zulu milk and beer, and admired the Amatonga, whose closely woven baskets could hold 9 gallons of beer. He breakfasted when the hunting was good on cold bush pig and wild mushrooms, and ended the day with a dinner of stewed eland marrow, pumpkins, sea-cow (hippo) stew, rhino hump baked in a hole or an elephant trunk steak. The marked difference between British hunters and their Boer counterparts is tellingly contained in Baldwin's comment: 'To me all places are alike. I have nothing to gain by pushing on, and it riled me to hear them [the English] everlastingly talking of "getting home".' He then made a significant observation: 'the colonies are only refuges for destitute social suicides.' Baldwin travelled 14,000 miles in his six-year career as a hunter and amassed 5,000lb of ivory, but it was stolen from him by another wagon driver! And he was a long way from being the biggest killer in the country.

Roualeyn Gordon Cumming of Altyre, who also arrived from Britain in the mid-1800s, concluded that the Boers had absolutely no 'sporting sentiments' when it came to wildlife and quoted the example of the Boers continuing to riddle the bodies of lions after the cats had safely been brought down – 'until the heads were shot to pieces'. The Boers, who unlike Cumming had farms and families to look after, regarded lions, which were numerous, as cattle-killing vermin and shot them on sight. By 1842, however, there were no lions left at all south of the Orange river, which marked the border of the old Afrikaaner Orange Free State.

In 1854 the British conceded the establishment of an independent Boer republic, the Orange Free State, between the Orange and the Vaal rivers. To celebrate, the jubilant Boers organised the largest one-day hunt in Africa's history for Queen Victoria's second son, Prince Alfred, known as the 'sailor prince'. Around 1,000 Sotho tribesmen (several of whom were trampled to death) were dragooned into a massive circular game drive that finally enclosed some 20,000–30,000 antelope, wildebeest, zebra and ostrich. Such was the confusion that details of the bag are sketchy, but certainly between 500 and 5,000 animals died that day and were carted away on 300 pack oxen. Not a single elephant was found or taken.

Gordon Cumming got to know the Boer hunters and the best places to find big tuskers by cashing in on the Boers' anti-British paranoia. Meeting them in their long wagon trains, he would offer the hunters a great goblet of gin, explaining that he was a 'mountain Scot' (not an Englishman). He wore his green and yellow Gordon kilt even when out elephant hunting. This ruse allowed him to cross-examine the Boers about the origins of the ivory in their ox wagons. He admired their skill with oxen and learned from them how to hunt from ox-back, oxen having a better survival record than horses in tsetse-fly areas. David Livingstone had already learnt this lesson: his favourite mount was his ox, Sinbad.

The native people hunted but played almost no part in the extinction of the big game, which was by now going on all around them. The Bantu, even those who could afford rifles, preferred their traditional weapons, because the killing of game remained either a specialist occupation (tribes dedicated to the hunting of elephants with specialised bows) or ritualistic (lion hunts as part of manhood-proving). Neither of these activities made any significant impact on the wildlife population.

The Matabele leader, Mzilikaze, had been driven out of Zululand and had built a little empire of vassal states among the tribes to the north. A generation later, however, his successor, Lobengula, had apparently still not really recognised that Africa would soon be ruled by the rifle and its wildlife decimated by the new smokeless cordite ammunition. When the grand imperialist, Cecil John

Rhodes, obtained an extremely dubious charter to exploit the mineral wealth of Mashonaland (where I grew up), Lobengula accepted as part of the deal 1,000 Martini Henri rifles. These were the new breech-loading rifles that had recently been used to bring down the old Zulu empire, and Lobengula must have heard of their killing power. Nevertheless, when the rifles arrived he put them in store and left them there even when Rhodes and a tiny force of whites marched a Pioneer Column through to take over Mashonaland in defiance of the terms of the charter.

Matabele and most other native hunts were ceremonial occasions and consisted of several thousand men forming a vast circle of many miles diameter. When the circle had tightened sufficiently round the frenzied animals, the Matabele fell upon them with their spears, displaying, as one white hunter put it, 'the most daring and dangerous sport that can be conceived'. He also noted that hyenas were spared as the Matabele believed they had magical powers. Vast areas of Matabeleland, including the savannahs leading to the Zambesi and the Victoria Falls, known today as the Hwange National Park and still one of the best elephant habitats in Africa, were set aside by Lobengula as royal hunting preserves. Without his permission you hunted there on pain of a very unpleasant death.

Big game such as rhino and elephant were only ever hunted in very small numbers using traps and spears. These animals usually gave as good as they got, and the impact of native hunting was negligible, indeed may even have been beneficial. Indigenous hunters invariably took out immature, infirm or elderly animals, assisting the natural selection processes of the African ecosystem. The Tswanas of Botswana used the same technique as Spanish matadors. Each hunter carried several spears and a long stick topped with a mass of ostrich feathers, which was used to distract the prey, mostly lion, while others speared it. Invariably the lions, and sometimes elephants and rhinos, did as well as the hunters, and these hunts were more manhood ceremonies than serious animal slaying. Sadly, among whites the 'sport' of big-game hunting was gaining popularity, and elephant extinction began, like a lethal carpet, to roll up the African continent from the south.

The fossil record shows that there have been elephants in southern Africa right down to the tip of the Cape of Good Hope for at least 30,000 years. Thanks to the San People (the once prolific Hottentot and Bushmen-like rock artists of southern Africa) there is an extensive pictorial record covering the last 2,000 years.

The forest areas of the Eastern Cape, like Knysna, Addo and the Great Fish River, are said to have swarmed with elephants, and there are reports of elephant paths into the Little Karoo and Outshoorn. In 1824, ivory markets were still flourishing at King Williams Town and at Fort Willshire, where we have records of 22,928lb of ivory being traded in seven months (which represents about 1,061 elephants.)

In the land of the Zulus, now know as Kwazulu-Natal, elephants existed in their thousands, probably hundreds of thousands, in the valleys of thickets and forests. The estimate before 1650 of elephants in the original tiny Cape Colony was 25,000, with 100,000 postulated for the whole area that now comprises South Africa.

The African people had what has been described as 'low-level ivory usage' – turning it into bracelets and ornaments – and gave it little commercial value. On the other hand, by 1702 the Europeans had embarked on serious slaughter. This 'sport' serviced a growing demand for ivory billiard balls, piano keys and, among many other highly prized items, false teeth.

Extinction became a reality, indeed an inevitability, for the elephants in the populated parts of the Cape just fifty years after it was colonised, and by 1775 all the Knysna Forest's elephants were in hiding. Today they are literally ghosts, kept alive only in the imagination of tourist promoters (who claim on the Internet that this vast and beautiful forest still has two elephants left).

This is a very dubious claim. My friend Clive Walker when he was Chairman of the South African Elephant and Rhino Foundation spent a lot of money and time trying to find the ghost elephants of Knysna. He brought spare elephants from the Kruger park and released them in the fringe forest at Knysna, hoping their presence would lure the ghosts out. Sadly it did not, and, as the Kruger elephants were not happy with the forest either, the project folded.

The Knysna elephant went the way of all flesh under British royal patronage. Knysna Forrest was the favourite hunting ground at the beginning of the twentieth century for England's King George V. He termed it the 'most exciting hunt in all the world', and the thunder of his guns was muted only when Knysna elephants became too difficult to find and Cape elephants in general were on their way out.

By the early 1920s, the extinction carpet had rolled another 1,000 or so miles north to the Transvaal. In 1920 an elephant count in the area now protected as the Kruger National Park revealed that there were only 200 left there and that this was probably the last viable population in the whole of South Africa.

The Kruger, as it is known, has since proved (largely as a result of draconian Afrikaaner policing that President Mbecki's regime inherited and has had the sense to maintain) the most stable elephant sanctuary on the continent, all but free of poaching, for half a century. It now produces an excess of elephants over and above the 6,000 the Kruger's own ecosystem can support and, with Addo, is a model for the future of the African elephant. I should add that these are models with which East African conservationists are very uncomfortable. More of that in future chapters.

Addo is a place of strange spiky thickets growing on rich agricultural soils and by 1918 these acres were intensively cultivated farm land. The whole area is immensely rich in plants – indeed the Cape *fynbos* (fine bush) is unique. The Cape Peninsula is known as the 'Cape Floristic Kingdom' and is the original wild garden of some of our most familiar domestic varieties including cotoneasters, heathers and geraniums. But these soils could also grow grapes, oranges and lemons, cereals and strawberries in vast commercial quantities. What were then known as Knysna rogue elephants were given to sneaking out of the remaining thickets to forage on this succulent produce. They were doomed.

A famous 'great white hunter', Major Jacobus Pretorius, was commissioned to eliminate 'problem elephants', and he made a careful and meticulous survey of the target and the terrain. It was known that the elephants of the Addo thickets were dangerous. They had killed several peasants. What nobody had told Major Pretorius was that the thickets were impenetrable to any creature not blessed with the thorn-proof hide of an elephant. There was no question of him riding down the elephants on horseback, judged then to be the most effective method for this 'clearing operation'.

Pretorius concluded that he would have to move on foot, cutting his way through the dense tangle of undergrowth intertwined with thick trees, aloes and cycads. The plants had one thing in common – thorns of every shape, size and sharpness – so Major Pretorius ordered an elephant-hide suit of armour. It covered him from head to toe, complete with a face-mask, leather hat and thick leather gaiters. He also realised that in this close cover he could be tripping over elephants and might need to bring them down at very short range, so a special elephant gun with the bore of a small cannon (4.75cm) was built for him. It could take bullets charged with the new cordite.

Temperatures in this part of the Cape average 30°C in the summer when the fearless major elected to make his onslaught on the thickets, but the rainy season presented an even worst prospect – downpours of driving rain to reduce visibility, mists to hide cunning little elephants (Addo elephants are typical of the smaller forest-dwelling species although still regarded as savannah elephants) and the ground very slippery underfoot for a man hefting so huge a gun.

So here we have the intrepid Pretorius hacking walkways through the thorn thicket in his perspiration-blackened elephant suit, eyes running with sweat, heavy rifle slippery in his gloved hands, every elephant for miles aware of his noisy approach, matriarchs and bulls able to remain invisible no more than a few feet from him, and all of them ready to fight to the death for their young in this their last retreat. It was a hunter's hell because it emerged that there were many more elephants in Addo than anyone had ever thought. After four months he had killed 114 but they still kept coming at him out of thickets.

Pretorius would have gone on until the end (part of his pay was the elephant spoil – ivory, specimens to museums and any young orphans to zoos), but the local administration sickened of the slaughter and ordered him to leave the last few beasts alive – just fourteen of them. This rump population became effectively the last remaining gene pool of elephants in the tip of Africa and was given sanctuary by a pioneer conservationist, J.T. Harvey, who had acquired land in the lower reaches of the Addo valley. In 1926 territory adjoining his to the north was proclaimed the Addo Elephant Park.

Even then the fate of the elephants was far from secure because their sanctuary quickly became ringed by farms – and there was the problem of getting the elephants into their tiny park. The first warden of Addo, Harold Trollope, inspected his charges and observed that they were a nasty little lot, 'made vicious and wary by the constant hunting by man'. He stopped them walking off in search of better fodder (and perhaps revenge) by feeding them lucerne and providing abundant water.

The new pocket park did not have a single natural spring or river, but within weeks Trollope renovated an old windmill serving a borehole and cleared the dam below of mud. The drive of the Addo elephants to their new home was successfully completed by making 'the greatest noise possible' (using shotguns, Chinese crackers and other fireworks) and lighting fires. The beaters carried torches made from the local Spanish moss soaked in tar, which also disguised the men's scent. It took two weeks to move the animals, and in fact Trollope lost one, a rogue bull. When the beaters went in search of him, they were charged. Trollope dropped the bull with a single shot fired when the elephant was 3 metres from one of his men.

For the following year, Addo's 'stroppy' elephants were persuaded to stay within their boundaries by bribes of lucerne, pumpkins, citrus and even pineapples. Nonetheless, he had to drive them back no fewer than four times that year. He realised that Addo had to be fenced – but how do you build a fence strong enough to contain elephants? An electric fence was tried as early as 1936 after a group of Addo elephants terrified Africans at the local station. Trains were forced to wait at the points for several hours until it was safe for the station staff to emerge. Then in 1938 two elephants were killed by trains and everyone knew that Addo either had to be fenced or abandoned as an elephant sanctuary.

They gave up on the electric fence after the elephants worked out that the support poles were not electrified and knocked them down. The task of finding an answer to the containment problem fell to the new warden, Graham Armstrong. He had already tried a number of bizarre elephant repellents. His most inventive was tripwire that fired a gun igniting a bottle of benzine. The elephants learned to walk round areas decorated with benzine bottles. Finally the warden conceived the structure that was later copied throughout Africa and became known as the Armstrong Fence. It consisted of old tram rails sunk 2 metres into the ground, strung with six strands of steel-wire rope, compliments of the City of Port Elizabeth, which was abandoning its tram system. The Waygood Otis lift company supplied Addo with a matching contribution of large quantities of used steel cables. Armstrong put up 750 metres of his fence round his own house and set up a large pile of oranges on his side as a lure. That night several bulls and a cow made repeated attempts to push over the fence and failed. Armstrong reported jubilantly: 'At last the elephants are beaten.'

Over the next four years a boundary path was cleared through 'hunters' hell' and 4,000 holes were dug (with a pole-digger borrowed from the Post Office). The City of Johannesburg also dumped its trams, adding more track and kilometres of used lift cable to the Port Elizabeth pile.

The fence finally closed round the Addo herd in 1954, but only just in time. A young girl had been trampled to death some months previously and the *Port Elizabeth Herald*'s editorial had questioned whether elephants should be allowed to remain in what was now an intensively farmed area. But the fenced park held and thrived, attracting a lucrative tourist trade because Addo is within a few miles of Port Elizabeth. Today more than 800,000 people visit this, the rarest, indeed most miraculous population of elephants in the world.

Addo is not far from Knysna, and the two groups may once have been one, migrating between Knysna's hardwood forests and the sharp and spiny protection of the Addo woodlands. The following time-line from a comprehensive report compiled by biologists at the University of Port Elizabeth shows just how threatened the Addo elephants had become by 1918:

Date	elephants in Knysna
1650	1,000
1876	400–500
1884	200
1905	20
2001	2

A closer examination of these records shows that the real damage was done in an incredibly short period of some three decades between the 1830s and the 1860s, when the British 'great white hunters' discovered Africa's big game and arrived with their guns blazing.

Several famous serial slaughterers, such as Oswell, Baldwin, Cornwallis Harris, Baker and Mungo Murray, became known as the 'old Africa hands'. Almost all were well brought up – Cumming had been to school at Eton and Harris at Rugby – and they usually mounted safaris that cost a fortune.

Cumming epitomised them all. I am the proud owner of a beautiful matched first-edition set of his legendary *A Hunter's Life in the Far Interior of South Africa*, published hugely successfully by John Murray in 1850, in which he described the 'overpowering excitements' of his favourite sport.

Roualeyn Gordon Cumming was larger than life: 6ft 4in tall and weighing 196lb, he sported shoulder-length red curly locks, a vast beard and moustache, and was a walking arsenal. His favourite gun was the heavy smooth-bore he had owned since boyhood, but he also had an equally mighty German 12-bore, a Purdey Double (barrelled) rifle, a light double rifle by William More and a two-grooved 'most perfect' double by Dickson of Edinburgh, plus three heavy double-barrelleds to be used on horseback. To fire off this armoury Cumming packed 400lb of gunpowder, 300lb of lead, 10,000 prepared bullets, 20,000 flints and 50,000 percussion caps for his safari.

Dressed for the hunt, he wore two wide leather belts to which were tied his loading rod (cut from rhinoceros horn), four otter-skin pouches loaded with percussion caps, a powder flask, balls and patches, two clasp knives, a compass, a flint and steel, and a loading mallet. For elephant hunting he usually carried his Dickson double in his right hand. On his feet were *veldschoen*, the buckskin shoes worn by the Boers, and a pair of huge spurs. Pity the horse that did not go where this wild second son of a Highland baronet pointed it! The Afrikaaners once described him as 'escaped from Bedlam'.

One simply has to suspend judgement and see Cumming as a man of his time to understand him. His account, almost 800 pages long, is littered with paradoxical reflections on his life and motives. Once he killed a lion then tucked a tuft of its hair 'in his bossom' out of respect for the dignity of its dying. A large sable bull brought on warm appreciation of 'the magnificence of the old black buck', but he vowed 'in my heart to slay him although I should follow him for a twelvemonth'.

Wild animals existed for him to use and abuse as it took his fancy. His most outrageous encounter was on the Limpopo when he spotted four hippopotamuses, three cows and a bull. He killed one of the cows with a single ball, 'knocking loose a great plate on the top of her skull', and then fired on another one, the ball entering the skull and passing out through the eye. His fear of losing this prize led him to ignore the numerous crocodiles, so he shed his trousers and, armed only with a knife, dived in after the wounded but still lively beast.

I seized her short tail attempting to incline her course for land but she continued to splash and plunge and blow, and make her circular course, carrying me along with her as if I was a fly on her tail.

Finding her tail gave me a poor hold, as the only means of securing my prey, I took out my knife, and cutting two deep parallel incisions through the skin of her rump, and lifting this skin from the flesh, I made use of this as a handle.

Holding on to her rump like grim Death, eventually I succeeded in bringing this gigantic and most powerful animal to the bank. Here the Bushmen quickly brought me a stout buffalo-rhein from my horses neck, which I passed through the opening in the thick skin, and moored Behemoth to a tree. I then took my rifle and sent a ball through the centre of her head, and she was numbered with the dead.

The next day he came across thirty hippos lying on rocks in a pool. 'I wounded seven or eight of these in the head,' he reported blithely, 'and killed two, a bull and a cow both of which we found next day.'

Gordon Cumming's book, we should remember, was a runaway best-seller in Victorian England and it brought several young men out to Africa to try their hand at being a 'great white hunter'. Most of them were after elephants whose ivory could be sold for 5 shillings a pound (which was real money in those days and helped meet the costs of a safari). There was something to be made from big cat skins (but they were hard to cure and transport in good condition), from hippo ivory (which was initially used for false teeth) and particularly from ostrich feathers, which at this time were fetching £7 a pound, quite literally more than their weight in gold. But about ninety large ostrich feathers were needed to make up a pound weight.

By 1850 Cumming had grown tired of blasting the hell out of lion and antelope in the Cape. He decided to head north in search of elephant, the 'mighty monarchs of the forest', and travelled to the territories of the Bechuanas (Botswana) to the south of the Matabele. By now Cumming had learnt that the elephant is an 'animal which entertains an extraordinary horror of man, and a child can put a hundred of them to flight by passing a quarter of a mile to windward; and when thus disturbed, they go a long way before they halt'.

Finally, in the land of the Bamangwato, he found himself on the spoor of big elephants. 'Before us stood a herd of mighty bull elephants, packed together beneath a shady grove.' The elephants promptly ran away. In the light of the distance he had travelled Cumming decided, however,

> that at least I would do my duty and, dashing my spurs into Sunday's ribs I was soon too close to their rear for my safety. Cantering alongside, I was about to fire when [the patriarch bull] instantly turned and, uttering a trumpet so strong and shrill that the earth seemed to vibrate between my feet, he charged furiously after me for several hundred yards in a direct line, not altering his course in the slightest degree for the trees of the forest which he snapped and overthrew like reeds in his headlong career.

Cumming then chased this bull all over the bush and (an indication of the low muzzle velocity of the old rifles) fired ball after ball into the elephant.

> I let fly at his shoulder but on receiving the ball the elephant shrugged his shoulder, and made off at a free, majestic walk. . . .
> He charged again and I saluted him with a second bullet in the

shoulder, of which he did not take the slightest notice. . . . At length exasperated, I became reckless of danger and springing from the saddle I approached the elephant under cover of a tree and gave him a bullet in the side of the head, when, trumpeting so shrilly that the forest trembled, he charged amongst the dogs.

I walked up very near as he was in the act of charging, stood coolly in his path and let drive at the hollow of his forehead. . . . The shot served only to increase his fury and continuing his charge with incredible quickness he all but terminated my elephant hunting forever. An enormous thorn ran deep into the sole of my foot, the old Badenock brogues which I had worn that day being worn through. . . .

My elephant kept crashing on at a steady pace with blood streaming from his wounds. It was long before I fired again as Sunday was extremely troublesome. At length I fired sharp right and left from the saddle: he got both balls through the shoulder and made a long charge after me, rumbling and trumpeting. . . . Mollyeon, a swift and active Bamangwato, was holding my fidgety horse's head while I reloaded and then fired six broadsides from the saddle, the elephant charging almost every time, and pursuing us back to our main body in the rear, who fled in all directions as he approached.

Riding up to him I dismounted and, approaching very near, I gave it to him right and left in the side of the head, upon which he made a long and determined charge after me, but I was now very reckless of his charges, for I saw that he could not overtake me, and in a twinkling I was loaded and again approaching, I fired sharp left and right behind his shoulder. Again he charged with a terrific trumpet which sent Sunday flying through the forest.

This was his last stand and he now stood at bay beside a thorny tree. Having loaded, I drew near and fired right and left at his forehead. Again I loaded and fired my last shot behind his shoulder: on receiving it, he turned round the bushy tree behind which he, and I ran round to give him the other barrel [*sic*]. But the mighty monarch of the forest needed no more: before I could clear the bushy tree he fell heavily on his side, and his spirit fled.

Cumming's feelings were of triumph and elation: 'My feelings at this moment can only be understood by a few brother Nimrods who have had the good fortune to enjoy a similar encounter.' And his dinner that night was 'a piece of flesh from the temple of the elephant'. The next five pages of his book are devoted to a detailed description (which I will spare you) of how his Bamangwato spent days cutting up and gorging themselves on this enormous mass of flesh, fat, offal, skin and marrow bone.

I must apologise to my readers for so long and gory an account, but Cumming's story (and it is one of many in an utterly fascinating book) says all that needs to be said about the 'sporting' attitude which resulted in the virtual extinction of the South African elephant. Loving every thrilling moment of it, Cumming fired at least twenty huge balls or bullets into this one elephant for no better reason than the thrill of the hunt or, if you like, bloodlust.

I know that this kind of hunting has been widely justified by descriptions of the excitements of the chase, as a test of a man's courage, even as a way of feeding local people, but in the end it remains for me a matter of simple cold-blooded killing. Cumming would go on to shoot virtually everything in sight, happily abandoning carcasses as he careered across the bush, red locks and yellow kilt flying, rifles blasting, in the saddle of a terrified and panicky horse.

I have spent most of my life wondering what kind of men came to Africa to slaughter mindlessly the most beautiful objects in an idyllic landscape. Most of them, like Roualeyn Gordon Cumming, were intelligent individuals who wrote books which they believed eulogised Africa; in fact their words describe the systematic destruction of everything they claimed to admire. Admittedly conservation attitudes were very different then.

So perhaps we should remember these old hunters not so much for their bags but for the love of Africa that the continent imbued in them as it has somehow imbued itself in me. They hunted mindlessly, but Africa's extraordinary beauty exerted itself inexorably, and it has to be said that it was this factor, as we shall see, that eventually bred the African conservation movement and the last-ditch rescue of the African elephant.

'There is a fascination to me in the remembrance of the free life,' wrote Charles Baldwin, fifty years after he left Africa and shortly before he died:

> The self dependence, the feeling as you lay under your *kaross* that you were looking at the stars from a point on earth whence no other European had ever seen them; the hope that very patch of bush was the only thing between you and some other strange scene – these are with me still. Were I not married with grandchildren, I should head back to Africa again, and end my days in the open air. It is useless to tell me of civilisation. Take the word of one who has tried both, there is a charm in the wild life.

And back at home in England there was still a glorification of the old 'Africa hands' who had pioneered an empire on which the sun never set. 'It was his creed', wrote Cotton Oswell's son, 'that a man should be able to bear any pain, trouble, worry or privation, without murmuring: act in any emergency, go out in any weather, walk any distance, eat anything, sleep; and he was unmerciful to petting, coddling, or talking about one's self.'

I dislike jingoism, although I am sure the old Africa hands were hard men with ethics of their own that are inconceivable now. Their problem was, however, that confronting all white hunters in pursuit of southern Africa's last remaining elephants was a truly hard black man, the Matabele chief Lobengula. I know the Matabele well, having lived among them for several years, and they had means of dealing with their enemies that made even Boer atrocities seem tame. They enslaved a whole tribe, the Shona, and pitched the dissident opposition off cliff tops (to mention just one of their milder sanctions). Lobengula, who has been portrayed as an astute, noble savage, was in fact a paradoxical despot typical of his time: cruel, simple, bribable and a drinker who preferred champagne, he enjoyed practical jokes, was easily seduced with trinkets and was no match for western entrepreneurs such as the sly John Rudd, Robert Moffat the missionary *manqué* and the truly single-minded imperialist Cecil John Rhodes, who easily stole his country from him and who had by this time also brought the greatest white hunter of them all, Frederick Courteney Selous, into 'the Great Game'.

Rhodes (whose company included a great number interested only in ivory), with Selous scouting ahead of him, drove straight through Lobengula's kingdom with a Pioneer Column of 700 adventurers who numbered among their ranks ex-Indian fighters from America, military conscripts from all over the empire, the soon-to-be-founder of the Boy Scout Movement, Robert Baden Powell, and the man who would go on to write *King Solomon's Mines*, H. Rider Haggard. They were all, at heart, treasure hunters (and really did think they would find King Solomon's mines and the biblical land of Ophir), but, when the gold failed to glitter, many of them, particularly Selous, reverted to hunting that more reliable African treasure – ivory.

FOUR

Across the Limpopo

At Rugby School in 1865 a rich teenager was writing his own curriculum: bird-watching, fishing, egg collecting and 'bunking out'. He commonly spent the night sleeping in the forest. None of Rugby's infamous disciplinary regimes frightened him. He explained his nocturnal outings to the headmaster: 'I am going to be a hunter in Africa and I am just hardening myself to sleep on the ground.'

He was Frederick Courteney Selous and he would keep that promise to himself, becoming the most deadly elephant hunter of all time. He read and hero-worshipped Gordon Cumming and Cotton Oswell, another Rugby man, labelling him 'the ideal of the roving British gentleman'. His 45-year career in the wilds of Africa would put all the other hunters in the shade. Selous, hunting largely alone and on foot, killed more elephants than any other man daring to use this technique. He would go on to be a famous writer, an explorer who made it possible for Rhodes to establish a new colonial country, a diplomat, the bosom pal of American president Teddy Roosevelt, and the model for Allan Quartermain in H. Rider Haggard's worldwide best-seller *King Solomon's Mines*. At sixty-five, when most men would have retired, Selous was still in the bush, fighting with the British Army in East Africa, when he was shot by a German sniper in what was to prove the last week of the First World War. The Rugby School Natural History Society is now named the Selous Society.

Selous finds a place in our story because he forms the bridge between the old 'great white hunters' of Africa and the groups which followed in their bloody tracks: the commercial hunters and, as elephants grew ever more scarce, the safari hunters and the game park rangers.

Selous lasted at Rugby until he was seventeen thanks to an observant housemaster who spotted in him acute senses – 'he could disentangle voices and listen to one, as a dog can follow one scent among many' – which would later serve him well in the bush. His family, rich Norman émigré Huguenots (who gave Selous a shared common ancestry with the first white settlers in the Cape), then sent him to Europe to become a doctor, but by 1871 he had quit all that and was in Africa, intending to hunt anything. He was just nineteen and literally loaded – with a fine modern Reilly Double breech-loading rifle costing £400 in cash (about £8,000 in today's money), a very large sum indeed for a teenager.

This was no longer, however, the old Africa of Cumming and Oswell. In 1450 just 15 per cent of the continent had been thinly occupied by whites. By 1850 80 per cent was under European occupation. The Afrikaaners had their own independent Boer republics – the Transvaal and the Orange Free State – and by the time Selous got there elephants were almost extinct south of the Limpopo. To find elephants in sufficient numbers to cover the cost of an expedition and to make a little money at it, the hunters of the late nineteenth century had to be more dedicated; they needed to be skilled loners who knew how to use the new high-powered rifles that were coming on to the market, knew what kind of weight and shot would bring down an elephant most efficiently, and were clear about exactly where to aim.

There was also beginning to be the vaguest whiff of concern in the air about the number of animals, especially elephants, being killed – between 1888 and 1902 more than seven million pounds of ivory was sold on the Antwerp ivory market. Such murmurings did little more than encourage the last of the old commercial sport hunters to find elephant country 'where no man had ever been before'. Harry Neumann vanished into the thick forests of the Mathews Range in northern Kenya, where he shot anything in sight 'because even smallish tusks were better than no ivory at all'. Another legendary killer, James Sutherland, worked the Portuguese territories and German East Africa armed with bullets that used the new, smokeless explosive, cordite and were capped with copper. But Selous literally outpaced them all. He made the decision to hunt on foot and alone.

Earlier southern elephant specialists, like Henry Hartley, had simply quit hunting when elephants learnt that they could retire to the safety of higher ground where they were protected by the tsetse fly. Tsetse fly killed horses (and people) if they were not 'salted' by previous bites. 'The Fly', as it was known, had effectively drawn a line across Africa south of the Limpopo beyond which most hunters did not go, but if, like Selous, you were prepared to walk or run all day after elephants, access to the rich lands of the Shona behind the lines of the Matabele empire became possible.

Mashonaland was thick with elephants in those days and the records of the old elephant auctions reflect the holocaust upon which the dedicated professional killers were now embarked. In 1850 the tusks of 30,000 elephants were sold on the markets in East Africa, mostly in Zanzibar. Thirty years later that number had doubled. Figures from the London ivory salesroom of 1880 record the passing of some 65,000 elephants.

Back on the frontier Selous had his smart Rigby rifle stolen and he was forced to head north with two heavy Boer *roers* weighing 12½lb and firing a 4oz bullet. He spent the rest of his money on a wagon, oxen and a string of horses, and could then afford only the 'common trade powder that is sold to the Kaffirs in five-pound bags' (black powder) – a box of which, ignited by a friend's pipe, blew up on their way into Matabele territory and burned off much of the skin of Selous's face.

Lobengula treated him with friendly derision when he announced his desire to hunt elephants. 'You're only a boy! Have you come to hunt tiny elephants?' Selous shocked the chief even further when he admitted that he hadn't actually ever seen an elephant. Lobengula agreed to let him go ahead, however, which came as a pleasant surprise to Selous, as he knew that earlier white hunters had angered the Matabele chief by trading guns for ivory with the Shona.

Selous soon realised that much of Mashonaland and the north-east of Matabeleland, while rich in elephants by comparison with the south, was infested with tsetse fly, and hunting them from a horse, the traditional method, was simply not viable. So he went off into fly country on foot, wearing a pair of sandals made of animal hide. He hunted with a single Hottentot elephant expert, Cigar. He lived off the land, walking after monster animals that were complete strangers to him through country infested with lethal beasts like lions, rhinoceros, buffalo, snakes (including the deadly black and green mambas) and leopards. Even the bush pig, with its razor-sharp tusks, or the hyena, which can bite through a thick tree branch, could easily have killed him.

This is veld that I grew up in and later filmed in extensively, particularly in Whange with David Shepherd, who can paint elephants better than any man I know. In addition to the animals, this country is infested with deadly insects such as ticks, scorpions and poisonous centipedes. There are still tsetse fly and lethal malarial mosquitoes. But the young Selous frankly did not know any better and he was, it must be remembered, still only twenty, supremely fit and light on his feet. On these hunts he wore what he called 'light running order' – a long thick shirt, *veldschoen* (light boots favoured by the Afrikaaner hunters) and a felt hat.

Hunting elephants on foot meant running after them, often for hours. His ancient *roers* (older even than the weapons used by his heroes Oswell and Cumming) had to be loaded on the run if he was not to lose prey. Selous made his own 'hardened' bullets by adding zinc and quicksilver to the lead balls, but the muzzle velocity of the *roers* was so low that even a 4oz bullet into the brain would not bring an elephant down. Selous found he had to run for miles even when one of his prey was mortally wounded. But his bags soon matched those of the finest in the trade – as many as five elephants a day. He justified this carnage with the excuse that elephants were so scarce he had to shoot anything he could find.

Selous has been lauded as a fine naturalist (he had several commissions to shoot specimens for the British Museum of Natural History), but in these early days the force that drove him was still the excitement of the chase. Even so these were not the great days of huge elephant bags (remember Oswell's 60,000lb of elephant and rhino meat for the Bakaa from a single day's shooting). Nonetheless, Selous shot sixty-eight elephants on his first safari.

The library at my club, the Travellers, has a first edition of Selous's most successful book, *A Hunter's Wanderings in Africa*, of 1881. It is a wonderful thing to hold as there is a real possibility that the hand that placed it on our shelves was Selous's own. It is full of incredible, adventurous detail and what today would be regarded as shocking claims:

In the course of four months I killed to my own gun 42 elephants, eleven of which were big bulls, whose tusks averaged 44lbs. apiece; I also shot several fine cows whose tusks weighed 15lb. to

16lb. The tusks of the largest bull I killed, when thoroughly dried out, weighed 74lbs. George Wood shot about 50 elephants and our Kaffir hunters shot nearly 49 more, so that altogether we made a very profitable hunt.

Selous also recorded that because he had only the *roer*, 'which were altogether unfitted for the destruction of the smaller game – I shot this season but a goodly number of elephants, rhinoceros and buffaloes, seldom fired at anything smaller'. He described how it was possible to hunt on foot. 'We made a permanent encampment, building a strong lion-proof enclosure for our cattle and erecting a small hut under the shade of a wide-branching Goussi tree, and from here we made raids on foot in search of elephants into the "fly"-infested country to the north-west, our stays varying from a fortnight to ten weeks in duration.' But it was very hard work. In an illustration from *A Hunter's Wanderings in Africa* we see Selous, as he described it, completely 'knocked up'. He and his 'Kaffirs' loll about waiting for the cool of night, oblivious to the dying elephants all around them.

Selous, as he grew older, came to regret the style and extent of his killing. He described as 'dreadful' the times when he shot elephants expediently for any ivory he could get and as a 'grievous sin' the shooting of rhinoceros for their meat, although he always justified his sport by claiming that it kept his safari on the road and that the meat from his slaughter was avidly consumed by local Africans.

A Hunter's Wanderings in Africa (published almost 100 years after the first petitions to ban slavery were presented to American legislatures) has a blood-chilling description of slaving and elephant hunting by the Portuguese, Swahili and Africans on the Zambesi river. Selous was pursuing elephants along the Zambesi valley when he came across a local warlord who had taken the name Basungo Canyema – 'a full-blooded black man from the Lower Zambesi whose sons have been educated by the Portuguese and both read and write that language'.

He has a great deal of power in these parts, having a very great number of men all armed with flintlock muskets, over whom he seems to exercise the most despotic power. He seems to be constantly making raids upon any people in the neighbourhood of the Zambesi who have anything to be taken. Sometimes he sends large parties of his men – two or three hundred – all armed with flintlock muskets, to hunt elephants. When he wants to make an attack upon a tribe he sends a letter down to the Portuguese governor of Tete, complaining of the injury done to Portuguese trade and Portuguese subjects, and asking him for a *permis de guerre* or licence to make war on them.

On 13 December 1877 Selous was staying with a Portuguese acquaintance, Señor Mendonca, when Canyemba, in full Portuguese dress uniform and carrying a sword, paid them a visit. Mendonca remarked afterwards that he was a friend not of Canyemba 'but of his ivory', which, he added 'is the friendship of the white man for the black man'. Señor Mendonca, it emerged, was still dealing actively in slaves as ivory bearers.

The first thing that jarred against my consciousness as an Englishman was the sight of ten Batonka women, just captured in the last raid, all chained together. Each had an iron ring round her neck and there were about five feet of chain between each. Whilst I was there they were never loosened from one another and from the verandah depended three raw hippopotamus-hide sjamboks [whips], the lower part of each dyed with black blood.

Two girls later escaped, were recaptured and 'cruelly beaten, and one of the sjamboks, dyed afresh with crimson stains, told its own tale'.

Large logs are cut up by the slaves from nine inches to a foot in diameter and in these logs are chopped holes sufficiently large to allow a man or woman's foot being put through; other holes are then bored, and wooden pegs driven in, which pass through the holes through which the feet have been pushed and only just leave room for the ankle, rendering it impossible to withdraw the foot. In this manner five or six slaves are safely fixed up in each log. By day they march with the forked sticks round their necks.

A year later he was back in Mashonaland happily slaughtering elephants. He killed two, chased a third and despatched that too, then found one of his bearers, Quarbeet, torn into three pieces by one of the elephants he had wounded earlier. 'There is little doubt that the infuriated elephant must have pressed the unfortunate man down with his foot, and then twisting his trunk under his body, wrenched him asunder.' However, as his wagon driver had managed to miss picking up 'a sable antelope's head I had placed in a tree', he decided to pause and attend to a 'small, worthless lot of cows. Of these we shot the six largest.'

Onwards again, this time trying to avoid tstetse fly (in fact deliberately giving up on several elephants who were heading for the fly), until he came upon a herd of sixty. 'As there was now but an hour of sunlight left, we could spare but little time for admiration, and so we rode towards them with murderous thoughts intent.' Shouting and hallooing he drove the panicking herd into a large circle, and, ignoring an infant 'knocked down, trampled on and half stunned', he finally dismounted and gave a young bull 'a bullet behind the shoulder as he came broadside past me. After this I killed two more with five shots. The fourth I tackled cost me six shots.'

His friends then arrived driving what was left of the elephant troop. He turned them back again. 'The poor animals were now completely knocked up, throwing water over their heated bodies as they walked slowly along, swerving first one way and then the other as the cruel bullets struck them. My friends had fired almost all their cartridges. As the elephants were now only walking and sometimes stood huddled together in a mass offering splendid standing shots, I felt sure of killing three or four more with my cartridges.' In fact he was robbed of this bag when the cow he had fired at turned to defend her infant – and then charged.

Horse and all, I was dashed to the ground. The first thing I became aware of was the strong smell of elephant and was pressed down on the ground in such a way I could not extricate my head. I threw my body over sideways, so that I rested on my hands, and saw the hind legs of an elephant standing like two pillars before me. She was on her knees, with her head and tusks in the ground, and I had been pressed under her chest.

One would think he would now have had enough of this encounter, but no. Borrowing a gun from a bearer he went back to the wounded elephant and shot her behind the shoulder, 'which bought her to the ground with a crash. Then I ran up and gave her a shot in the back of the head to make sure of her.' The party did not return to count or 'make sure of' the other elephants until the following morning. They had killed twenty-two.

This mindless slaughter of elephants and other animals continues for pages and pages of Selous's book. In spite of his inhibitions about killing rhinoceros, he happily brought home and took to the Natural History Museum a trophy of a horn measuring 2½ft. Then there were innumerable buffalo, antelope, wild pigs, hippos, giraffe: you name it, Selous shot it.

'Elephants are now so scarce that one cannot afford to leave even smallish ones alone,' Selous actually confessed to his readers. In this sense Selous has me completely confused. He knew his sport was rendering elephants extinct, but towards the end of his career he was told by his great friend, Teddy Roosevelt, 'nobody can write the natural history of game as you can', and he went on to pen *African Nature Notes*, which might be regarded as a pioneering attempt at a conservation treatise. It may be that he believed, as he often said, that large game in Africa was on its way out by the time he got there; he, living off the residue, allowed himself a few good years of hunting. It was certainly true that this cleaning-up operation would have gone on without him.

By the later nineteenth century Arabs and trader-warlords like Canyemba were employing small armies of Africans to hunt down elephants and rhino, whose tusks and horns were used in Europe for knife handles. There is a record from this time of an Arab dealer arming 400 Matabele with guns to kill rhino. Lobengula himself grew worried at the shortage of game available and fined Selous, along with three other European hunters, a sum equivalent to £1,500 in today's money. Smaller game was also being overhunted, as lucrative elephants and rhino vanished from the landscape. One Boer dealer in the Transvaal exported almost two million antelope hides in two years.

Selous and others needed to find a new way of staying, and shooting, in Africa, and in Selous's case his huge fame pointed the way. Roosevelt was now in the White House and had written the foreword to *African Nature Notes*. Other tyros of their time, like Cecil John Rhodes, had met and talked with Selous, particularly about Mashonaland.

In Rhodes's mind Mashonaland was not a backward little slave-state of the Matabele but Ophir of the Bible, the lost land of King Solomon's mines. His obsession was spawned by the German-Afrikaaner elephant hunter Willie Posselt, who had sold Rhodes an enigmatic stone bird from 'Ophir', and by the elephant hunters Mauch and Hartley, who had actually found ancient mines. Rhodes determined to take Mashonaland. But it was not uncontested territory. Indeed, it was claimed absolutely by the Portuguese. Selous now began to play a double game every bit as dangerous as his elephant hunting, the object of which was to undermine Lobengula's claim to Mashonaland.

In 1889 a group calling itself the Northern Goldfields Exploration Society employed Selous, ostensibly for his unique knowledge of the region; in fact he was tasked to support their claim that they had a valid concession from a local chief, Kgama, and from the Portuguese to exploit a gold-rich valley in Mashonaland called Mazoe. They renamed the society the Selous Exploration Group.

Writing in the London *Fortnightly Review*, Selous described Mashonaland as a place of numerous tribes who 'were in no wise subject to Lobengula'. When he returned to Cape Town he discovered that the Portuguese had cancelled the gold concession. Now posing as an elephant hunter (no doubt bagging a few along the way), Selous travelled up the east coast and the Zambesi to Tete (the town where my family also first entered Mashonaland when we went out overland) to get the Mazoe concession endorsed by the local chiefs. He was successful. Two headmen of the Korekore signed a paper stating that they were entirely independent and had never paid tribute, directly or indirectly, to the Portuguese. Selous again returned to Cape Town, this time to find that the mighty Rhodes had decided to take over the Selous Exploration Group. Waving his by now bottomless purse, Rhodes simply bought Selous out for an undisclosed sum and the promise of a 100-square-mile property in Mashonaland.

Rhodes later told his own version of this skulduggery to the Duke of Abercorn, claiming that he had convinced Selous that supporting the claim of the Korekore chiefs that they were independent would play into the hands of the Portuguese. He said he paid Selous only £2,000 and offered him a job – he was required to find a way into Mashonaland for the little army of occupation. Selous, again in the guise of an elephant hunter licensed by Lobengula, abandoned the idea of going by the most direct route through Bulawayo, as that would indubitably have incensed the Matabele and their well-disciplined army of at least 5,000. He did another reconnaissance up the Zambesi but decided to reject that route too, as the river inland was not navigable and the Portuguese would resist any such invasion of their sphere of influence.

Rhodes had by this time worked out how he could bribe a concession out of Lobengula by making him an offer he could not refuse: 1,000 of the new Martini Henri rifles, a gunboat on the Zambesi (which was delivered in pieces without any assembly instructions) and £1,000 in gold (which was stolen back from Lobengula's emissaries by two troopers of the Pioneer Column). Lobengula later publicly rejected this concession. The whole affair was duplicitous in the extreme. The legislation of the Cape, where Rhodes was about to become prime minister, had laws specifically banning the sale of rifles to natives, but Rhodes, using ordnance from his warehouses at the Kimberley Diamond Mines, went ahead anyway. In addition, the concession itself lied as to Rhodes's real intentions. At best Lobengula had conceded rights to exploit minerals in Mashonaland, not to rule the country, and in the event Lobengula cancelled the concession out of hand when he got wind of Rhodes's true agenda. Rhodes had also agreed to recognise Lobengula's hunting rights, but in fact the Pioneer Column lived off game meat, and a good number of its members were professional elephant hunters.

These pioneers were supposed to be miners, but several of them were literally hostages to fortune. Ever cynical, Rhodes told his recruiting officer, Johnston:

Do you know what will happen to you? You will probably be massacred by the Matabele, or at least one day we shall hear you have been surrounded and cut off. And who will rescue you, do you think? I will tell you – the Imperial Factor. And what do you think will bring pressure to bear on the Imperial Factor and stir them to save you? The influential fathers of your young men!

Johnston took the point and hired a lot of sons of influential men. The Matabele, thanks only to Lobengula's caution, did not attack the column, but the chief did make two attempts in subsequent years to throw the colonialists out. Both of these wars failed bloodily, and Lobengula died (it is said of hypothermia) in a swamp, on the run.

On 7 December 1890 Johnson signed a contract with Rhodes by which he undertook to 'raise in South Africa an auxiliary European Force of about 500 men for service under the British South Africa Company', which agreed to

carry by sudden assault all the principal strongholds of the Matabele nation and generally to so break up the power of the Amandebele as to render raids on surrounding tribes impossible, to effect the emancipation of all their slaves and further to reduce the country to such a condition as to enable the prospecting, mining and commercial staff of the BSAC to conduct their operations in Matabeleland in peace and safety.

Johnston planned either to kill Lobengula or to take him hostage.

Selous met Rhodes in Kimberley to propose his alternative scheme – a road that avoided Ndebele towns. Rumour has it that Rhodes adopted Selous's scheme only when the more aggressive Johnston plan had been leaked by another of Rhodes's henchmen, Heany, when he was in his cups. Selous was now at the heart of the whole crooked adventure to take over Mashonaland. As the historian Arthur Keppel-Jones has said of Selous at this time: 'The readers of *Travel and Adventure in South-East Africa* would never guess what lay behind the Selous expedition to the Mazoe – it was a rewriting of history after the manner of the *New Soviet Encyclopedia*!'

Rhodes's column of occupation also demonstrated the need for a new kind of hunter-guide in Africa and Selous pioneered that role. If you think of the column as a huge safari, Selous was in fact inventing the next stage (one might argue the final stage) of the process that would restrict African elephants to tiny, beleaguered populations in need of full-time protection. Selous addressed for the first time the logistics of a safari led by an expert hunter-guide. Previously he had been responsible for himself, a few Africans, a couple of wagons and a string of horses. That company was now multiplied at least five-hundredfold. This was the biggest safari anyone had ever organised, a huge expedition mounted at massive risk, and while Selous's morality in the context of his hunting may have been questionable even by the standards of the time, there could be no doubting his courage.

He had first to decide on a route for the Pioneer Column to follow and then to cut a road along it. If he made the wrong choice, hundreds of his compatriots would die on Matabele spears. In his decision to take Mashonaland in this way he was the voice of reason. Others close to Rhodes had suggested he employ 500 Boers, giving them farms as compensation, and form a police force of 1,500 men to protect the miners. Leander Starr Jameson (of abortive Jameson Raid fame) claimed Rhodes had told him he had made 'the decision that we will never be able to work peaceably alongside the natives, and the sooner the brush is over the better'.

Selous's scheme involved huge risks. He gambled that Lobengula would be able to restrain his hot-headed young warriors eager to 'wash their spears' in battle, and, extraordinarily, he was right. In addition, he had to cut a wagon road through almost 700 miles of thick bush and find a pass up which the wagons could struggle to reach the Shona plateau at 5,000ft. He did that too – Providential Pass is so named to this day.

On 17 March 1890 Selous went north to start his road, only to discover that Lobengula was violently opposed to it. 'If the road is good for you it will also let in Boers,' Lobengula told him. 'You have this road [through Bulawayo] which is already made.' Selous returned to Kimberley with the unwelcome news.

The Boers had also started stirring, and on the first day of 1890 a prospectus was issued in the Transvaal inviting farmers to join a 'Great North Trek', offering 3,000 *morgen* (the traditional area of a Boer farm) on easy terms. This prospectus said also that it would recognise any European government that was found to be established in the area. This meant the Portuguese. The Portuguese consul in Pretoria immediately pointed out that Mashonaland belonged to His Most Faithful Majesty, 'who would gladly welcome immigrants who acknowledged this fact'. Selous warned Rhodes that it was time to get a move on.

Rhodes decided to put the plan into action. Few good words have been used to describe his motives in recent times, but it should be said that he believed as strongly in British imperialism as an evangelical force as he did in making a fortune. By this time his fortune was anyway so immense (he controlled both the gold of the Johannesberg Rand and the diamond mines of Kimberley, not to mention vast areas of agricultural land) that he was more interested in the glory, and, as he also had heart trouble, he was a man in a hurry. 'So much to do, so little done' is the inscription on his tombstone in the Matopos where I used to take my children on picnics. A little like the Mad Hatter in *Alice's Adventures in Wonderland*.

Selous's safari assembled in Mafeking south of Matabeleland. There were 2,000 oxen, 117 wagons, uniforms of brown corduroy, 'digger' hats, rifles, revolvers, a searchlight with a dynamo and steam engine, 'salted' horses at Selous's insistence, medical supplies and Maxim, Gatling and Nordenfeldt guns. But the official strength of the column (less the police from Bechuanaland who would turn back once the plateau had been scaled) was still only 186 officers and men. Lobengula's army numbered at least 20,000. But Lobengula remembered the defeat of his relative the Zulu chief Cetshwayo, who was crushed by the British with a massively reinforced army after a tiny force firing Martini Henri rifles held out against several thousand Zulus at Rorkes Drift in Natal. Lobengula actually told his *indunas*: 'I promise you the white men soon. Go home, take your cattle to the white men and buy powder and lead, make all the preparations for war.' But he never gave the order to attack. And Selous was able to find and climb Providential Pass, which put him and his vast safari outside Matabeleland, psychologically at least.

Mashonaland may initially have seemed like Shangri-La – the elephant hunting was fabulous. And it did indeed contain a mysterious stone city (whose African origins were instantly questioned) and many ancient, worked-out gold mines, but in many ways it was untenable as a sovereign state. Most of the new white settlers suffered desperate poverty when it was revealed that the remaining gold was mostly on the surface and that the ancient, vanished miners had taken most of the deeper deposits. Many reverted to elephant hunting to feed themselves and large areas of Mashonaland, especially around the capital, Salisbury, where I went to school, saw elephants vanish, never to reappear.

Rhodesia, as Rhodes agreed the place should be called, was also land-locked and the road to the Indian Ocean was blocked by a Portuguese colony highly incensed by the occupation of the hinterland. Rhodes decided he would have to open a corridor to the sea and sent Selous and a Major Forbes to obtain a completely illegal treaty with the Manica chief, Mutasa, in territory even Britain recognised as Portuguese. A party of Portuguese diplomats arrived to reclaim Mutasa's loyalty, whereupon Selous and Forbes captured the lot and sent them as prisoners to Cape Town.

Selous returned to Rhodesia carrying the Mutasa Treaty and a report that Mozambique was crawling with elephants. It also housed the ancient port of Sofala from whence came, according to the Bible, 700 tusks of ivory for Solomon. With the chance of such riches in his mind, Forbes decided to open a corridor to the sea before orders could be issued to stop him. A small Portuguese fort at Macequece was overrun by the Rhodesians without much resistance, and Forbes made a push for the coastal town of Beira. This was the final straw for Queen Victoria and the British government, who had been watching Rhodes's bandits with increasing alarm and really did not want yet another difficult British colony or a war with the Portuguese. Rhodes was forced to recall Forbes.

Selous mostly stood aside from all this carpet-bagging, concentrating instead on his bush skills and his ability to deal with natives. He had married in England and returned to Rhodesia in 1892 to run a vast estate in Lobengula's old elephant preserve in partnership with the military commander of the Pioneer force, Sir John Willoughby. He became a close friend of the head dance doctor, Mlugula, who acted as a kind of Matabele regent after the death of Lobengula and was later thought to be responsible for planning the first Matabele Rebellion.

Selous built fortifications 'which the whole Matabele nation will never take by assault' in Lobengula's old court of Bulawayo, which was now a European town. Indeed the defences were never breached. Later he led a commando group of 110 men against the Matabele, routinely routing opposition *impi* numbering as many as 4,000. In my day Ian Smith, the last white leader, formed a particularly murderous group of white shock troops trained by the British SAS Regiment to fight against Robert Mugabe *et al*. They were very aptly named the Selous Scouts. Mugabe in his turn 'Africanised' the unit and used them murderously against the Matabele.

Finally the race wars ended, but not without atrocities. Olive Shreiner, whose semi-biograpical novel *The Story of an African Farm* is the classic account of rural Boer life, wrote a lesser, now out-of-print book entitled *Trooper Peter Halket of Mashonaland*, which featured a famous frontispiece – a photograph of three Matabele hanging from a tree and seven whites standing watching. Selous was present at that hanging.

By this time, Selous was sick of war and had started to question his future as a colonial estate manager. His books had kept his name alive in the West, particularly with President Theodore Roosevelt, with whom he had corresponded regularly. In 1903 he had been invited as a guest to the White House, where the president asked him to recount African hunting stories to his children. Roosevelt, to the consternation of his staff, also took time off to go rock climbing, riding and swimming across the Potomac with Selous. The president eventually revealed to Selous his extraordinary dream: exhausted by his eight years in office, he had decided not to run for a third term but would go big game hunting in Africa with Selous instead.

The age of the lucrative, entirely commercial African hunting safari was about to begin. It would breed a new style of hunter and would move the killing of elephants on from the depleted wild lands of South and south-central Africa into the prolific savannahs of East Africa – Kenya, Uganda, Tanzania and the Sudan.

FIVE

The Lunatic Line

There is a legendary photograph, dated 1909, of President Theodore Roosevelt and Frederick Courteney Selous in Kenya perched on a bench seat mounted on the front of a specially imported Baldwin steam locomotive. That picture says everything about the way modern technology was employed in the pursuit of the African elephant as it grew more and more scarce across the length and breadth of the continent. For years this image graced every bar from Mombasa through Voi in Tsavo to the Norfolk Hotel in Nairobi and every little guest house or *dak* bungalow at which we stopped on our own long overland journey to Africa. I was nine years old at the time. It hung where nowadays you would find the face of a prime minister or a president and it symbolised the sea change that was about to engulf African hunting.

I have written elsewhere (*Bye Bye Shangri-La*) of that African journey, which was seminal for me. There were animals etching the whole horizon when I was sent to bed at sundown and a similar frieze greeted me when I woke with the dawn. It must have been the same for Teddy Roosevelt. Mounted on his train above a cow-catcher dented by a collision with a rhino, guided by the greatest hunter in the world, a man who had led white men to the mythical Land of Punt and discovered King Solomon's mines, Roosevelt described it thus: 'It was literally like passing through a vast zoological garden.'

I think I understand Roosevelt better than I understand Selous. He was a hunter because he enjoyed the excitement of the chase and he admitted honestly to his passion. Roosevelt was born with a golden spoon in his mouth and never had to worry about paying for anything. He could afford to believe in his enthusiasms and paradoxically this served American wildlife very well: the

American buffalo and the vast Yellowstone National Park are monuments to his interest.

Like Selous in his later days, Roosevelt was a considerable natural historian. However, he enjoyed the divine right of the king of an economy that was beginning to take over the world. Aged eight he had founded the Roosevelt Museum of Natural History in the bedroom of his New York apartment with the head of an Atlantic seal he had picked up as a bargain at the local greengrocer's. He kept mice and by eleven was writing extensive articles on ants and fireflies, bats and homing birds. By then his collection numbered more than 1,000 exhibits, all filed and indexed, mostly by Latin names. The collection expanded exponentially when he took up taxidermy aged thirteen and at fourteen he stuffed and mounted a prize piece, a crocodile bird. Like many other naturalists of his ilk and time, he was not inhibited by shooting live animals for his collection. This of course had its dangers. Two ornithologists who shot birds on an island off Madagascar at the turn of the twentieth century discovered later that they had killed the last known breeding pair of the Aldabra warbler.

Being a young Roosevelt meant that Teddy's opportunities were almost limitless. His first recorded bag was a warbler shot in Cairo; more exotic still was the red-tail chat he winged on a column of Rameses' temple at Thebes. This was also his first experience of Africa. His family spent two weeks hunting birds in the Nile delta from an Arab dhow, Roosevelt stuffing these specimens in front of the astounded sailors.

Almost all the great naturalists I have ever met, people such as Sir Peter Scott and the elephant experts Bill Woodley, Eric Balson and Myles Turner, were once great hunters or, as the saying goes, poachers turned gamekeepers. Scott used to mow down the birds he later came to preserve at his Slimbridge Wetlands Centre near where I now live in Gloucestershire using a baby cannon called a punt gun. Woodley and Turner were both employed when they were young men as government elephant killers, or, as they were euphemistically called then, 'control officers'.

Roosevelt was from this mould. In fact it could be said that he cast the mould. He loved nothing better than antelope hunting in the American west and as a young man was still putting the excitements of the hunt above the need for the conservation of wildlife, even the most threatened of wildlife. At twenty-five he grew concerned that he wasn't going to bag a buffalo 'while there are still buffalo left to shoot', so in 1883 he boarded a train for the Dakota Badlands armed with a Sharps .45 buffalo gun, which fired a huge lead ball. The result (because Roosevelt was never more than a poor hunter with bad eyesight who invariably loosed off too soon) was just one dead buffalo after six days of hunting. That debt was admittedly repaid to society with huge interest when some twenty-five years later, as president, he promulgated three vast American buffalo sanctuaries, including the National Bison Range in Montana.

Sadly I have not the space even to list adequately the achievements that had earned Theodore Roosevelt the title of the most pre-eminent conservationist in America by the time he went to Africa with Selous. This much-abbreviated summary is but a sample of his work for nature.

- During his period in office he set up fifty-five wildlife refuges.
- He helped found the Sierra Club and spent much time in the sequoia forests of Yosemite.
- He massively expanded the American National Parks structure to secure wildlife reserves along the length and breadth of the United States.
- He created the National Monument system.
- He almost single-handedly created the American mind-set that nature was a national asset that had to be supported by constant and active spending if it was to be preserved.
- When still governor of New York he demanded that nature monuments like the Grand Canyon be kept free of development, banned the use of bird feathers as fashion accessories, and called for laws to prevent the picking of wild flowers.
- He saw the dangers of deforestation years ahead of his time, more than quadrupled the acreage of public forest, and built the United States Forest Service.
- He is widely credited with saving more habitat and wildlife than any other individual in history.

Nonetheless, in March 1909 Teddy Roosevelt dumped politics, dressed himself in full hunting gear complete with solar topee and puttees, hired Frederick Courteney Selous and, with his own press corps, went off to see what the pair of them could bag in East Africa – from a train!

Let us stay with this train for a moment. It is a locomotive out of time, carrying Roosevelt and Selous from the old days of African hunting into a new, commercial future. The railway line had been built by the British to open up the interior, meaning Uganda. It seemed to most people that to spend £8 million, an outrageous sum at the time, on a line that would have to cross the worst lion country in Africa, climb 5,000ft up an escarpment that required a slotted track and special trains, bridge the Nairobi wetlands (Nairobi means 'cold') and then wander into uncharted Africa all the way to Lake Victoria was a lunatic thing to do. Indeed, the railway soon came to be called 'the Lunatic Line'.

A good many years after I first rode this Lunatic Line I discovered the real (if you could call it that) reason for the British interest. Apparently the French, in league with certain dissident Egyptian interests, had their eyes on the head-waters of the Nile, which by then was known to have its source in the Central African Great Lakes region. Were the French to control the Nile source (or so it was reasoned in Britain) they could then switch the Nile off and strangle the economy of Egypt. But if the British controlled Uganda and had a railway that could get troops in quickly and efficiently, the problem of the Nile and Egypt was solved. It is hard to think that anyone really believed in this conspiracy theory, but apparently the British government did – and was prepared to waste £8 million on the venture.

When you cast a stone into a pond as large as this the ripples reach out almost infinitely, and one of the ripples was that the Lunatic Line opened a new road to the sea for the ivory that was waiting to spill out of the Great Lakes basin – Uganda and the Congo, indubitably the greatest source of ivory on the planet. Moreover, the British soon recognised this and began to exploit it.

It should be remembered that at this time most of the country we know as Kenya (then the British East African Protectorate) was regarded as *nyika*, thorny wild-animal-infested wasteland between the lush coastal regions and the rich agricultural highlands far inland. However, as the Lunatic Line began to gobble up money, the British looked around for ways to recoup some of these costs and they discovered one – ecotourism. 'The Highlands of East Africa as a winter home for Aristocrats has become a Fashion' crowed a publicity poster for the Uganda Railway (as the line was called officially). 'Sportsmen in search of Big Game revel in this Field of Nature's own Making. Uganda Railway observation cars pass through the Greatest Natural Game Preserve in the World.' This was true. They did. What wasn't true was that the game pictured on that poster was not preserved – in fact quite the contrary; the area (later it would become Tsavo) was a long way from being a 'Game Preserve'. The poster depicts every wild animal under the sun (including a mountain gorilla) ripping up a station and terrorising the staff, and was an open invitation to the 'sportsmen' to blast everything in sight. It worked.

The aptly named J.A. Hunter (later to become an East African hunting legend) literally learned his trade on the Uganda Railway. He reportedly got a job on the railway as an armed guard but boosted his meagre salary by bagging lion and leopard, both of which were then regarded as vermin, from the moving train. He had an arrangement with the driver whereby he would pull the communication cord when he had made a kill and, with an African assistant, jump down to skin his trophies. The driver also used to toot his hooter for J.A. whenever he saw a lion, lion skins being worth £1 a time.

The 'aristocracy' were soon making Kenya their 'fashionable' wintering spot. The Duke of Connaught staged an early safari in 1910, which, while not equalling the splendour being planned by Roosevelt, did include a lady in waiting for his wife and fifty retainers, among them a Goanese head cook and a baker, and replaced the traditional enamel tableware with china and glass.

Britain also cast around for other ways to support the Lunatic Line and decided to encourage settlement in Kenya by issuing land leases at give-away prices. The first of the settlers arrived in 1903, among them the diminutive but hard-working Lord Delamere who had already had a taste of big game hunting in Ethiopia. A lion had also had a taste of him, leaving him with a permanent limp. Delamere found in the highlands of Kenya (later to be known as the 'White Highlands') 'the promised land, the realisation of Rider Haggard's dream of a rich and fertile country hidden beyond impenetrable deserts and mountains'. This promised land also had virtually no people in it. Occasionally groups of Masai wandered through, plus a few Wanderoba elephant hunters. By 1914, however, there were some 6,000 settlers and Delamere, by mortgaging his Cheshire estates, had cobbled together two vast properties, Soysambu and the Equator Ranch, totalling 142,000 acres, for which he paid a rent of £200 a year. They were located in the giant earth fault known as the Rift Valley.

I arrived in Africa almost half a century after Delamere, Selous and Roosevelt, but we alighted at the same station, Voi, where we stayed in the *dak* bungalows. A *dak* bungalow was a clean, thatched mud hut built for postal messengers and was much the cheapest and most cheerful accommodation available to travellers of limited means in those days. And it was at Voi in these same *dak* bungalows alongside the railway tracks that I first heard the story of the legendary man-eaters of the area. It was story I would retell half a century later in a film called *Man-eaters of Tsavo: The True Story* for the BBC's *Natural World* series.

Ten years before the presidential entourage got to Voi two lions – 'turned man-eater' – had been operating around the station, having developed a taste for human flesh. And not just any old flesh. They seemed to prefer indentured Indian railway workers who had been brought in to build the railway line up from Mombasa. A British expert, Colonel J.H. Patterson, had been imported from India to hunt the killers down. Two of the victims had been taken on the station at Voi. Twenty-one others followed in the next three months. Roosevelt and Selous actually met one of victims of the man-eaters' most famous attack which took place at a siding in what is now Tsavo East National Park.

Three hunters, a German, an Italian and an Englishman, had gone to the siding and were camped in a passenger carriage to wait for a lion which had terrorised the station-master. Come midnight they went to bed, waking to find a male lion standing on the Italian in the lower bunk while he savaged the Englishman on the upper. The German leapt into the adjoining toilet compartment, from where he heard the lion leap through the window taking the Englishman with him. His body was found the following day.

But presidential security was obviously much laxer in those days and the presence of serial man-eating lions was not allowed to disrupt the arrangements for a hunter as tough as Teddy Roosevelt. When the train pulled up at the siding of Kapiti Plains, some 300 (later increasing to over 500 thanks to a top-up grant of $30,000 from Andrew Carnegie) Swahili porters in bush uniforms were there to meet it – plus Kikuyu *saises* (grooms), gunbearers, soldiers, and more than sixty tents. On the move this safari stretched for over a mile. Supplies included five dozen barrels of salt for drying skins, tins of the president's favourite Boston baked beans, a set of books specially bound in pigskin to withstand the journey and hundreds of animal traps. The safari was officially sponsored by the Smithsonian Museum, which was building up its natural history collection.

The president planned his dream safari meticulously. Roosevelt went so far as to bring his son, Kermit, to stand in for him when the hunts were too hard. There was a row about native staffing so Selous stayed on as a friend and companion for the ageing president, and the administration of the safari was handed over to professionals from the company Newland & Tarlton. This again was to set a precedent for the future. The old stereotype of the crusty, reclusive hunter reluctantly taking a client off to bag a lion was soon replaced by suave, sophisticated party organisers who also knew how to handle a rifle. The most famous of these was the English aristocrat Denys Finch Hatton, made famous by his mistress, Karen Blixen, who would lead even more elegant safaris than the president's, some commissioned by European royalty.

The president's planning took two years. He fussed over every detail and was obsessive about his armoury, sending his handmade Winchester rifles back for work to the sights. 'They're useless to me,' he complained, which was true as he had been blind in one eye for some time, although he never admitted to it before going to Africa. He had a firing range built in the White House basement to test the various rifles he finally chose. These included the most expensive rifle money could buy, a 'Royal' Grade Holland & Holland double-barrelled .500/450 Nitro Express, specifically made for hunting elephant. Somewhat paradoxically this rifle, which could 'stop' anything, was presented to him by English sportsmen 'in recognition of his services on behalf of the preservation of species'. The president took great pains to assure the press, however, that 'he would not be doing any butchering'.

Rider Haggard was invited to the White House for lunch and the famous hunter, Karl Akeley, who had killed a wild leopard with his bare hands, was also a guest. Roosevelt even sought information from Colonel Patterson, who had despatched the famous man-eaters of Tsavo. Selous joined him on the steamship *Admiral* in Naples for the final leg out to Africa and they had such a rip-roaring time that the appreciative passengers published a shipboard journal, *The Lookout*, which carried a farewell article: 'How shall we miss the deck circle where under sunny skies we spent hours enthralled. Your tales will live for ever in our memory.'

When they came to count costs, however, the safari ran up a final bill of just under $1 million, although a good part of this was met with proceeds from the book, *African Game Trails*, that Roosevelt wrote about his adventure.

Why did our ancestors, even our caring ancestors, because both Roosevelt and Selous were certainly that, have values so different from ours when it came to the slaughter of wildlife? It would be easy to say, as many did, that there was so much of it, it didn't seem to matter. But that is not true, certainly not of these two. Selous knew that their activities threatened Africa's wildlife stocks – he wrote about it – and the president had to fend off criticism from his press corps about the size of his bags.

The writer Bartle Bull who, as a hunter himself, has, I believe, examined this paradox more thoroughly than most, suggests (quoting the Spanish philosopher José Ortega y Gasset's *Meditations on Hunting*) that 'man is a fugitive from nature' and we can only enter it by hunting. If that is universally true, and I fear it may be, then the elephant is in more trouble than I thought.

Somewhat less palatable than the extraordinary presidential safari (it is ungracious to suggest, even by today's standards, that Roosevelt hadn't earned it) was the reality that middle Africa and its fabled elephant grounds had indeed been opened up and the ivory was now streaming out to markets in Zanzibar. Those professional hunters who had not turned their hands to farming or ranching, to the embryonic safari business or to the trade and industry that had started to grow in Nairobi, had to find new sources of income. As these became ever harder and more expensive to reach, a hunter needed to concentrate on the high-yield product – ivory.

Most typical of these last great white commercial hunters was indubitably Karamojo Bell, who made a science of elephant hunting and wrote several highly successful books illustrated with diagrams of himself demonstrating the likes of 'Brain shot quartering from the rear', a shot he had invented for bringing down elephants while they were running away. Karamojo (he is named after the elephant grounds he opened up in north-eastern Uganda) admitted to killing more than 1,000 elephants in a career that took him from Ethiopia in the east to Liberia in West Africa. Like Selous he hunted mostly on foot and is said to have covered 60,000 miles in the course of a twenty-year career.

His books (they were all best-sellers) demonstrate how dramatically morality with regard to wildlife, particularly elephants, has changed over the last century. 'Elephant had to be slain for their ivory to make at least the expenses of the expedition,' Bell wrote in *Karamojo Safari* in 1949,

> buffalo for their meat and hides for making sandals (as there were 40-odd boys to feed) and giraffe for their meat, fat and hides to trade off to the natives for making shields. All the common antelope like kudu, hartebeest, topi and eland had to be killed for meat and skins, the eland being used to make donkey saddles for packing flour, water bags and of course, ivory teeth when, and if, we got any.

Admittedly this sounds more like the accounts of a grocer than a sportsman-adventurer.

> The day's work then began and became not so much a matter of picking out the largest tusker from the bunch of bulls but rather a matter of how to manoeuvre so that the whole lot was laid low

... the little .256 Mannlicher-Schoenauer [especially lightened for him in Scotland so that it weighed only 5lb] laid them low (12 bulls) with a shot apiece – all brain shot. Was I delighted?

Few hunters, if any, would equal this record. But finding elephants in these numbers was no longer easy. Bell was forced to try out West Africa where he was disappointed by the size of the elephants but noted wryly that the freed slaves of Liberia were now supplementing their incomes by enslaving local Africans for plantation work.

He ordered an assemble-it-yourself steamboat from England and in it he went after the elephants on the islands of the Ubangui river, a branch of the Congo. His most profitable day's shooting in the Sudan was when he brought down nine elephants with an average of two bullets per beast. Their ivory weighed in at about 1,500lb and earned him £900, almost £18,000 in today's money.

In 1909 Bell joined, with virtually every other professional elephant hunter in Africa (including Quentin Grogan who later took over the hunting duties on the Roosevelt safari), a jamboree of killing in an area called the Lado, previously a Belgian royal hunting preserve, between the Sudan and the Belgian Congo. Law, order, the protection of wildlife and the licensing of hunting had been suspended in the area when its administration passed from the Congo to the Sudan on the death of King Leopold. Amid scenes of wild partying, Lado elephants died in their hundreds.

It was to the Lado that Grogan bought President Roosevelt and it was here that the president finally blotted his copybook. They were in Lado to add a white rhino to the president's and the Smithsonian's bag – but he ended up killing *nine*, including four cows and a calf, and he wounded two other calves. The president's first shot was at a sleeping rhino. Lord Cranford, a friend of Roosevelt's, later commented: 'Do these nine white rhinoceros ever cause ex-President Roosevelt a pang of conscience or a restless night? I venture to hope so.'

The press did not like it either. Associated Press had a large safari party of their own tagging the president and he was forced to justify the 'slaughter' (Lord Cranford's description) and the heavy shooting in general as being 'for science' and for meat for the staff. He and

Kermit, the president wrote, shot only out of necessity. This was not even vaguely true. He fired indiscriminately, pumping off shots at animals he spotted often 600 yards away. Indeed he wrote of his belief in the 'Ciceronian theory, that he who throws the javelin all day must hit the mark sometimes'. Other hunters, including the pioneer conservationist Sir Frederick Jackson, thought Roosevelt's hunting notes made 'most unpleasant reading'.

And so, with what today would be regarded as an atrocity, one era ended and another began. In the course of his safari, which closed with Roosevelt sailing down the Nile to Egypt, the president met virtually every man who was still earning his living from elephant hunting – J.H. Cunninghame, Bell, William Judd, Sir Alfred Pease, Delamere, Leslie Tarlton, Berkeley Cole, Quentin Grogan, Harold and Clifford Hill, Lord Cranford, Philip Percival, J.A. Hunter, Denys Finch Hatton and half a dozen more. A few – Bell, Grogan and Philip Percival certainly – would hunt elephant for a living for a few years more but all would eventually, and reluctantly, become part of a new safari-tourism industry. Roosevelt met some of these hunters when he reached the Lado, and although they threw a party for him on New Year's Eve 1909 the President was not too impressed: 'They're a hard-bit set, these elephant poachers.'

Let me end with a description by Bartle Bull, from his excellent book *Safari: A Chronicle of Adventure*, of the last days of the great elephant hunters, specifically of Karamojo Bell arriving back at the coast with a great hoard of ivory:

The return of a Karamojo Bell safari, among the last of their kind, was a spectacle even in the ivory centres of East Africa. Sparkling in brightly beaded robes, a hundred men paraded to the ivory market, proudly bearing the teeth of 180 elephants. Escorted by Bell's six armed askaris, the donkey men kept 180 donkeys in order. Each of the great tusks, so hot that it blistered the shoulders, its empty nerve hole filled with the bearer's belongings, was carried by one of the thirty-one hand-picked Karamojoan porters. Blood red ostrich feathers and the manes of giraffes, lions and baboons bedecked each man's head. Averaging one elephant per day over the six months of hunting on a 14-

month safari to Uganda and the Lado Enclave, Bell returned
with a hoard of treasure. The magnificent Karamojo tusks
averaged 53 lbs. each, the Lado tusks 23 lbs. The total cost of
the safari was £3,000 (about £90,000 today), of which wages
were about £600. The ivory sold for £9,000. In today's money
the safari realised a profit of £181,000.

While the old Africa hands were shooting out their swansongs in
east-central African countries where British rule prevailed, the
lethal carpet of elephant extinction I have referred to previously
continued to roll inexorably northwards. The further north it
went, the more it was influenced by Islam where the enslavement
of ivory porters remained an important element in financial
equations.

Arabs were slow to give up slavery, especially in remote
hinterland areas like the Sudan, which as late as the nineteenth
century continued to trade in slaves and spill copious quantities of
ivory. It is frankly impossible to say how many elephants have
been killed in the Sudan because no one knows how many were
there originally. My guess would be, based on casual references
from hunters' diaries of sightings, that there were in the Sudan
acres of seemingly endless elephant habitat which was home to at
least as many elephants as there are today in the whole of Africa.

A decade before he died I made a film (*The Last Great Explorer*)
with the man who has been named as the greatest western explorer
of the last century, Wilfred Thesiger. Wilfred is the only man ever
to be awarded all five Gold Medals for Exploration from the
Royal Geographical Society. We met in Maralal in northern Kenya
where he had been living very happily in a tiny hut for several
years – but he also kept a house with a housekeeper, a vast travel
library and his unique photographic collection (which can now be
seen at the Pitt Rivers Museum in Oxford) in Tite Street, Chelsea.
Wilfred was from an influential family which included his uncle,
Lord Chelmsford, who had been viceroy of India.

First and foremost Wilfred loved Africa. He was born at the
British Legation in Addis Ababa, Abyssinia, where his father was
the British consul, and in his early days he had been a formidable
hunter. As a young district commissioner in a remote province

of the Sudan (having traded in his government horse and uniform for a camel and Arab dress) he killed sixty-five lions in five years, often shooting with a small Rigby rifle from camel-back. 'Mostly on control operations,' Wilfred told me, not quite meeting my eye. 'We viewed things differently in those days.' How differently is reflected in a passage from Wilfred's extraordinary *Arabian Sands*, where he considers the appeal of hunting and exploration:

> this perverse necessity which drives me from my own land [England]. Perhaps it lies in the background of my memory: in journeys through the deserts of Ethiopia; in the thrill of seeing my father shoot an oryx when I was only three; in the smell of dust and acacias under a hot sun; in the chorus of hyenas and jackals in the darkness round the camp . . . a way of life from which there could be no recall.

Or perhaps it comes from the time when Wilfred stood as a young man and counted more than 1,000 elephants in one day on the banks of the Sudan's White Nile. Today there are no elephants there at all.

Wilfred greatly admired the Arabs. He took the trouble to live among the more primitive tribes in the mosquito-infested wetlands on the borders of Iraq and Iran (see *The Marsh Arabs*). And it was from Wilfred, who wrote the introduction to my book *The Lost City of Solomon and Sheba* (Sutton Publishing, 2003), that I discovered a little known fact about Arab attitudes to slavery, one which had a considerable impact on the elephants of sub-Saharan Africa. The Qur'an does not actually condemn slavery as a ubiquitous sin, arguing that only the people of Islam may not be enslaved. Thus when Arab caravans travelled south into British Christian-influenced Sudan, they found not just a huge abundance of elephants but a vast labour force which could be obliged to carry the ivory home without the slavers offending their God. Whether you accept this tenuous justification or not, the killing of elephants north of the Equator now shifted out of the hands of white professionals in south central Africa to Arab northerners who had been in the trade a great deal longer.

Ivory had, since time immemorial, been the major source of export revenue from the Christian southern Sudan. But the trade has always been controlled from Khartoum, the northern capital (which actually means 'elephant'), and when in later years an attempt was made to license the ivory trade, all the licences continued to be issued in Khartoum, not in the southern capital, Juba, where the elephants came from.

Britain, in the late nineteenth century, made one last effort to regain control of the political situation and of what amounted to the last great source of ivory on the planet. The Sudan at this time was an Egyptian condominium, technically a territory in limbo within the Egyptian sphere of influence, but at this point Egypt was actually under British control. Britain had effectively taken over Egypt when the Egyptian army revolted in 1882 and the country was under the *de facto* administration of the British Pro-Consul, Sir Evelyn Baring.

A clutch of Victorian 'heroes' now entered the ring. The hunter Sir Samuel Baker (accompanied by his mistress, a Turkish beauty whom Sir Samuel had actually bought) was, under pressure from Britain, made a pasha – a lord of the Ottoman Empire – and a major-general and sent to Sudan to 'suppress the slave trade'. This, of course, would have returned the lucrative ivory trade to British hands. The Islamic Arabs fought back. The Mahdi, Mohammed Ahmed Ibn el-Sayyid Abdullah, and his 'whirling dervishes' defeated the Anglo-Egyptian Army in 1883 and murdered General Gordon who had been sent out to 'save the southern Sudan from Islam'. Islam then ruled for fifteen years, funding their revolution with ivory, under the Mahdi's successor, the Khalifa Abdullah. Finally, in 1898, they were put down by Kitchener at the battle of Omdurman.

Thus began an ivory trade which has essentially never changed. The Kenya trade ceased to be significant, excluding, as I have said, the island port of Zanzibar which was essentially the Arab entrepôt for central African ivory spilling south rather than north. (Bagamoyo is actually closer to the southern Sudan and Uganda than the nearest Arab controlled entrepôt of Port Sudan.)

So in terms of the ivory trade it did not much matter that the old Africa hands south of the Equator had virtually shot themselves out of business by the beginning of the twentieth century. There were still vast areas of Africa, much of it under British 'influence', which could be exploited for elephants if you had a taste for a hard, dangerous and lonely life. In Kenya the hunters began instead to have fun. It was the start of an era when elephant hunting was no longer a matter of necessity but the quest for a 'big bag' on a safari holiday. Only the very rich could afford these trips and they were soon to become infamous, indeed notorious, for the level of 'white mischief'.

SIX

White Mischief

Kenya, billed as the 'big game paradise', had by now been successfully hyped as a winter playground for the very rich. Great numbers of affluent Europeans and Americans as well as rich potentates of the East heard the siren call of the best 'sport' in the world. The word 'safari' acquired a new, exotic meaning, as indeed did the term 'great white hunter'. (It was said of one of the most famous of the elephant hunters, Count Bror von Blixen, that if you took your wife on safari with him it was advisable to bring a spare.)

The 'anything goes' attitude in this new Kenya colony was the result of its being modelled on the feudal England of several centuries before. It was run, and standards of colonial morality were set, by émigré blue-blooded Brits like Lord Delamere, with his two vast ranches in the Rift Valley, and Lord Cranford, who had a beautiful farm in the rolling foothills of Mount Kenya; and influential men like the second son of the Earl of Winchester, the Rt Hon. Denys Finch Hatton, a remarkable character who was eventually immortalised by his love affair with Karen Blixen. Karen Blixen, who chose the pen-name Isak Dineson for her book *Out of Africa* which tells of this affair, was herself a minor Scandinavian aristocrat married to the Swedish Bror von Blixen.

That is not to say that all four men were not tough, industrious and totally wedded to Africa. Lord Delamere, for example, made huge contributions to the development of Kenya and convinced the British government, which was treating the whole place rather nervously, that the country was a wonderful location for settlers to live and work. Initially Delamere lived by hunting, but as his enormous African estates grew he became a hands-on farmer, breeding disease-resistant sheep and cattle and experimenting with irrigation. He and his wife lived for years in a group of mud huts without window glass or doors.

Things improved a lot for the Delameres as the colony grew. Lord Delamere was a founder member of the famous Muthaiga Club and a legendary hell-raiser. He and his cronies, all raised in English public schools, played rugby in the bar, shot up the town after drinking it dry, hunted furiously (for jackals), solemnly attended with full pomp the meets of the East Africa Turf Club (Delamere was its first president) and, of course, played serious all-white cricket. Delamere staged a famous party in 1926 at which about 200 guests consumed some 600 bottles of champagne. He is said to have coined the term 'white hunter'. He employed two hunters on his ranches to shoot problem animals – Alan Black whom he called his 'white hunter', and a black Abyssinian whose name has vanished into history.

Lord Cranford, who was carried ashore at Mombasa in 1906, was also a professional hunter. He went on to found a variety of Kenyan businesses including the first safari outfitter, Newland & Tarlton, which by 1914 was employing more people than any other firm in Kenya.

The well-bred Denys Finch Hatton was the most complex character of them all. A hell-raiser and hard drinker whose special party piece was a forward dive across a room that ended up with him sitting facing you in an armchair (or collapsed in a heap beside it), Finch Hatton was also a widely read intellectual who taught Karen Blixen to love classical music. Some years later while training with the Royal Flying Corps in the Middle East he met a young American military pilot, Kermit Roosevelt, and discovered with him a shared love of poetry. Finch Hatton is reputed to have made a special air drop when Kermit ran out of reading matter – of *Plutarch's Lives*! Some years ago I prepared a film script on Denys, having unearthed some little-known information about early conservation work he was secretly engaged upon at the time of his death in his little yellow Gypsy Moth aircraft. This work has been completely lost in the background noise of his affair with Karen but it is an important link in our story and I will return to it later.

Standing squarely alongside all these adventurous men were at least as many intrepid women pioneers. The legends have it that they were as promiscuous as alley cats, but I am convinced that this is another judgement which has been warped by time's changing value systems. Karen Blixen has gone down in history for her outstanding *Out of Africa*, a bitter-sweet love story. In fact it is a book about the white obsession with the unique, closeted and inevitably doomed lifestyle of colonial Kenya. It was nicely filmed with Meryl Streep and Robert Redford, the movie making much of her love affair with Denys. In fact Denys jilted Karen for Beryl Markham, having found the former an obsessive neurotic, and in truth she wrote much better when Denys was dead and she had left Africa to live a long, sad life in Scandinavia.

Karen Blixen is not remembered as one of the great libertines of Kenya's white mischief era, nor was she. Those standards were set by a friend of hers, Lady Diane Broughton, who had been married five times and was having a flamboyant affair with another serial libertine, Joss Hay, Earl of Erroll. Joss Erroll was found in his car shot to death, but he had so many enemies among Kenya's husbands that the identity of the murderer is still a profound mystery.

Karen Blixen was no more than a girl of her time, but she was married to a great philanderer and thus became associated with the white mischief club. She arrived in Kenya on 13 January 1914, newly married to Baron Blixen and very worried about her social status (especially as Sweden had initially supported Germany in the First World War). Karen had married on the rebound after a failed affair with Count Blixen's brother. By common consent Bror was a charming chap, but his great love was elephants, particularly dead ones, and his wife always took second place to his hunting. He had a taste for native women and is said to have given Karen syphilis. As he commonly slept with Masai girls among whom gonococcal syphilis is endemic this seems likely, but Blor never displayed signs of the disease himself. Karen was forced home to Sweden for years of painful arsenic-based treatments. Her marriage, even though she did not acknowledge it or ever sue for divorce, was essentially over, but by then she had met and been fascinated by the odd aesthetic presence of Denys Finch Hatton. The story has it that Denys took her off on an elephant safari, taught her to shoot lions and seduced her – legend has it to the sounds of Strauss, but I think it is much more likely that the African night got to them as it has to so many people, including me.

Whatever the case, Denys was soon sharing a bed with another remarkable Kenya pioneer, Beryl Markham, who was actually born in the country (her father trained Lord Delamere's horses). Beryl's place in history has been secured by the fact that she was the first woman to fly the Atlantic solo from east to west. She is also rumoured to have had an illegitimate son by the king of England's brother, the Duke of Gloucester.

The hills around Nairobi up to Lake Naivasha became known as 'Happy Valley'. But Bartle Bull reminds us, 'to see the Happy Valley set as representative of Kenya settlers, however, is historical perjury. As Lord Cranford put it "their existence means nothing to the real life of the colony".' This I somewhat disagree with. They gave Kenya an exotic flavour which no other African tourist country possessed and you can still smell a whiff of it today. It was also no easy place to carve out a living, even if much of the country did look like paradise. Karen and Bror's coffee farm 'under the Ngong Hills', at which they worked industriously, went bankrupt. Denys ran several little businesses to make ends meet. For years and years Lord Delamere did 'work like a black'. But they also drank an ocean of champagne, seduced all the interesting, sexy women, and lived life to the full – or rather, until it overflowed. Suffice it to say that Kenya in its pioneering days produced some extraordinary men and women.

Part of the process was, sadly, to clear the wilderness of its wildlife and in this the settlers were assisted by the local dominant tribe, the Masai. It is not that the Masai actively dislike wildlife, but it takes second place to their cattle. The *raison d'être* of any Masai is to possess as many cattle (and as much grass for them to graze upon) as he can lay his hands on, and as a result the outlook for wildlife was not good when the Europeans arrived. Today the effects of these tribal attitudes can be clearly seen in parts of modern Kenya. The Masai also refused any work with the settlers except in cattle- and camp-guarding.

Masai *moran* believe that they have been placed on this earth by god to protect cattle. Unfortunately this means any cattle, so cattle raiding, cattle rustling and the general succouring of cattle can be considered a kind of divine work for a Masai. Anything interfering with this process was simply eliminated: lion that killed cattle, elephants that might knock down a family *manyatta* and, in the old days, Kikuyu, Kamba, Luo and white farmers who should have known better than to keep cattle. Today, the Masai, still one of Kenya's most successful tribes, are also one of the most influential thanks to their obdurate attitude towards cattle, reality politics and, by extension, to wildlife. As I will explain later, paradoxically this attitude could contain the seeds of the only long-term plan for wildlife which is ever likely to work in Kenya.

While Happy Valley played, the modern stereotype of the great white hunter was being forged from a new realisation of what wildlife actually represented for Kenya – a *sustainable* resource. The mould from which this realisation emerged was cast largely by one individual, yet another Scot with a love of the great outdoors, the aptly named J. A. Hunter.

In 1905 Hunter went to work as a security guard protecting the Lunatic Line from man-eaters. This gave him the right to hunt from its carriages and he was soon bagging lions, leopards, antelope, giraffe and even the odd elephant. Rich tourists travelling to Uganda, including a few with the money to contemplate an expensive safari, soon got to hear of him and Hunter began to accept commissions to take these amateurs out. For example, he led the first ever paid safari to the fabulous Ngorongoro Crater in Tanzania.

At about the same time real concerns began to be expressed at the huge bags turning up at the ivory markets from the likes of Karamojo Bell. As the twentieth century opened, 'the need to conserve' was a phrase in circulation even among professional elephant hunters. In 1900 an international conference for the protection of wild animals was held in London. Admittedly its main outcome was a call for a ban on the export of ivory tusks weighing less than 10lb at a time when the average weight on sale was nearer 20lb, but it was clearly a signal that the harbingers of change were in the ascendancy. There were already a few embryonic 'conservationists' around, like the British High Commissioner in Uganda, Harry Johnston, who condemned the 'ravages of European and American sportsmen as the greatest blot on our twentieth-century civilisation'. Visiting America just before Roosevelt set out on his safari, he also commented publicly: 'If I had my say, I would present a telephoto camera instead of a rifle to the President.' This, as future safaris were to demonstrate, was a suggestion of some prescience and in the years ahead it would be taken up by many.

Some of the desire to control hunting in the lost regions of the African interior stemmed also from opposition to Arab-managed slavery which was still going on apace in these primitive places. Sir Harry had been very active in opposing slavery, and slavery and the ivory trade were, quite rightly, still seen as one. But the truth was that Africa still had millions of elephants and most of the western angst expressed against hunting and slavery disguised a dislike of Arab control of the ivory trade and in a sense of primitive Africa. This was reflected earlier by Livingstone's plaints against Arab slavers and ivory traders (upon whom he was often entirely dependent, indeed several times owing them his life) when he himself was happy to turn a blind eye to slavers like the Batonka, among whom he attempted to set up a mission, provided they operated under a British (or his own) sphere of influence.

If there is one home truth that will spill inexorably from these pages it is that there will only be elephants left alive in Africa if Africans have a vested commercial interest in keeping them alive. I have come to realise that unless this reality underscores western plans to influence the conservation of wildlife and wildlife habitats in Africa, such plans are not worth the paper they are written on.

For almost as long as elephants have been hunted there has been a tenuous awareness that stocks have to be managed. Lobengula practised a form of conservation in his elephant hunting reserve, so did the Egyptians and so, 700 years previously, did the Emperor of all the Tartars, Kublai Khan, who by then controlled three-quarters of the world and had come to appreciate the value of elephants for sport and war. He also knew that their numbers were finite. The Great Khan, according to Marco Polo, planted grains to feed the wild birds he hunted with hawks while seated on an elephant, and the penalty for neglecting a royal elephant was death. Lobengula once fined Selous and two other hunters when they killed elephants against his rules.

Successive governments in southern Africa, where the extermination threat to elephants was first recognised, sought to rein in
hunting to little avail until, in 1883, professional hunters formed the
private Natal Game Protection Association. Their motives were not
entirely altruistic – they wanted first call via a licensing system on
what little game was left – but at least it was a start. America had
made an earlier and better start, setting up the Yellowstone
National Park in 1872 to protect the last buffalo. South Africa
introduced a similar emergency rescue of the southern elephant in
1898 with the creation of the Sabi, later Kruger, Game Reserve.

But this was not conservation as we know it. That was still three
decades away. Hunters were essentially still in control and the
motivation behind all of these initiatives was to sustain a valuable
African resource which was rapidly falling below levels which could
support a booming industry, the safari business. The most valuable
unit in this business was still the elephant, both for hunters and
wilderness enthusiasts, and a growing number of people booking
safaris were keen to shoot with a camera rather than a gun. The
mighty elephant was of course the animal everyone wanted to
record on film, and within a very short period the embryonic
cinema industry began to realise that elephants and 'great white
hunters' (with the odd redhead, blonde or brunette hanging
decoratively on their chest wigs) were what the cinema-going public
wanted to see. Here was a resource that really was unique to the
African continent and to Kenya in particular.

The first wildlife picture, the business in which for thirty years I
earned a good and very interesting living, was reportedly taken in
1863 by a German explorer using glass coated with 'negative'. Not
surprisingly it was of a group of elephants. 'Photographic
apparatus' was, according to Frederick Courteney Selous, carried by
a French client of his on a safari to the Zambesi valley in 1886.
Serious wildlife photography using Goerz lenses (comparable at
least in acuity to almost anything used today) arrived in the shape
of Herr C.G. Schilling and a safari of 170 porters carrying 60lb
loads. I have seen some of the original Schilling plates and although
they are only monochrome, the resolution he obtained from the use
of oversized negatives measuring 16 × 20in is incredible. Schilling
took hundreds of elephant pictures. He also used techniques to

restrain the game he photographed, such as heavy metal leg traps, which would not be accepted today, and he baited for predators with other animals. That is not to say, and I speak from experience, that the morality of the film-making community has changed much.

The man who first publicly promoted colour photography was the future King Edward VIII of England, then David, Prince of Wales. He mounted a very famous safari to Africa in 1928 and is known to have taken with him one of the very first Eastman Kodak colour movie cameras. David was as much interested in photographing game as shooting it, which surprised most safari leaders of the time, although not the man he chose to lead the royal expedition, Denys Finch Hatton.

Movie photography was first introduced professionally by an American couple, Martin and Osa Johnson, who in 1924 brought state-of-the-art equipment (although the cameras were still hand-cranked) including camera-cars and two Sikorsky aeroplanes to make a professional film. George Eastman, founder of the Eastman Kodak Company, put $10,000 dollars into their project, a huge amount in those days and one that reflected how Africa was becoming popular with the general public. He went on a safari in Kenya with the inventive Johnsons (it was Osa who did most of the hunting for the pot) and supervised their use of new film stocks. These movie pioneers built the foundations for a hugely profitable industry which kept the safari industry in the black for years and greatly enhanced the cause of elephant conservation.

In later years perhaps the most famous film ever made in Kenya, *Born Free* (1966), produced – as a direct consequence of the treatment of an elephant in the film – one of the most active elephant conservation ginger groups around today. Pole Pole, as this actor-elephant was called, was shot at Regent's Park Zoo in controversial circumstances after allegedly going 'berserk'. The stars of *Born Free*, Virginia McKenna and the late Bill Travers, were so angered by these events that they formed Zoo Check, which later became the Born Free Foundation and today is run by their son, Will Travers.

In the early years of the twentieth century the focus of Europe's commercial interest in African ivory shifted north, first to the territories of East Africa (Kenya, Tanganyika and later Uganda), then even further up the continent to the Great Lakes and the Sudan. The south was regarded as 'hunted out', although by today's standards there were still large herds of elephants lurking behind 'the Fly' in western Rhodesia (Zimbabwe) and Bechuanaland (Botswana).

The pioneer hunter turned safari leader J.A. Hunter led his first ever party of paying travellers to the Ngorongoro Crater in Tanzania. Some eighty or so years later in 1984, I made a film for ITV in Ngorongoro with Solomon Ole Saibul, a young Masai and the first African to be given the awesome task of running the Tanzanian National Parks Department after decades of white administrators. For the very first time an indigenous black man (and a Masai at that) was given a platform to present African views about the wildlife of Africa – and these views raised a lot of eyebrows.

Ngorongoro is essentially a vast game trap and truly the eighth wonder of the world. The crater of an extinct volcano, it is thick with animals, resident and visiting, who have one thing in common: once in the crater they are too lazy to climb the steep walls out (only the elephants are the exception to this rule). Over the centuries the bowl has achieved a natural balance of predators and prey, foragers and browsers, and hunters and scavengers. The whole thing is surrounded by an extraordinary, misty mountain forest draped in Spanish moss.

The crater is 10 miles in diameter with a typical crater lake at the centre of it. All the big cats can be found on its floor including leopards and a good population of cheetah. Lion numbers hover around 100. Some 2,000 buffalo call the place home. Elephants come and go, culling the trees as elephants do, so that some years there are 50 to be seen, other years none. A further 25,000 grazing animals and their associated predators pack every foot of crater left. All this in a piece of land that can be driven across in less than half an hour!

'Few areas in the world are left with such a variety of animals in such large numbers', Saibul told me. 'It is different from the rest of Africa, indeed from the rest of the world.' Ironically, indeed sadly, that might have been true back in 1984 but it is not true today.

Indeed Ngorongoro has become the African conservation problem in microcosm. What evolves here may be a model for the rest of the southern continent and help us in our search for a long-term solution to the plight of the African elephant. The writing was on the wall, however, all those years ago.

Saibul first saw Ngorongoro as a young student when he was already deeply committed to African nationalism. 'At the time there was a controversy between the Masai and the colonial administration who wanted to protect Ngorongoro as park. My reaction at that time was that protecting an area for animals rather than people was wrong. That, coupled with the fact that the quarrel was between the colonialists and my own people, put me definitely on the side against the park.' I cannot tell you what trouble this statement got us both into when I transmitted it on British primetime commercial television in a series of programmes called *Nature Watch*, presented by my good friend Julian Pettifer. There was literally a shock-horror reaction from the World Wildlife Fund and from the emerging *enfants terribles* of the conservation movement, Friends of the Earth and Greenpeace. Was this Saibul creature really going to take over Ngorongoro – the brightest jewel in the crown of the mighty Tanzanian Game Department whose territory included the vast Serengeti and Selous National Parks? (It didn't help that Ole, as he liked to be called, was, like his boss President Julius Nyerere, quite patently a Communist!)

The controversy smouldered on. Saibul was at university when an official committee of inquiry came out from Britain to resolve what had become known as 'The Serengeti Question' (Ngorongoro is part of the Serengeti ecosystem). Five years later a compromise was reached which Saibul, now a rising civil administrator, thought might be 'a lasting solution'. I wrote in the *Nature Watchers*, 'It was agreed that the animals would be protected but that the Masai would continue to live in the conservation area, which encompassed Ngorongoro, at peace with the animals. So the stage seemed set for an ideal experiment in cohabitation, a test that conservationists badly needed then if they were to resolve similar problems of confrontation the length and breadth of Africa.' It is a very salutary thought, though, that I wrote that line more than thirty years ago and the problems of cohabitation have still largely to be resolved.

One of the most hopeful projects in Kenya (Ol Pejeta) is about to try to address it as I go to press.

Initially, Ole Saibul admitted, all the signs pointed to success in Ngorongoro. With their nomadic lifestyle and mobile food supply he was confident that the Masai would not farm the bush and kill the game that invaded their crops, as other tribes were doing all over Africa. Nor would they set up permanent houses that would grow into villages, towns and cities, ousting wildlife. Finally, the experiment was to be monitored by a Masai – himself, the young nationalist Saibul, who loved his country and its wildlife heritage but was sympathetic to political realities.

This young man then found himself in an extraordinary position. Tanzania became independent from Britain and Saibul was offered the job of conservator of the whole huge conservation area; he was to take over from a long line of chief game wardens who had ruled the Ngorongoro and the Serengeti with a feudal autocracy which the naturally well-disciplined Masai had resented but respected.

'I came here to take over about ten years after I had first visited the place as a boy', Ole recalled. 'I immediately found it very attractive and started getting interested in wildlife and conservation. At that time I had no background at all in these things. I read everything I could find on the Ngorongoro and started spending a lot of time in the crater itself. That interest has just gone on and on; even today I can stay in the crater all day and still find something new.'

By the time of this conversation some years later Ole had become a government minister and had started to face up to the questions of whether man, especially the rural Masai, could cohabit with animals. Saibul decided to make the parks for which he was now responsible his first priority. He and his ranger force fought the first of what would become known as 'the wildlife wars', involving a number of characters who will feature large in this book. The rangers were almost all white, however, and Ole, still climbing the Masai hierarchical system, had to tread warily to avoid alienating himself from his people.

In the beginning he tackled the first waves of heavy commercial poaching, which would later become endemic in Kenya and

Tanzania, launched from neighbouring Somalia. Here in the Horn of Africa intertribal war had been going on for years and Somali fighters, known as 'shifta', constantly spilled into neighbouring territory, often just to get away from the fighting but always to pick up some easy loot in the form of rhino horn or elephant ivory.

'It became necessary to station a special, highly mobile force on the floor of the crater to keep track of these poachers', Ole told me. He was very pessimistic about the highly threatened animals, such as black rhino, and he was right. In the mid-1980s white rhino (they are not really black and white: one is a grazer and the Afrikaaners named this animal *weit* (wide) mouthed) went completely extinct in Tanzania and the black suffered the same fate in Ngorongoro.

Saibul wanted to make the crater a no-go zone for poachers but soon came to realise that commercial pressures were at work on elements of the Masai who still resented sharing their grazing lands with wild game. 'The crater is really like a fortress. It's not easy for any poacher to enter undetected, but we continued to lose rhino. I was forced to accept that the killers were already in the fortress and that we were in real trouble.'

While not accepting this killing (it was essentially against their tradition), the Masai in general closed ranks when it came to protecting the renegades just as they had always done. It used to be said that they were the only major tribe in Africa who were never colonised. Both German and British rulers in Tanganyika more or less left the Masai to go their nomadic way. Even the missionaries made little impact, and the fabric of Masai culture has remained largely intact to this day. This fierce independence is the product of the Masai's singular lifestyle. They are cattle herders living on a highly nutritious diet composed largely of blood and milk, both taken from live cattle, giving the Masai an assured source of food and great mobility. You can't starve the Masai out any more than you can box them in. Game, which they did not need to kill for food, had survived well in their company.

Furthermore the Masai homeland is located to the north of the Serengeti National Park, and had thus always been a dangerous place for intruders from other tribes, especially trespassing Somalis. But when rhino horns began to fetch huge sums on the black market because of the Arab tradition that the Prophet Mohammed's dagger had a rhino-horn handle and the Chinese belief that the horn has aphrodisiac and medicinal qualities (even today it is as least as valuable as gold), Ngorongoro's ancient saurians were doomed. 'The truth is that the Masai cannot be frozen in time, insulated against all temptation, in order for them to remain part of the tourist landscape,' Saibul concluded, and he decided to evict the resident Masai from the Ngorongoro and the nearby Empakai Crater.

The Ngorongoro Masai, more used to the ways of the world, moved on without much trouble, Saibul remembered. 'I think they had grown tired of the daily tourists relegating them to the role of the wild animals they lived among.' But with the seven families living in the Empakai it was a different story:

> My father had died the year before and one of the elders came up to me and asked, 'Where is your father?'
>
> I replied, 'He is dead.'
>
> 'We know,' the elder told me, 'and this should be the last time you come to this crater, otherwise we will make sure you follow your father.'
>
> At the same time this man had started to shake like an elder, and the ranger who was with me cocked his rifle! I asked the elder, 'If you, an elder, are going to shake with rage, what should this warrior (my ranger) do now?'
>
> The elder said, 'He may do as he pleases!'

Ole backed off. '"Warriors obey elders", I conceded. He repeated that I should not come back to the crater and I told him he had until Saturday to leave.'

Come Saturday they were still there and Ole, at the head of a detachment of the army, went into the crater throwing thunder-flashes and flares. Some of the Masai moved but the die-hards just sat tight and armed themselves. When he went forward to arrest them one of them came at him with a *panga* (a short sword). 'One of the sergeants raised his rifle and ordered him to stop his arm, which thankfully he did. I took away their spears and swords but left them their sticks. It is very bad to disarm a Masai and take away everything.'

I have told this story of thirty years ago because it contains a lesson for Africa which conservationists failed to hear then and are still failing to hear now. Moreover, it has occurred to me in the telling that if we had better respected the experiences of the first black conservationists we would not have made many of the mistakes committed since. More simply, the West, tainted with the colonial legacy, cannot tell Africa what to do. In this case Saibul's reputation with the Masai was damaged by his becoming effectively a colonial game policeman.

J.A. Hunter, hunting elephant for a living back at the beginning of the twentieth century, went about all this in another way and enjoyed amazing relations with the Masai for which he has never been properly recognised. As a start he sat down and listened to their tales of woe. Ngorongoro lions, he was told, were wreaking havoc on the 'divine cattle'. J.A. studied the large black-maned beasts that had only collected in the area because there were so many juicy cattle around. He hunted them mercilessly with a pack of 'kangaroo hounds', eventually killing several hundred. The delighted Masai told him to regard himself as one of them and invited him back to hunt the crater whenever he wanted. (I should remind my readers that there is an abundance of fine lions in Ngorongoro today.)

By the 1920s he had been working as a government control officer for several years. He was still very sympathetic to African attitudes and, recognising that times were changing, he knew colonial wildlife policies had to change too. The Masai came to him again and pointed out that their herds had grown but were once more being decimated by an excess of lions and leopards. Again J.A. stepped in, this time for the government, but shot only eighty-six lions and ten leopards over a period of three months. Nonetheless, the Masai were delighted with his selective cull and they asked the Game Department to sell him to them for 500 head of cattle.

The Wakamba had a similar problem with black rhino on their Machakos range – J.A. 'took out' 163. This is many more rhino than there were in Kenya as a whole in the mid-1980s, but all these animals were culled on government-authorised control programmes. J.A. is credited in his lifetime with having killed 350 buffalo, 1,000 black rhino, hundreds of lions and 1,400 elephants. (Control officers kept one of the tusks as their pay and could buy the other one at a concession rate of 1 shilling per pound.)

According to the conservation values of today all this reads like a horror story, but it may also be the African reality. J.A. Hunter was practising reality politics at least seventy-five years ahead of his time. Behind the scenes in game departments across the whole of Africa wild animals which persistently destroy crops (usually elephants) or threaten or kill people are quietly being shot: this was a major theme of my 2002 film for the BBC's *Natural World* series, 'Man-Eaters of Tsavo'. We filmed the shooting of a renegade lion by control wardens. What seemed to shock my viewers, however, was not so much the shooting of this rogue animal but the revelation that it was an everyday event around Tsavo. On the adjoining Galana cattle ranch a professional hunter was called in two or three times a year to 'keep down' the lions. Much the same rules applied to aberrant elephants. Again I would ask, have western conservation policies essentially failed in Africa because they were colonial in their nature, perceived as anti-African and took little, if any, account of African priorities?

J.A. Hunter had the interests of Africa and Africans in his blood. While still obliged to take clients out on hunting safaris, he often held them in contempt. He wrote of Americans who shot until the barrels of their rifles were too hot to handle as having 'trigger itch'. Wild beasts were not the problem, he said, far more dangerous were the clients. On his first Ngorongoro safari an American client shot a large impala and afterwards asked J.A. if he 'would mind steaming the horns to stretch the ferrules and get a record', a proposal J.A. rejected with contempt.

Sadly, Kenya's wildlife professionals could not do without these foreigners. They gave African hunting, or to put that more accurately the slow destruction of Africa's wildlife, a new lease of life. Every boat from Europe bought dozens of would-be hunters to Kenya. Safari outfitting boomed and in its peak year before the First World War, Newland & Tarlton welcomed 300 clients. But as I have said, a new idea – indeed a new word, 'conservation' – was blowing in the African wind of change.

The man who brought modern conservation in its widest sense to East Africa was Captain Arthur Ritchie. He is widely regarded as the father of the East African national parks network. A woman who knew him well is Daphne Sheldrick, wife of the famous chief warden of Tsavo and today, through the David Sheldrick Memorial Trust, the leading propagandist for Kenya's elephants. When Arthur Ritchie died his young rangers, including David, the man who went on to fight the anti-poaching war in the Serengeti, Myles Turner, and I think Daphne's first husband, the poacher–hunter Bill Woodley, of whom we will hear more later, took Ritchie's remains (I presume at his own request), tied an engine block to the body and buried him at sea off Mombasa.

Ritchie was what you might call 'old school', the type of Kenyan whom Lord Cranford was trying to describe when he pleaded that not all Kenya's white settlers were Happy Valley hell-raisers and serial philanderers. It took about a decade for East Africa to get most of the white mischief out of its system, and during that time Arthur Ritchie set up a 'modern' structure of game 'sanctuaries', which saw hundreds of thousands of acres essentially taken away from Africans and handed over to wildlife, which was then protected and policed by paramilitary colonial wardens and rangers. On these lands wildlife interests took absolute priority. It was a situation the rest of the world applauded. Arthur Ritchie was a paragon and the game system he created worked well. But the price was that across the length and breadth of British Africa many dedicated hunter-tribes were rendered landless and severed from their cultural wildife-based traditions. Some, like the Waliangula, would eventually almost die out.

For a brief time after the First World War the young men left alive – the 'precious few' – especially the young men with money and titles, partied as if there was no tomorrow, particularly in Kenya which by southern African standards was cosmopolitan, sophisticated and what my father used to call 'louche'. These were the aptly named Roaring Twenties. Teddy Roosevelt had started the precedent with his six months of elegant, indulged safari-ing in 1909. He had followed in a tradition already established by British royals and sub-royals like Winston Churchill's father, Lord Randolph Churchill, the Duke of Blenheim. The duke spent an estimated £70,000 on his safari, hiring one of the first professionals, Hans Lee, as his hunter-guide. The total cost for the dozens of black staff was only £100 a month and Lord Randolph was forced to lighten his loads when his safari reached Salisbury in my native Rhodesia. Notes of the trip record that among the luxuries disposed of were copious quantities of *eau de toilette* and trade beads on which he made a profit of 250 per cent from the natives. Lord Randolph, in fact, had all the qualifications for a rich safari client of the time, not least that he too was a serial philanderer suffering from terminal syphilis. Thankfully he was an indifferent hunter and shot very little.

He wrote articles on his safari for the *Daily Graphic* at 100 guineas a time and, while notoriously bad tempered, was a gifted, acerbic writer like his son. Months of the most elegant travel that money and influence could buy generated comments like: 'The idea of galloping at full speed on a second rate horse through the thick bush, chased by a lion was singularly unpleasant to me.' He stayed with Cecil Rhodes, loathed him, but confessed he had tolerated the experience because it was 'the only place in this God-forsaken country where I can get Perrier-Jouet '74'. But he was more subtle in his observation of people, forecasting that 'upon the pages of African history the Transvaal Boer will leave a shadow of a dark reputation and an evil name'. That name, of course, would be known and eventually vilified worldwide as apartheid.

In 1907 Winston Churchill, then the very young British Colonial Secretary, was a guest of Lord Delamere at Soysambu and also enjoyed riding at break-neck speeds across the open veld, but the shift away from the mindless killing of wildlife had already started. Winston was both relieved not to have to kill a lion himself and a trifle mocking of Delamere: 'Nothing causes the colonialist more concern than that his guest should have been provided with a lion.'

However, by 1928 Kenya had a sophisticated tourist–hunter safari infrastructure running round the clock. It provided employment for at least a dozen fully professional hunters as skilled in diplomacy and people management as they were with a rifle, and as many again who combined safari work with diverse businesses and farming. The industry was about to enter its halcyon days and it did so in style with the future king of England, indeed with the 'heir' and the 'spare' – David, Prince of Wales, and his brother, the

Duke of Gloucester. They tried to hire J.A. Hunter to lead their safari but he was out with rich American clients who refused to give way to the British royals. Denys Finch Hatton was engaged in Hunter's place. A celebratory dinner was held at the Muthaiga Club attended by, among others, Captain Arthur Ritchie, who was heard to utter a famous admonition which rather epitomises where this story has got to: 'There is a limit, even in Kenya,' Ritchie exploded. 'When someone offers cocaine to the Heir to the Throne, something has to be done about it, particularly when it is between courses at the dinner table!'

SEVEN

The End of the Game

The Prince of Wales's two expeditions in the late 1920s introduced seminal changes to the safari scene. It was certainly the end of the era in which most white hunters regarded tourist safaris as an activity they were obliged to engage in only when there were too few elephants left to seek out in the accessible part of Africa. This was, to a degree, a result of the royals' decision to hire the intelligent Denys Finch Hatton to lead their safaris in 1928 and 1930. It turned out to be an inspired choice. It also put the winter safari on the map as the fashionable thing for rich Europeans to do.

Four years earlier in 1924 it was the prince's brother, the Duke of York, and his new young wife Elizabeth who paved the way. There was much talk about whether Elizabeth would wear shorts on safari. Little did the Kenyan royal-watchers of that time realise that in a few years it would be this shy pair who would rule England, not the dashing Prince of Wales.

David, Prince of Wales (later Edward VIII) has been much vilified down the years for his seeming arrogance in choosing Mrs Simpson in preference to the throne, and for his leanings towards Hitler and Hitler's English groupies, some of the Mitford girls. I once spent several weeks in the company of Diana Mitford while making a television documentary with her husband, Sir Oswald Mosley, and she convinced me there was more to David than these wartime judgements suggest. It took enormous moral courage, she thought, given the forces raised against him, to stand by the divorced Mrs Simpson and remain her devoted husband until his death. Be that as it may, it was David, as a result of the joy and excitement of his first safari, who pushed through the British House of Lords a Finch Hatton proposal which amounted to the first modern conservation plan to control the hunting of elephant and other animals in East Africa.

Denys recorded that David was an extraordinarily fit, tough and brave man on safari, as interested in photography as he was in shooting with a rifle, although he did both well. The high point of the prince's second safari, for which Denys had called in Bror von Blixen to help with the hunting, was a long and arduous elephant hunt. Blixen was amazed at the young prince's endurance. 'He makes the greatest demands on himself', Blixen wrote in his autobiography after watching David cheerfully track elephants through thick bush for 20 miles near Mount Kilimanjaro without getting in a single shot. 'He is one of the three or four toughest sportsmen I have ever been out with, perhaps the toughest of them all.'

Finch Hatton turned out to be a safari leader of genius. Indeed he cast the mould for future safari planning. His attention to detail was legendary. 'Method', he wrote, 'maketh the man.' He told J.A. Hunter (who was no slouch himself) that the real secret of ordering stores was to be able to 'estimate the life of a tin of sardines'. There was a 'law of averages, the mathematics of which will teach you that one pound of tea will last one man a fortnight, the same man a week to finish a pound of marmalade, and ten days to finish a tin of plum jam'. A polymorph as I have said, he combined this almost pedantic efficiency with extraordinary and eccentric personal behaviour. Denys, tall and very handsome but losing his hair, was famous for his collection of hats – topees, a blue bowler which he wore quite casually, double terais, homburgs and a silken collapsible opera hat. He regularly flew to England to attend a single performance of a beloved opera when such flights could take days. Lord Cranford described him as 'possessed of more gifts than one man has a right to'.

During the course of his affair with Karen Blixen he taught her to read Latin and Greek, played the guitar and sang to her. He bought her a Graphonola and played records of *Don Giovanni* and Schubert's 'Trout' Quintet. Handel's 'Where e'er you walk' was her favourite record. He also outlined the plots of the plays of Shakespeare for her. She responded with her own story ideas. One of Denys's favourite poets was, surprisingly, the socialist Walt Whitman, whom he could quote verbatim, particularly one piece from 'Song of Myself' that reflected his own ideas about animals.

I think I could turn and live with animals, they are so placid
  and self-contain'd.
I stand and look at them long and long.
They do not sweat and whine about their condition,
They do not lie awake in the dark and weep for their sins,
They do not make me sick discussing their duty to God,
Not one is dissatisfied, not one is demented with the mania of
  owning things,
Not one kneels to another, nor to his kind that lived thousands
  of years ago,
Not one is respected or unhappy over the whole earth.
So they show their relations to me, and I accept them,
They bring me tokens of myself, they evince them plainly in
  their possession.

On safari with the Prince of Wales, Denys soon learnt that he was
dealing with a man very used to having his own way, and this led to
a famous encounter which seems to have laid the grounds for the
relationship they later enjoyed. Knowing very little fear, David
insisted on getting close-up photographs of animals, especially the
more formidable big game. Denys was standing behind him while
he photographed a black rhino that was getting much too close.
Eventually Finch Hatton dropped the beast with a well-aimed
bullet.

'How dare you shoot without an order?' David demanded. 'I
wanted him close.' Denys told the prince calmly that if the heir to
the throne was killed on his safari, he would have no other option
but to go behind a tree and blow his own brains out.

They became extremely good friends and when Denys's fears
about the future of African wildlife grew serious he turned to the
prince for help. These concerns became public when Denys wrote a
letter to *The Times* in May 1929 protesting at what he called 'the
apathy displayed by the Tanganyika authorities towards the
wholesale slaughter from motor cars which has been going on for
over two years in flagrant infringement of the existing Game Laws
of the country'. He went on to quote from a professional hunter,
Andries Pienaar:

Last year a certain American entered an African territory with a film operator. The tales he [Pienaar] told of shooting by this gentleman are absolutely disgusting. Animals are raced down by the car before being shot. The buffalo bag alone was thirty-seven head, bulls, cows and youngsters being killed indiscriminately. Besides having the word of a reliable man who confesses to have got sick of the butchery, I also saw photographs of the dead animals.

Two years ago I met yet another party of Americans in East Africa. They had already killed 21 lions from the car. One morning they left camp with the words 'Let us shoot every living thing that we can find today and see what is possible in one day.' These words were repeated by the party's professional hunter and he might be accused of not being over-sentimental on the subject.

And what shall we say of the two gentlemen who entered the Serengeti by motor car and killed between them eighty lions? Can one think of anything more nauseating? No, worse than that, these men find circles abroad where they are admired. They figure in magazines as 'Famous Big Game Hunters'. The party who had the 37 buffaloes filled the American magazines with their pictures and tales of prowess for weeks on end. These are facts not fancies. I have no hesitation in saying that the truly revolting picture which his letter gives of the methods and manners of these licensed butchers are not exaggerated in any way.

I find it difficult to assemble words to express an opinion of an Administration which has had full knowledge of this disgraceful state of affairs for over two years, and which, though provided with the necessary legal machinery to deal with the situation and with officers whose express duties are the maintenance of game laws, persists in abstaining from the simple and inexpensive measures required to put an end to this hideous abuse.

Denys Finch Hatton, Mombasa, 1929

This arrow was aimed straight and true at the heart of the British colonial administration and it had an immediate effect. Denys had timed his letter to coincide with a visit to a conservation committee of the League of Nations by Douglas Jardine, Chief Secretary to the Government of Tanganyika.

Jardine replied via *The Times* in July 1929. He decried, 'as a sportsman myself', excessive hunting of animals from cars but he condemned as 'reckless' Denys's statement that his secretariat had done nothing to 'prevent such outrages to the sportsman's code'. He pointed out that the Serengeti, where it was said to be happening, was the size of Scotland and that the outrages were the work of 'tourists with more money than taste' slipping across from Kenya in 'swift and sometimes armoured cars'. Some people had already been caught and fined, Jardine pointed out, but fines were not an effective deterrent to wealthy offenders. 'Mr. Finch Hatton complains that the Tanganyika Government is inclined to adopt a policy of wholesale game destruction and that we will allow natives to kill as much as they like. This insinuation is definitely untrue.'

It is interesting to note what a change of opinion, public and official, this letter represents. Ten years previously no one, let alone a hunter like Finch Hatton, would have thought to stir up such a hornets' nest and I seriously doubt that *The Times* would have bothered to print it. (There were forty professional lion hunters operating out of Nairobi in 1906.) The newspaper exchange showed that conservation was at last coming, albeit kicking and screaming, into the hunters' world.

Denys replied to Jardine the following day. He pinpointed the area where the slaughter had happened (an area of open bush near Lake Natron), claiming it would be impossible for a party of 'shootists' operating from motor cars to remain undetected by the game ranger. He had discussed the issue with the game warden of the Tanganyika Territory who, while sympathetic, doubted that the government would agree to close the area for hunting. (This, so far as I know, is the first time a professional hunter had called for an area of famous game country to be closed to hunters.) Denys went on to outline repeated efforts he had made to have a native ranger he had trained sent to the area. The ranger, said Finch Hatton, was still waiting in Nairobi for transport to the Serengeti, proving his previous allegation that the Tanganyika government had known for more than two years of the 'wanton destruction of lions and other game taking place in the Serengeti plain'.

'These are not, as Mr. Jardine pretends, reckless statements', Denys declared, pulling no punches. 'They are indisputable facts which are well known as an open scandal to most people interested in the Preservation of Game [his capitals] in East Africa.' And as his *coup de grâce* he told Jardine that the bloodbath was not going on in territory the size of Scotland but in 'a small definite area, about the size of Greater London'. Finally, he countered Jardine's denial that the natives had been given the right to kill all the wildlife they liked by quoting a report made to the League of Nations in 1927 in which Tanganyika declared that it would not prosecute natives for breaches of the game laws 'unless in flagrant and exceptional cases'. (The Serengeti is Masai country and as I mentioned earlier even in those days the colonial administrators had decided that it was all but impossible to control the tribe.) 'It has been my experience and that of several of my friends that since the issue of the instructions mentioned in this quotation in many districts there has been no sort of control of the killing of game by the natives, who are able in fact to kill as much as they like.'

Here, most interestingly, Denys revealed his hand, the issue that was really concerning him. Fifty years later I would go to the Serengeti and make a film called *The Animal War* in which the legendary anti-poacher warden, Myles Turner, made *exactly* the same statement. 'Before I left Africa', said Denys, way back in 1927, 'I was authoritatively informed that it was the intention of the [Tanganyika] Government to introduce amendments to the Game Ordinance in which the principle would definitely be laid down that game was considered to be the property of the natives. This would in my opinion be the beginning of the end.'

Before doing the research for this book I had never come across Denys Finch Hatton's prescient observation and it really is hard to believe that the stumbling block of African compliance on which, in my opinion, all of modern conservation has foundered was being raised, indeed debated, by the British Parliament almost 100 years ago. Admittedly Denys, a latent conservationist, did not accept that African game really is the property of Africans to do with as they wish, but I doubt that any settler of those days, especially those involved in the game industry, would have accepted that statement.

The story of Finch Hatton has a bitter-sweet ending but it is not the one that Karen Blixen wrote in *Out of Africa*. Anyone can tell you that tragic tale: Denys had planned a trip to Voi in Tsavo in his little yellow Gypsy Moth aircraft and Karen, or so she claims, had asked if she could go with him. He refused.

'It was the first time', she wrote in her whimsical style, 'that I had asked Denys to fly me in his aeroplane that he would not do it. When he started in his car for the aerodrome in Nairobi and had turned down the drive he came back for a volume of poems that he had given me, and that he now wanted on his journey. He stood with one foot on the running board of his car, reading out a poem that we had been discussing. "Here are your grey geese," he said.'

Denys flew to Voi, crashed and burned. Karen, distraught, buried him in the Ngong Hills near the farm and read the 'The Grey Geese', a poem written for him by Iris Tree, at the graveside.

> I saw grey geese flying over the flatlands,
> Wild geese vibrant in the high air,
> Unswerving from horizon to horizon
> And the grey whiteness of them ribboning the enormous
>   skies
> And the spokes of the sun over the crumpled hills.

Denys's family placed a brass plaque on the grave in the Ngong inscribed with a line from the *Rime of the Ancient Mariner* by Samuel Taylor Coleridge:

> He prayeth well, who loveth well
> Both Man and Bird and Beast.

Thus died one of Africa's more cultured elephant hunters, but what Karen Blixen's account does not say is that he left the world the most extraordinary legacy. Denys Finch Hatton is remembered as an aristocratic fringe member of the Happy Valley set and the lover of a writer who went on to become world famous. He should also be remembered as the founding father of what was once the greatest gathering place for plains elephants in Africa, Tanzania's Serengeti National Park.

Denys's acrimonious exchanges in the London *Times* led to a white paper being introduced in the House of Lords promoted by the Prince of Wales. It established a very early form of elephant conservation in the Serengeti area, leading a few years later to the promulgation of the Serengeti National Park and arguably to the creation of other famous parks like the Selous and the Masai Mara in Kenya.

The unlikely concept of hunter as hero was ideally suited to the media phenomenon which was packing American and European custom-built palaces, odeons, and alhambras housing a device called a cinematograph. These cinemas (which quickly proved to be gold-mines) showed movies made mainly in a town of tar-paper shacks in the desert of California, Hollywood.

Rich Americans like President Roosevelt who had learned their big game hunting in East Africa's rich wilderness had so raved about the place that it started to attract beasts more lowly on the social scale, including one who fancied himself a great hunter. In 1934 the young, affluent American writer Ernest Hemingway went to Kenya for the first time, talked an old but famous hunter, Phillip Percival, out of retirement and so fell in love with the country that he would write two excellent books about it. *The Macomber Affair* and *The Snows of Kilimanjaro* would change the image of Kenya for ever and would upgrade the African elephant from the status of prime bag to national star attraction.

Both books were quickly made into star-studded films with Gregory Peck (in both), Joan Bennett, Susan Hayward and Ava Gardner playing the leads. The films literally set Kenya apart from the rest of Africa. Other countries with almost equal wildlife attractions like Zimbabwe and South Africa cannot to this day quite comprehend why Kenya was always the place tourists thought of first when contemplating a trip to Africa. The answer is these films.

Later *Mogambo*, starring Ava Gardner, Clark Gable and Grace Kelly, went on location to Tanganyika to stir the public's interest in the 'real' Africa and by then (1952) huge picture budgets were the order of the day. *Mogambo* was filmed from what amounted to a satellite tent-city employing hundreds of safari organisers and their native staff. Bunny Allen, an elephant hunter turned safari organiser, set up 300 tents, built an 1,800ft airstrip, installed a generator so that the stars could run their hair dryers and watch MGM films in the evening, and supplied the place using a convoy of 50 Bedford trucks and an airlift operated by three Dakotas. Frank Sinatra had recently married the 21-year-old, hard-drinking Ava Gardner and, concerned that Clark Gable was recently divorced, he flew in to keep an eye on her. While they argued in their tent, however, Gable was quietly consoling himself next door with Grace Kelly.

Ernest Hemingway himself sadly appears to have succumbed to Kenya's other safari addiction, the 'sundowner'. Consistently 'under the weather', he sought out Phillip Percival again (Percival was still shooting cattle-killing lions on his seventy-sixth birthday!) but rapidly alienated the old hunter by shaving his head, wearing ochre-coloured Masai clothes, hunting with a spear, doing Annie Oakley shooting tricks with a .22 rifle, and having a fling with a young Wakamba. Percival finally told Hemingway that his behaviour was a disgrace. (There is a small plaque on the wall of a hotel in Schruns near Gargellen in Austria where I go skiing which records the spot where Hemingway finally brought his troubled life to an abrupt end.)

It is at about this time that this history begins to connect intimately with my own. One dark winter's morning in 1947, an extraordinary vehicle drew up at the front door of our bungalow in Brighton and stood (from the perspective of a boy of nine) breathing smoke and fire like a dragon. All the neighbours rushed outside to see it. I can remember wondering what an object so alien could possibly be doing there. In fact it crossed my mind that perhaps the Germans weren't beaten and had invaded sleepy Brighton after all. The vehicle was certainly military and still painted camouflage green but, peeping from behind our front lounge net curtains, I saw that 'Uncle' Ken Stowell was sitting grinning at the wheel and beside him, grinning even more fiercely, was my dad.

This was my first meeting with 'Shaky', the American Dodge Desert Command Car which a few months hence would carry me overland to Africa. Ken Stowell and Len Brown had bought it 'war-surplus' in Bristol. They were both slightly wounded veterans, my father from the RAF and Ken from the British infantry. Len was at that time a lowly meter-reader with Brighton Council, the only job he could get in poverty-stricken post-war Britain, Ken an electrician.

It was the worst winter ever experienced in England. The sea froze between the piers in Brighton and fuel was strictly rationed to a few lumps a day. We went out looking like Russian peasants, wrapped to the ears in hand-knitted woollens, collecting wood on a sledge my father had built for me.

My mother regarded my father's job, because of the state of the meters he was inspecting, as far more dangerous than his RAF experiences. He frequently suffered severe electric shocks. Both men had had enough of post-war Britain and, taking four quite young children with them (my brother Peter was only two), they decided to emigrate overland to Africa. Just where in Africa they hadn't quite decided. Like the ostrich eggs they would buy in Tanganyika, they were going to 'suck it and see'.

We got to Tanganyika by accident. Our route was supposed to be down France, across the Mediterranean, then down North Africa, the Sudan, Kenya and so on. In the event there was no cross-Mediterranean shipping to be had in the wake of the war, and North Africa had been closed to overlanders because a bunch ahead of us had been blown up by rogue Italian minefields. So we took a converted Great Lakes steamer of 1,000 tons on a voyage to Mombasa. It was a nightmare of sea-sickness. Peter was tied on a short rope to my mother's arm while she heaved away for all of the three weeks we were at sea. I spent most of my time sleeping on deck in the canvas cover of a lifeboat. My father accepted this course of action because most nights the sink in our cabin gushed oily black bilge water over our floor and he was worried about typhoid. Typhoid was the only one of at least half a dozen foreign diseases we had not had painful injections against.

I have puzzled long and hard about why my parents (who had never been abroad) took on so long and potentially dangerous a journey. My mother was terrified for the entire three months while my father, when questioned, grinned and said we were going looking for King Solomon's mines. Ironically, we eventually settled in Rhodesia which I think is the land of King Solomon's mines and I started the research which resulted almost half a century later in my book *The Lost City of Solomon and Sheba*.

But it was only when I sat down to research this book that I came to realise that, for people of my parents' age who went to the pictures as often as they could afford (indeed saw more films than they read books), the 1940s were the decade when East Africa and its elephants burst into the limelight to fill the silver screens. The most famous and impressive of those films was of course MGM's *King Solomon's Mines*, which came out a little later, in 1950, and starred two of the great British heart-throbs of the time, Deborah Kerr and Stewart Granger. I have a photograph of my mother from that time with the same haircut as Ms Kerr. Indeed aged ninety-five and living independently in Cape Town, she still has it!

There had already been two films of the Rider Haggard book, one produced in South Africa in 1920 and a more ambitious attempt starring Cedric Hardwick as Allan Quartermain and the American singer Paul Robeson as Umbopa, the gun bearer, made by Gaumont British in 1938. The MGM film was producer Sam Zimbalist's dream project and he was determined to shoot everything on location, no matter what the cost. Eventually he spent about $2 million dollars in Africa, ten times what anyone had ever invested on an African location before. The crew and cast travelled some 14,000 miles by safari car, steamboat, aeroplane and on foot. Film stock was stored in two refrigerated vehicles and a set of unique five-gear safari cars was built for the high-speed animal chases. There were fifty film-makers involved, hundreds of Africans, and the safari work was looked after by four professional hunters.

Zimbalist was blessed with his choice of cast; Kerr's cool 'English' persona fitted well into the tale of a Denys Finch Hatton-type great white hunter and Stewart Granger was in reality a very good hunter. My parents must have read avidly about how Kerr and Granger personally stalked elephants in temperatures well over 100°F. On Mount Kenya 'looking for Umbopa's lost tribe' they filmed in a blizzard so severe that Zimbalist decided not to use the scene in the final film because he thought no one would believe it could have been shot in equatorial Africa.

Kerr was required to wear a hot Edwardian costume which included a long skirt, petticoats and a boned corset – probably so that Granger could engage in a little bodice-ripping and deliver one of his more famous lines: 'You're all sealed up like a can of peas.' (It is most likely coincidence but my mother wore a woollen Gor-ray skirt for most of the time on our trip and I had brown corduroy shorts just like Allan Quartermain wore.)

Zimbalist allowed himself a little more licence when it came to the African cast, replacing Rider Haggard's émigré Zulus (Haggard based his 'lost tribe' on the Matabele who fled to Rhodesia from Zululand in the nineteenth century) with 500 Watutsi from Rwanda-Urundi, spectacular-looking people. Umbopa was played by a Tutsi called Siriaque who was 7ft 8in tall. Zimbalist may have chosen the Tutsi with greater historical accuracy than he realised: I was able to show in my own book on King Solomon's mines that the Tutsi may have played host to, and some of them intermarried with, the diffused tribe who ended up in modern Zimbabwe and built the stone cities which guarded the ancient gold mines of Solomon.

The film also featured a vast cast of Kamba extras at a specially staged *ngoma* (fertility feast dance) but nobody told the girls about American censorship and their excited bare-breasted performances had to be thrown out.

That aside, the film opened to packed audiences and was a huge critical success, much praised for its veracity. 'British Grit Overcomes Horrors of Savage Africa' raved *Life* magazine, while the *Saturday Review of Literature* lauded it as 'one of the most remarkable pictures ever made'. It won an Oscar that year for Best Color Photography.

When we arrived in Salisbury, the Rhodesian capital, we took to going to the cinema (the Palace on First Street) at least once a week, my father always wearing a tuxedo jacket on these important social outings. *King Solomon's Mines* was followed by another Rider Haggard tale, *She* (an RKO picture), and, my personal favourites, the *Tarzan* films of which some thirty were made. The first natural history films, the genre in which I would later earn my own living, also came along at this time with *Savage Splendor* presented by Armand and Michaela Denis; it was shown in 1949.

Although obviously I did not realise it at the time, my long safari through some of Africa's richest elephant country was made at a moment of unique calm in the troubled history of the continent.

Innocently ignorant of the holocaust which was about to descend on these paradisiacal places, we trundled along *murram* roads at an average speed of 30mph through the small hill country which would later become the mighty Tsavo National Park (it was promulgated in 1948). It still contained a mass of elephants at that time. We also travelled across the Serengeti plateau which was indubitably the most accessible giraffe, antelope, elephant, leopard and lion habitat on the planet; past Ngorongoro tucked away in its misty Spanish-moss forest; through Northern Rhodesia (now Zambia) where the Luangwa Park area adjoining the Zambesi river crawled with elephants; across the Victoria Falls, over what was then a comparatively new bridge; and across Wankie National Park in north-west Southern Rhodesia which once housed the largest herd of black rhino in Africa and a mighty herd of elephant, many of which are today crowding into northern Botswana because there, at least for the moment, they are safe from poaching. I was quite literally dazed with wonder for all of the three months it took to reach Salisbury (now Harare) where my mother decided she had had enough and I had been out of school too long. Little did she know that short exposure to a real school of wildlife had changed me for ever. It has directed my footsteps ever since.

The places I have described above are very different now and reflect the dramatic changes which have overtaken African wildlife in the last half century. The Rhodesian Game Department is no more and even its successor, the Zimbabwe Game Department, which struggled valiantly for several years, has now collapsed into Mugabe's starving, derelict state. Tsavo was the epicentre of massive, almost apocalyptic poaching in the 1980s. Serengeti, where a famous documentary, *Serengeti Shall Not Die*, was made, did almost die in the same decade and its game is now a pale shadow of former days. In Luangwa black rhino were hunted to extinction. Poachers from Luangwa paddled across Lake Kariba into Zimbabwe and there quickly reduced a large rhino population to zero. In 1987 I made a film of this story called *Black Rhino: The Last Stand* for Granada Television.

Sadly there are almost no exceptions to this tragic list. In my lifetime Africa's teeming wildlife (as I and a few other lucky travellers, film-makers and writers knew it) has been obliterated. Arguably the best African conservation book of all time was written by Peter Beard under the title *The End of the Game*. People still refer me to this book, but it was actually published almost forty years ago. The end of the game is not a state of affairs that should be taking anyone by surprise.

In Kenya in the 1950s a tight, militaristic (native accommodation in Tsavo was known as 'the Lines') game department, many of whose wardens had been officers in the war, divided the country into eighty-eight hunting blocks with two or three areas significantly, and quite strictly, set aside for conservation. A large part of Tsavo West fell into this category and could only be used for scientific research. Hunting in the remaining blocks was tightly controlled and earned the administration substantial income. By today's standard these fees seem cheap – 400 Kenya shillings for a lion, 2,000 shillings for a rhino, and a first elephant for 1,500 shillings (the second would cost you 2,500). These licence fees represented a material contribution to the tiny national economy. It was the pioneering prototype for what today has its own politically correct description – 'resource management' – and it may well be, were it ever to be accepted by the mass of the general public who fund conservation and conservationists, a prototype for the future. We will return to that large subject later.

Hunters were also required to pay a fee which went to the local community. Fees escalated rapidly if a hunter chose to shoot more than one of the 'Big Five' and the controls were quite strict. It was unlawful to spot elephants from aircraft, nothing could be shot within 200 yards of a safari vehicle, and you could go to prison if you shot and wounded a large animal without taking every action possible to put it out of its misery. Certain animals like hippo were banned outright from being hunted. Photographic safaris increased in popularity, not least because they cost about a third of a hunting safari.

Britain was destitute after the war so there were no more royal safaris, but Americans continued to come in great numbers. (Bing

Crosby came seven times.) Tony Dyer, the last President of the East African Professional Hunters' Association, once told Bartle Bull (a serious hunter himself): 'I had thirteen years of the most perfect hunting. I would wake up in the morning, drink my tea, and just decide then, thinking about my clients, whether I was going to hunt in Kenya, Tanganyika or Uganda. We could even go freely to the Sudan.' Moreover, within such a tightly balanced eco-political system there was still more than enough game. The professional hunters had state laws with which to keep their clients on tight reins and these laws caused the hunting parties to act pretty much according to Darwin's laws of natural selection: everyone wanted a big trophy and big trophies were only to be found on old (in the case of elephants, very old) animals.

The professional hunters/safari leaders had all seen the game stock shrink dramatically in their lifetime. In fact many of them whom I knew had fathers who had committed the slaughter. Sons now employed in the professional game business ruefully called these old Africa hands the 'when-we's' for the way they tended to dwell on the past.

In 2001 I hired a professional hunter with an unashamedly 'when-we' background, Tony Seth-Smith. Tony's immediate ancestors had all been elephant hunters and he had a contract to control the lions that were plaguing the huge Galana ranch adjoining Tsavo. He regularly shot a dozen or so a year when they were found guilty of persistent cattle raiding or man eating. Everyone knew that lions that lived next door on the protected acres of Tsavo stalked off to Galana for a quick meal of oxen (knowing they did not require much hunting) and then carried their prey home to the safety of Tsavo. My *Man-eaters of Tsavo* film made the point that it is no longer acceptable for dangerous game to predate on the expanding human populations which now surround all of Africa's national parks. In other words the control officer, with duties not that far removed from J.A. Hunter a century ago, is back with a vengeance.

Kenya has an annual population growth rate of well over 3.5 per cent, which means that the population doubles every 18 to 20 years. Lord Delamere estimated that the native people of Kenya numbered about two million in 1897; fifty years later there were about seven million, thirty-eight million in the year 2000 and by 2020 the count is expected to reach eighty million. Forget about poaching. If anything is going to render the African elephant extinct it is this inexorable march of the naked ape.

Tony Seth-Smith's father was the famous pioneer hunter Donald Seth-Smith, who came to Kenya in 1906 when it was all about making a go of it as a professional hunter. A year later in a letter home he described Kenya jubilantly as 'crawling with big game shooters. Thirty more parties are coming in the next boat or two.' Today, almost a century later, Tony is still wedded to Kenya but increasingly less sanguine about the future. 'From a wild, proud, free man the African has become homogenized man, like us. Everything we love is being destroyed.'

Tony Dyer, who is in his eighties, still runs a large wilderness ranch near Lewa under Mount Kenya and gave me great help with this book. He believes there is increasing evidence that Kenya made a serious mistake in banning professional hunting. Leaving aside the money a country can make from the activity, Tony believes responsible government wardenship in partnership with licensed hunting provides a system of game monitoring that has never been equalled. It would not surprise me (as with the reintroduction of the control officer) if commercially significant legal hunting returned to Kenya in the near future.

The wind of change ('wind of doubt' might be a better phrase) was first recognised by the avuncular Harold Macmillan who applied it to the changing politics of Africa. Macmillan then made it clear that Britain would not interfere in these changes, indeed would smooth their way, which, as those, like me, who lived in the British colonies quickly and harshly recognised, made it a self-fulfilling philosophy. Suddenly it was all change. Africa, singularly unprepared, raced to independence in Ghana, Nigeria, the Congo, Zambia, the Rhodesias and Nyasaland, Tanganyika and Kenya. If you had looked at a map of Africa as a traffic signal, most of the pink British lights suddenly went out and the green lights of Africa came on. Sadly these signals had no amber pause period and there would be a lot of crashes on the road ahead. The most disastrous was the abrupt withdrawal of British finance for game management, which included the British abandoning their responsibility for game wardens' pensions. This coupled with the 'Africanisation' of game department jobs resulted in an exodus of much of the skilled, white game hierarchy. Such was the enthusiasm for *uhuru* (freedom) and all its works, Africans seem not to have been aware of a yawning elephant trap which was opening up before them. Over the next three decades the continent became understandably mesmerised by the excitements of self-rule and change, and sadly change is always bought at a price.

EIGHT

The Last Stand

Imagine 1,000 elephants (as described by Wilfred Thesiger) standing by the banks of the White Nile in the Sudan. Now imagine the same view utterly emptied of elephants by unrestricted poaching. It is unimaginable but it is what has happened in the Sudan and in other parts of Africa in the past seventy-five years. We have suffered an elephant holocaust. The ultimate paradox of this situation is that everything that all those gung-ho great white hunters, all the Waliangula bowmen (or more accurately the Wata of the Tana river, Taita and Kwale districts) for whom elephant hunting was a way of life, all those trigger-happy 'sportsmen', had little or nothing to do with this holocaust. Africa's elephants could happily have shrugged off their piffling attrition. The elephant has reached its present parlous state, a limbo in which the beast has lived for several decades, simply because of often quite innocent occupation and destruction of its habitat by indigenous people. In several such places the indigenous people did not wait for destruction to happen. They got rid of the elephants when the conflict of interests became evident. This has been most graphic in the Great Lakes region, particularly Rwanda and Uganda. The 'Heart of Darkness', as a prescient Joseph Conrad once described it, has been something of an object lesson for the whole of Africa on the issue of reality versus conservation. Indeed in situations of 'extreme reality', as was the case in Rwanda in 1994, wild animal conservation simply ceases to exist. On this I speak from personal experience.

Just a week after the majority Hutu turned on the aristocratic minority Tutsi and murdered a million of them, I flew into blood-stained Rwanda to research a film on mountain gorillas for National Geographic. The act of genocide was committed mostly with *pangas* (bush knives) on men, women and children, and mostly by Hutu women. The local radio station egged them on and the French, who had military responsibility for the country, dithered and watched it happen.

When a Tutsi army came in from Uganda and overthrew the Hutu government, those who had committed the genocide fled across the border in their millions and set up forest hovels the like of which I never thought to see (and I am used to African slums). Several gorillas and almost every other wild thing in the vicinity of the camps was chopped up for bush meat. Then the refugees turned on the forest itself, destroying the equivalent of a football field a day to fuel their cooking fires. Within the year some of these Hutu had formed the Intrahamwe and were dominating the camps, kidnapping tourists (six from a camp near Bwindi Gorilla Reserve in Uganda where we had been filming just a few days previously) and, daubed in white paint, had allegedly started to eat people. If all this was not enough, a disease called Ebola, which killed in a fortnight by literally rotting human flesh, broke out in these jungles. Space-suited physicians who heroically treated the Ebola patients speculated that the initial scourge could have resulted from people eating the flesh of wild monkeys.

This was the first time I had ever seen conservation *entirely* collapse as a result of human overpopulation and habitat destruction. The mountain gorilla, of which there are just 600 left, was now the subject of one of the longest and most successful conservation operations of modern times. Started by Dian Fossey under the direction of Richard Leakey's father, Louis, a large and committed team had been watching over these animals for three decades and, in spite of the difficulties of the high terrain, volcanic forests and an ever-present demand for bush meat, their number had remained stable. But here we were, six years before the millennium, watching this model conservation initiative simply collapse under the human onslaught. Thankfully the gorillas quite literally 'took to the hills' and survived. I was forced to cancel my film schedule because there was simply no safe way for a film crew to work safely in those mountains.

Elephants, as we shall see in a moment, had been the first to go from Rwanda, victims of what have today come to be known as 'biodiversity conflicts'. Antelope in the forests were also constantly hunted using snare traps. These were the bane of Dian Fossey's life; because baby gorillas also got caught in the traps, they were the subject of many bitter battles with the forest people. Finally, after Dian lost her famous temper and had two poachers beaten with giant stinging nettle vines by her game wardens, members of the victim's tribe killed her favourite silverback, Digit. Dian should have known better. Rwanda is after all a revenge-based culture. But Dian's story from this tiny backward volcanic state where she was murdered in 1985 rings like an echo from the past. It was perhaps a harbinger of the conflicts which were about to break out around almost every game park in Africa.

In 1972 Rwanda's human population explosion was used to justify shooting out almost the whole of the country's elephant population. The cull was paid for by Russ Train's America-funded African Wildlife Foundation. The elephants were judged to be a destructive nuisance to the African settlers who had crowded out the area and also to the gorillas which needed forest trees. Mr Train felt he had to choose between the elephants and the mountain gorillas. It should perhaps be pointed out that the conservation of mountain gorillas was very popular indeed with the brigade of emotional conservationists (sometimes unkindly known as bunny-huggers) who brought in millions of dollars to AWF. The shooting was done by a former Kenya game warden by the name of Ian Parker, who will feature large in our story a few chapters on. Parker's Wildlife Services company shot all but twenty-five of what amounted to the last elephants in Rwanda and parked this rump population in the Akagera National Park. But in 1997 this park also succumbed to yet more human population growth when two-thirds of it was excised for settlement. Elephants adieu.

So Rwanda really does seem to be the African elephant problem in microcosm – too many people on too little wilderness with too many hungry mouths waiting in the wings. It is now the most densely populated place on earth with more people – 99 per cent of them poor – packed together more tightly than inhabitants of the suburbs of London. While Parker's cull is hard to condone (an outfit as rich as the African Wildlife Foundation could surely have found a safe place for 150 quite rare forest elephants), the reality is that then, as now, there was no place for elephants in Rwanda.

How long before climate, habitat change and a population explosion like the one going on in Kenya renders that country untenable for elephants too? And then the Sudan, Congo and almost anywhere you care to name in West Africa.

So how about native Kenyans? Are they happy with this state of affairs? A few middle- and upper-class *wabenzi* still mouth the conservation clichés but if you were to call a referendum asking the *watu* (the people) to choose between allocating land to wildlife or to people I am certain they would choose for the people.

I find it frankly incredible that anyone who knows Africa could have been naive enough to think that it was ever going to be any different. Certainly not a single old Kenya hand of my acquaintance ever thought it was going to turn out another way. They saw the unrestricted expansion of the African population as a threat and decided wild animals could only be saved by draconian methods, employing ex-soldiers and paramilitary forces to keep the *watu* and the wildlife apart. One statute in particular, passed by the British colonial administration, drove this point home. Game might only be hunted with guns, but it was illegal for Africans to carry guns. Catch-22 with a bang! And it was all done under the umbrella of a holier-than-thou attitude to Africans. Ian Parker, writing of the company he joined as a fledgling game ranger, says: 'We were a band of gentlemen. There was always a general acceptance that game and park wardens were in some way special. As with religion's priests, padres, ministers and imams, the western public accorded them an exalted *moral* status. . . . What they did seemed spiritually *good*' (emphasis in original).

By 1956 all the land in Kenya was controlled by the Wild Animals Protection Ordinance (WAPO) which administered the Game Department, and the Royal National Parks of Kenya Ordinance which had a Board of Trustees who administered the national parks and made them somewhat independent of government.

The country was divided into ten game ranges ruled over by some very famous rangers who were mostly old hunters like J.A. Hunter at Makindi, Jack Barrah at Nanyuki, and the man who would become a legend and the archetypical game warden (a title all the rangers acquired in 1958), George Adamson.

I met George Adamson when he was in late middle age, at his headquarters for the Kora Game Reserve up on the Tana river overlooking Somaliland. This comprised a number of thatched shacks and 'guest sleeping accommodation' with walls that reached only to waist height. George told us that there was a black mamba in the ceiling but I was not to disturb it as it was in labour, and that he would also prefer that the bats hanging under our bed were not disturbed. The loo was a line of elephant skulls poised precariously over three 'thunderbox' earth toilets. His brother Terence was in residence at the time we were there, a sweet and gentle African eccentric whom my wife fell in love with when he taught her how to divine using two wire coat hangers. Terence only owned one suit which he kept buried, soldered into a large tin, against termites, and they went searching for this coffer with their coat hangers. Terence limped, having recently been mauled (for the umpteenth time) by one of the descendants of George's famous lioness, Elsa, the subject of his wife Joy's international best-seller, *Born Free*.

By this time (the early 1980s) George had become one of Kenya's protected tourist assets in his own right. *Born Free* and a later book, *My Pride and Joy*, edited by my friend and former publisher at Collins, Adrian House, had made George and Joy the icons of the emotional conservationist school of wildlife welfare. The truth is another story. Suffice it to say that when gentle George was seduced by the predatory Joy it proved not unlike being run over by a 10-ton truck. He also became obsessed with his lions in later years, a devotion that did much to undo his earlier reputation as a game warden. I personally found his obsession rather endearing, if a little scary, because George had no fear at all of the disturbed lions, which kept chewing on the people all around him. Dressed in a pair of khaki shorts and safari boots he visited them daily armed only with a .22 pistol. He took my wife and me, with two other visitors, to see an observably irritable lioness called Grow. He allowed us to approach to within 200 yards then squatted down himself just 10 feet from the lactating lion. As I had by then filmed several dozen lions in various parts of Kenya hurtling across distances of that kind in a matter of seconds I led Heather quietly away to the safari car. George came

back eventually and we all drove home. A few days later Terence
was badly mauled again.

I know a number of people in Kenya today who believe that
George and his custodianship of remote Kora Park was a cover for
Kenya's best-kept secret – that most of the descendants of Elsa
were born-again man-eaters. But George, with his reputation
unsullied, died as he had lived, racing to the aid of a friend who
was being attacked by Somali bandits.

Somali bandits had been a problem for a long time. The Chief
Warden in the 1940s was Captain Arthur Ritchie and it was
Ritchie who first warned his staff, including George Adamson, that
the country's elephants were in serious trouble from this threat.
Professional bandits or off-duty soldiers from Somalia (*shifta*) were
starting to operate in the territory and Somalia was rapidly
becoming a major illegal ivory entrepôt state.

George made several forays into Somali territory, writing to
Ritchie in 1943: 'I came across many places where leopard traps
had been set along paths. I gather [there is] considerable trade in
giraffe skins and leopard skins with the Somalis . . . the leopard
traps are probably supplied by Somalis from Jubaland.' And a
Kenya Police report was circulated to game wardens: 'Captain
Corfe. Assistant Political Officer, Mismayo, estimates that about
3,000 elephants were shot in the Garissa District and the Somali
District adjoining Garissa from March 1941 to March 1942. As
regards leopard skins [more valuable than ivory in those days] the
Political Officer, Lugh, in Jubaland told me recently that the trade
in them was officially encouraged in Somalia.'

This obscure memo was the harbinger of a dramatic change
that was about to happen to Kenya's wildlife. It forecast, at least
fifty years before the reality was to become obvious, that a
neighbour state (which had been trading ivory up the East African
coast to Arabia and India since Solomon's time) was breaking
ranks with British East Africa and would in future trade wildlife
products as an important national resource. Much has been
written about the evil Somalis but this shift was really no more
than a recognition of an African economic reality, one which has
prevailed in Somalia ever since. It should have warned the
Kenyans what to expect.

Instead WAPO responded by conferring on its white game wardens extraordinary policing powers aimed largely at indigenous Africans. It even gave stop and search powers to 'honorary' game wardens who had the right to set up roadblocks, arrest and charge anyone for infringements of game laws, and then prosecute them. It was a policy guaranteed to alienate the rural Africans.

The holocaust of ivory poaching is commonly thought to have hit Kenya and Tanzania in the early 1970s, rising to a crescendo of attrition in the 1980s. In fact the Governor General of Kenya, Sir Evelyn Baring, was so worried about it in 1956 that he launched an anti-poaching campaign calling for a concerted effort by all the branches of government: the police, the army, the air wing, the Game Department and the Parks Department.

Moving to occupy centre stage in this animal war were characters who had replaced George Adamson as the quintessential game wardens, David Sheldrick and Bill Woodley, and, by association, Daphne Sheldrick. Daphne has appeared in several of my films and is, among my best friends in Kenya. We have known each other for a quarter of a century, talking always about elephants. She introduced me to both Iain Douglas-Hamilton and Ian Parker.

With his wife-to-be Oria, Iain Douglas-Hamilton wrote what in my view is the definitive book on Kenya's elephants, *Among the Elephants*, a sweet saga of love and elephant behaviour. The couple featured in probably the best *Nature Watch* programme we ever made. His daughter Saba, conceived in Amboseli, is now a BBC Natural History Unit presenter. Ian Parker, as I think will become apparent, is the historian of the African elephant ivory trade.

Daphne's description of Iain when I first met her was: 'Iain's a good bloke but he's a boffin at heart.' In those days Daphne was very wary of boffins because of what they wanted to do to elephants in her beloved Tsavo. Ian Parker was also a 'good bloke at heart' because all he ever thought about was elephants, even though his views were often diametrically opposed to her own. If you are writing a book about elephants, Daphne is definitely the gal to know. She has either argued elephant destinies with everyone who is anyone in East African conservation, or she has been married to them. She has no academic qualifications of any kind but her knowledge has been learned from the school of life in the bush, although she proudly (and with a rather evil grin) told me when I saw her in Nairobi in 2005 that she was now an 'honorary boffin' herself, having been given an honorary degree.

Daphne is driven by her loving memory of her husband, David Sheldrick, Chief Game Warden of Tsavo, who died of a heart attack or, as Daphne sometimes puts it, overwork, fighting poachers. She started the David Sheldrick Memorial Trust from scratch and today it is a powerful international pressure group for elephants. It has branches and a steady flow of money from at least three countries, particularly America.

Daphne is a white African from an old mould, her parents having trekked to Kenya from South Africa in an ox wagon to join the Afrikaaner community at Eldoret. When David was out hunting poachers, Daphne set up an extraordinary elephant orphanage for the baby animals her husband was bringing home from the poacher-ravaged Tsavo bush. Hands on, twenty-four hours a day, Daphne learnt the hard way what baby elephants need. She invented a formula for tiny orphans which had coconut milk as its main ingredient. She got up every four hours to feed her babies personally from a huge bottle which had the finger of a washing-up glove as a makeshift teat.

The first orphan to survive and grow to adulthood was Eleanor, featured in a programme we made with Daphne in 1982. Julian Pettifer did an interview with Daphne standing under Eleanor's stomach. Eleanor was Daphne's close friend and media tool. During our interview Eleanor reached her trunk over Julian's shoulder and turned on a garden tap for a quick drink. Daphne pretended not to notice. Eleanor of her own volition eventually returned to the wild in Tsavo and since then Daphne has reintroduced dozens of elephants to her late husband's park, most of which I have filmed at one time or another. In my view Daphne has achieved hugely more than she realises but she has difficulty recognising it because, paradoxically, she has become subject to 'boffin' intellectual discipline in recent years.

Daphne's elephants are in fact a new breed, although there is no way she will ever admit to it. She has actually produced a small group of animals whose memory of the human race is slightly more favourable than their parents'. Daphne's animals are hand-raised as infants at her popular Animal Orphanage in the Nairobi National Park. They then go to Tsavo with their attendants, walk around with them, and get used to the bush. At night they come home to sleep in the old Tsavo Lines. There was a famous occasion when Eleanor, who was by then living wild in the bush, came to these stables, unlocked a hasp and spent the night with the babies.

The process of familiarising the elephants with Tsavo, known as 'hacking out', goes on until the new arrivals have met, grown used to, and finally joined the wild herds. Although I have slight doubts about how these 'humanised' elephants are going to work out in the long run (Daphne Sheldrick is an unrepentant emotional conservationist when it comes to elephants), the scheme is certainly working now. More important to the huge park is the fact that Daphne regards Tsavo as the place where her heart lies. It is her personal sphere of influence. She will defend it against all comers (and that includes at least one former chief game warden of Kenya) and is directing ever larger sums of conservation money into it. She pays for dams and boreholes and maintains a mobile vet service.

Admittedly she has an intensely personal relationship with Tsavo, where, in the dangerous days of the mid-1950s, David Sheldrick and Bill Woodley were told to do something about the heavy poaching that had descended on the park. David was the chief warden of Tsavo East and Bill held a more lowly position in Tsavo West. Daphne was Mrs Woodley at that time, and had a daughter, Jill, who went on to help her with the Elephant Orphanage. But in Tsavo Daphne fell head over heels for David and soon became Mrs Sheldrick. The Parks Department only tolerated this wife swap, it is said, because Daphne, Bill and David remained such good friends. Bill later remarried and had three sons, Bongo, Danny and Ben, all of whom followed their father into the wildlife business – Bongo and Danny as game wardens (they are now chief wardens) and Ben as the manager of the famous Kukie Galman's Likipia Ranch, a sanctuary for black rhino.

The anti-poaching campaign that David and Bill launched had, as I have said, 'royal' approval from the Governor General, Sir Evelyn Baring, and in a sense it was a new departure for the Parks Department, which had always leaned on poaching but had never thought it possible to stop it. For example, in the eleven years from 1938 to 1949 George Adamson's reports show he arrested just 447 Africans on the huge Isiolo Game Range.

The news of serious elephant and rhino poaching had started to filter through to the Colonial Office in Britain and Sir Evelyn decided that he would make this his personal (and valedictory) crusade. He brought together all the arms of government and told them to apply themselves to the problem. The police were told to give no quarter to poachers, and magistrates were ordered to hand down deterrent sentences. A light aircraft was made available to Woodley and Sheldrick by the Kenya Air Wing, and Chief Inspector of Police A. Child was sent to run the anti-poaching operation out of Voi, while Superintendent R. Potgeiter targeted illegal ivory and rhino buyers. It was, until Richard Leakey came along in the late 1990s with his units of SAS-trained poacher-killers, the biggest operation ever mounted; indeed Leakey modelled his units on Sheldrick's 1950s field force.

Sheldrick was the planner and organiser, a martinet when it came to operational detail, while Bill Woodley was an exceptional woodsman. Born in Kenya, he spent three years in the Kenya Regiment where he rose through the ranks to captain and was awarded the Military Cross. He was actively involved in tackling the Mau Mau emergency and, with Francis Erskine, helped establish the 'pseudo-gangs' which were instrumental in putting down the insurgency. A pseudo-gang comprised young white Kenyans blacked up and backing up a few turned Mau Mau. Sometimes the pseudo-gangs contacted Mau Mau groups and arranged their surrender; other times they gunned them down and hacked off a hand for identification purposes. Young whites like Bill Woodley and Myles Turner, who will take his place in this story in the next chapter, literally metamorphosed into Mau Mau; dressing like them, even wearing the hair of their victims, living as close to the ways of animals as was possible, and eating only forest fare so that they and their excrement would smell the same as the Mau Mau's.

I knew several of these pseudo-gang members. Few of them are prepared to talk about what really happened in *this* heart of darkness. A feature of the work was the pseudo-gang's ability to run for days through Kenya's thick forests virtually without stopping. The Mau Mau gangs could initially always outrun their pursuers, but eventually the pseudo-gangs were fit enough and, with the help of aerial surveillance, the war began to go their way. The Mau Mau were defeated in 1960. Bill Woodley came home having learnt a whole lot about gathering intelligence from indigenous people, and the Mau Mau leader, Jomo Kenyatta, was arrested. But there is an ironic twist to this tragic tale. Mau Mau was the beginning of the Kikuyu independence movement which in 1963 brought Jomo Kenyatta to power as president. The Mau Mau generals who survived were declared state heroes and, as we shall hear in more detail shortly, were given licence to exploit the national elephant herd.

In Tsavo, Bill and David took up Sir Evelyn's challenge and went to work with a will, apparently utterly unaware that they were about to establish a lasting antipathy towards wildlife and wildlife managers in the indigenous people. Bill specialised in conducting lightning raids on dazed native communities and arresting anyone with a questionable game trophy. David planned each raid in meticulous detail and circled above in his spotter plane trying to catch poachers in the field.

Things came a trifle unstuck when the 'Dream Team' planned an operation outside Tsavo. Bill had spent weeks collecting information and intelligence, but when the Parks Department field force went in, they discovered that a junior Game Department warden had got there before them, thus alerting the community. That game warden was Ian Parker, who had just been appointed. This 'cocky little twerp' (Ian's own words) had a flaming row with Bill and David, but it was later shown that it was they who had jumped the gun by not telling Ian's Game Department of their plans. Parker went on to be employed by Sheldrick in one of two new anti-poaching platoons formed to beef up Sir Evelyn's operation. Ian being Ian, however, he soon got himself into more trouble, and David had him transferred out of the anti-poaching operation.

A serious paradox now begins to creep into this story. Bill Woodley was a soldier used to following orders. He obeyed the rules and prosecuted wrong-doers – 'poachers'. But in their hearts he and David had great respect and admiration for the native tribes who had a historic and intimate empathy with the Kenya bush. As the anti-poaching operation progressed, Bill built up an extraordinary rapport with his Waliangula trackers who were from a tribe that specialised in and was dependent on the killing of elephants. (I used Waliangula trackers in my film *Man-eaters of Tsavo* for the BBC as recently as 2003.)

The Waliangula (more accurately the Wata) shared their world with elephants in a relationship which was symbiotic. They have names for each beast and they know the habits and temperaments of individual animals. They have songs they sing when an animal is lying dying, poisoned by one of their arrows tipped with the black gum of acokanthera poison made from boiling scrub olive with puff adder and scorpion venom.

The Wata are short and muscular, and they traditionally hunted young bulls with smaller tusks that were less crafty than the old bulls and their tusks easier to carry. But in spite of their size (they have often been compared to the Kalahari bushmen) Wata hunters nevertheless hunted with a massive 7ft bow which few but they could pull. In 1953 the Waliangula (there are arguably two tribes so I shall stick to this name as a generic) numbered between 5,000 and 8,000, according to Bartle Bull.

There is some evidence that the tribe has extremely ancient roots and could have traded ivory with the Arabs of the coast in Solomon's time or even earlier. The *Periplus of the Erythraen Sea*, an anonymous geography of maritime activities in the Red Sea dating from about AD 50 which I consulted at length for my book on Solomon's central African gold-mines, says also that great quantities of ivory were exported from Middle Africa, or *Kaferia*. It specifically mentions that the ivory was produced by a tribe in the hinterland who employed bows so large they could not be drawn by one man. The only weapon I know which fits that description is a Wata longbow weighing more than 150lb. George Adamson had one and it was a party trick of his to challenge his guests to try to pull it. I am 6ft 2in (at least a foot taller than your average

Waliangula) and heavily built. I could not even bend it enough to notch the cord.

So when Bill and David stormed in to make Tsavo safe from poaching they could well have been invading an ancient hunting society which had supplied the art material for the oldest and greatest cultures the world has ever known. The world, however, was unaware of that history in 1956–7, and the anti-poaching campaign in Tsavo was a great success. Bill Woodley and David Sheldrick became very famous wildlife warriors and the darlings of a growing conservation movement. They also effectively destroyed the Waliangula, although Bill and David were genuinely concerned about this aspect of their campaign and tried to do something about it.

David went to see an influential wildlife enthusiast, Noel Simon, who had first raised a hue and cry in the local press about poaching in Tsavo, to discuss the plight of Waliangula elephant bowmen, and they debated a programme based on Canadian laws that allowed native people to hunt. Simon, David, Bill and the rehabilitated 'little twerp', Ian Parker, joined forces to propose the scheme to the Game Department, with David providing an addendum that clearly showed that he was also aware of the core conservation problem: 'There is no doubt that if the Waliangula were to think that this scheme was for the benefit of the European or other tribesmen it would fail.'

The Game Policy Committee thought enough of the scheme to give it a trial, and Ian Parker, who had been Warden of Kilifi, the main Wata area, was relieved of this post and told to work on the Waliangula scheme. Woodley and Parker made several visits to the Wata and in 1958 a report was submitted. It was quickly thrown out. Ian was told to go back to his job at Kalifi. Instead he lobbied other agencies, as did Simon, gaining the support of the influential International Union for the Conservation of Nature and Natural Resources (IUCN) and the Nuffield Foundation, which made a £10,000 development grant available. The project was now called the Galana River Management Scheme.

However, an earlier annual report (1954) to the Kenya Game Department by the Chief Warden, William Hale, boded ill for this enlightened scheme, which in my opinion could have made a real difference to the way game laws were interpreted in many Kenyan parks. Tsavo was one of the top elephant areas and if an entire tribe of 'poachers', the Wata, could have been converted to 'gamekeepers' with their ancient lifestyle and culture entirely invested in wildlife management, a lot more elephants would be alive in Tsavo today. But William Hale was one of several influential harbingers of doom. 'Every African is a poacher,' he wrote in his report. 'In Kenya one recognises no customary hunting rights. . . . Poaching must be stopped and, therefore, poachers must be prosecuted.'

There were other difficulties. The Game Department refused outright to give up the ivory the scheme might produce (all ivory in Kenya at that time belonged to the Game Department, a full-blooded arm of government unlike the semi-autonomous Parks Department) which meant the Galana Project was underfunded from the start. With insufficient funds and widespread opposition from several quarters (the East African Professional Hunters' Association said it would ruin the project's business) it was probably doomed from the start, but in 1959 Parker went off to set it up accompanied by Tony Seth-Smith, scion of a pioneer Kenya hunting family.

In 2002 I hired Tony to work on *Man-eaters of Tsavo*, and completely coincidentally we talked about this enlightened attempt to make a place for indigenous hunters when we were camped on the huge Galana concession adjoining Tsavo, now a cattle ranch. Another wildlife warrior from whom we will be hearing shortly, and who would go on to become the World Wildife Fund's chief elephant scientist, Dr John Hanks, also worked briefly as a young scientist on the Galana River Management Scheme.

Ian Parker claims the project was eventually strangled by the red tape that so restricted what the Wata could do. This, coupled with the refusal to allow the tribe to market its ivory, meant the project fell into the hole David Sheldrick had forecast – if the Wata did not believe that the scheme was for them it would fail, and it did. Parker quit the Game Department to begin his long and colourful career as a private wildlife entrepreneur.

In 2002 I found Tony Seth-Smith reluctant to talk about any of this other than to observe that there really was no Waliangula society now. It had effectively vanished as an identifiable and definable tribal group. Thus ended Kenya's first and probably last attempt at a rational game- and habitat-sharing scheme. From then on game – especially very valuable game like elephants, rhino and big cats – was seen by most rural Africans as something which had to be stolen from the whites. Moreover, the word *uhuru* (freedom from whites) was now something more than just a whisper in the wind, and most of these rural people, who were in the main law-abiding, stopped seeing poaching as a crime. The animals had been taken from them anyway and it was now glaringly obvious that the *mzungus* were never going to give them back.

NINE

Africa for the Africans

Why did the whites of Africa and their descendants find it so difficult, so unreasonable when Africans demanded the return of their countries and their wildlife? The charitable answer is that the whites simply did not think Africans were ready for these responsibilities. The uncharitable one is that many thought they would never be ready. Realistically, they all feared it would mean the end of the good life. It was only happening, they claimed, because craven European governments were abandoning them as the colonies had now become more trouble than they were worth. This was probably true, but those of us who suggested it might democratically also be the *right* thing to do incurred the wrath of recidivist white regimes.

As a young journalist with my own television news show in Rhodesia I got myself into terrible trouble with Ian Smith's government and, faced with doing time for treason and subversion or leaving the country in a great hurry, I, with the responsibility for two young daughters, chose the latter. My friend Peter Nieswand was not so lucky. He ended up serving two years in a bush prison called Gonakudzingwa.

The subject of the 'treason and subversion' (a definition introduced under a draconian Smith law called the Law and Order Maintenance Amendment Act) was the basis of my first novel, *When the Woods Became the Trees* (1965), a tome so naive politically (the hero was a seventeen-year-old boy) that it is hard to see why anyone took it seriously. Out of the blue, however (having attracted a prominent and favourable review by Elspeth Huxley in *The Times*) it was nominated for a Pulitzer Prize and from then on my days were numbered.

The book's message, which seemed to me so glaringly obvious (and is another way of putting the issue with which I opened this chapter), was that if the whites went to war with the blacks, we, the whites, would lose. More simply, if we tried to keep Africa for ourselves, so much bitterness would be generated by the process we would lose it and probably all be kicked out. I take no pride whatsoever in the fact that modern Zimbabwe is the nightmare I foresaw and Robert Mugabe is a caricature of my fictional 'President'; a ludicrous, posturing despot who is now kept alive politically by an ageing ANC 'nationalist' faction as detached from rich, democratic, successful South Africa as Mugabe is from all reality.

Several decades after those traumatic times, however, I still find it hard to believe that the International Conservation Movement still looks and acts like colonialism *manqué* and still does not really accept that Africans do own Africa and have a right to do whatever they want with their wildlife, including killing it to feed hungry mouths. That after all is exactly what we of the West did. If you think this is an extreme way of presenting the matter, try this test question on International Conservation organisations or any of the other big charity fundraisers for nature: 'Do Africans have the right to eliminate wildlife – in particular elephant, rhino and all the big cats – in the interests of their becoming modern industrial and agricultural countries?' The *moral* answer is of course 'Yes, they do.' The answer you get runs something along these lines: 'Forgive them, for they know not what they do. We must stop them doing it until they have developed sufficiently to recognise that it would be a crime against nature and humanity.' But that is exactly the old colonial argument and still as patronising as ever it was.

I put this very question to the most famous wildlife warrior of them all, Richard Leakey, in Kenya, just a few months ago. 'No,' he said, reminding me that he was also a native Kenyan. 'We should work to prevent that happening. If the case is properly presented, the West is prepared to pay for the conservation of African wildlife.'

I have no doubt that Leakey, who has always been a consistent supporter of most other aspects of 'Africa for the Africans', could make that work. But he is virtually the *only* man in Kenya who could, as he has proved on several occasions in the past. The stop-go condition of Kenya's conservation finances over the past decade can be traced back to whether Leakey was in office at the time or not.

At the moment he is not and I doubt that he will now ever be fit enough to take on another major hands-on conservation appointment. As a result funds, particularly funds for the Game Department, are in desperately short supply. In other words, without his charismatic stewardship, the West is not prepared to shell out.

One of the ironies of the success of my novel in England was that when I arrived there pretty penniless in January 1965 it was assumed that I knew all about wildlife and I was able (provided I kept my mouth shut) to walk straight into a job in television.

But the city of Salisbury (now Harare) where I grew up is not unlike a mushroom which has grown overnight on the golf course. Any wildlife that survived the building of the place sensibly headed for the nearest hills as the suburbs grew. In the year before I left the country I interviewed David Attenborough on the local news show I presented for RTV. David was in the country poking about for animals in holes (as was always his wont) for his BBC series *Zoo Quest*, and happily I have worked with him at the BBC Natural History Unit in Bristol on and off ever since.

David appeared on a show in which I also interviewed the extreme right-wing Prime Minister, Ian Smith (a show which caused me to be accused of 'reeking run-to-seed-liberalism'). David watched Smith walk out rather grim-faced and slipped me his card with the comment, 'Come and see me if you need to.' Two years later, when David had just become Controller of the newly formed BBC2, I sent in that card and was invited to call on him at the brand new BBC Television Centre at Shepherds Bush.

In fact it would be some twenty years before I found my way back to the BBC. By then David had given up television administration and was back doing the presenting job he loved for the Natural History Unit in Bristol. I had been commissioned to direct a special for *Natural World* entitled *Incredible Suckers* (it was a film about squid) for which Attenborough agreed to do the narration.

The point of this rambling story is that because of my bogus qualifications as an African naturalist, in 1971 I was also invited by Bob Heller, Head of Factual Programmes at ATV (later Central, later still Carlton and now Granada), to make a documentary back in Africa! Heller was an extremely astute documentary commissioning editor who had an almost uncanny nose for a developing story, and he was on the lookout for someone who might investigate reports he had read about rhino being slaughtered for their allegedly aphrodisiac horns and a new market for ivory in East Africa. South Africa was then at war with all of its neighbours and the suggestion was that the illegal game spoil was paying for the destabilisation of its enemies. My credentials as 'wildlife expert' and refugee from a white right-wing regime made me the ideal candidate to make the film and Heller pulled the strings necessary in those days to get me a director's ticket.

So a month or so later I was on an undercover mission to East Africa with a film crew consisting of cameraman Mike Whittaker, who went on to run Granada's inventive drama department, and his assistant Dick Pope, who is today a successful feature film director. This story put me into direct bloody contact with the dying elephants of Africa and built contacts who have kept me up to date on that story for the past forty years.

We worked our way from Nairobi to the Serengeti taking random footage from the roadside of whatever wildlife presented itself and then waited five long days until the man Bob Heller had read about, an irascible character called Myles Turner, came Land-Rovering in from the bush at the head of a squad of rangers straight from the cast of *Apocalypse Now*. He took a few minutes off from refilling his petrol and water tanks to talk to us.

'Come on patrol with us,' he said. 'Come and see it as it is.' I accepted with alacrity but I sense even now, fifteen years after Myles had an early stroke, that all the long departed old Africa hands who knew how he operated were laughing their heads off at that moment.

Myles, like Daphne Sheldrick, was a graduate, as he liked to put it, of the 'African school of life'. He was born in Kenya and, after a perfunctory education, hunted a little and then joined the Game Department as a control officer. The life of a control officer was an extraordinary one. All very young, all paid a pittance, control officers were in a sense the government's hunters and in that role they killed an enormous number of animals.

'Control' was the way the government attempted in the old days to keep at bay the question I am attempting to answer in this book:

how do you stop a system of wildlife management structured by and for white folk from becoming so unpopular with the rural African that he will simply ignore it and exploit its loopholes at every opportunity? In the government's control officer system people had their place and animals theirs. If either crossed the line, they faced sanctions. In the case of people they were judged to be poachers and jailed. Any animals that broke out of their designated territory and inflicted mayhem on human territory were shot. Elephants, it has to be said, are among the most destructive animals on earth. Daphne Sheldrick gets round the problem by piously branding them 'nature's gardeners'. That is all very well if the garden is the size of Tsavo but not if it is a peasant's garden with his annual crop of ripe mielies.

So this young bushman, Myles Turner, travelled around Kenya 'controlling' such animals as elephants, rhino, lions, leopards and particularly buffalo. He slept mostly in native villages or in remote farmhouses, usually with his pack of semi-wild dogs. This extraordinary way of life bred an equally extraordinary state of mind.

> In my mind the rogue wildlife ceased to be animals and became instead a kind of criminal element which I was paid to hunt down. I was a policeman really. I would go to an area, sniff around with my dogs and get to know the kind of criminal, or the gang if it was buffalo, I was going to be dealing with. An old buffalo could be as cunning as any human being and twice as dangerous. Lions were brave and arrogant. They would move away from you at first, casting you a contemptuous glance, but if you went after them they thought 'To hell with this' and charged their heads off. Leopards were the most cunning of all. Whenever I went after a leopard, usually at night, I always told myself to remember that the leopard was also hunting me – and [was] better at it!

Elephants he saw as creatures so 'above it all' that people were no more than irritants to them. His technique with rogue elephants was first to try and scare them away from human settlements, saving more severe sanctions for persistent offenders. Nevertheless he admits to killing or 'controlling' huge numbers of elephants and buffalo. Travelling like a gypsy, risking his life sometimes several times a day, and often having no contact with other Europeans for days or weeks on end, Myles both loved and hated the life. Like all the committed hunters before him, he adored being in the wilderness but he was also aware that he was becoming more and more anti-social. When the Kenya Emergency came along in 1952 he and several of the other young control officers realised that their former lives had been an apprenticeship for an even more bizarre role, hunting Mau Mau.

'We had to become animals of the forest,' said Myles with the wry grin which was his trademark. 'The closer you got to being an animal, the longer you lived. We had to change what we ate just so as our shit would smell like theirs. I learnt more about animals in that time than I ever have since.'

As I have said elsewhere, few of these forest fighters from the Mau Mau days will discuss the gory details of their experiences. They were in fact fighting Kenya's independence war and, as we have heard, by 1960 that war had been won – or had it? The Mau Mau certainly was defeated, but some years later the Kikuyu led by Jomo Kenyatta formed Kenya's first black government and a lot of Mau Mau generals and field marshals (the Mau Mau leader Dedan Kimathi had promised that anyone who fought until the end of the war would be called field marshal) were still alive and expecting to be paid for their years in the forest. Was that so bad? Robin Hood was a poacher in the forest and put arrows through a goodly number of the Sheriff of Nottingham's soldiers, but when Richard the Lionheart came home, Robin left the forest and was rewarded with lands and estates well endowed with rich wildlife. A cyclone of change – that famous wind of change forecast by Harold Macmillan – was about to pick up East Africa's tightly controlled game management policies and throw them to the winds. Lost in this holocaust were the game and the game managers, people like Myles who found themselves spiralling into a limbo.

Jomo Kenyatta presented himself as a modern leader with one foot (and his famous fly-whisk) in the traditionalist camp. The Cold War world of the 1960s, particularly America, was relieved to have him. His one-party state and the murder of at least one opposition leader, Tom Mboya, were tolerated so long as he did not go down the Communist road as Julius Nyerere had in Tanganyika, Milton Obote in Uganda, and Moise Tshombe in the Congo, to mention but a few. In those days America put up with anyone who did not brandish the Red Flag, even the hammer-wielding psychopath Idi Amin, whom the US paid to topple Obote. Then there was the man I regard as the most corrupt egomaniac beleaguered Africa has ever produced, Sese Seko Mobutu, who with American support had Tshombe beaten to death in an aeroplane and then got on with the job of royally milking the Congo.

Nyerere in Tanzania, where the game lands were vast and elephants prolific (it had joined itself with Zanzibar island after a Chinese expeditionary force toppled the ages-old Omani sultanate), was watched nervously. Nyerere, fortunately, was a political theorist, a pleasant and intelligent man who had his heart in the right place. His Arusha Manifesto was one of the most enlightened conservation plans ever published:

> The survival of our wildlife is a matter of grave concern to all of us in Africa. These wild creatures amid the wild places they inhabit are not only important as sources of wonder and inspiration but are an integral part of our natural resources and of our future livelihood and well being. In accepting the trusteeship of our wildlife we solemnly declare that we will do everything in our power to make sure that our children's grandchildren will be able to enjoy this rich heritage.

But then came this little codicil:

> The conservation of wildlife and wild places calls for specialist knowledge, trained manpower and money and we look to other nations to co-operate in this – the success or failure of which not only affects the continent of Africa but the rest of the world as well.

Not to be outdone, Jomo Kenyatta issued the Kenya Government Manifesto:

The natural resources of this country – its wildlife which offers such an attraction to visitors from all over the world, the beautiful places in which these animals live, the mighty forests which guard the water catchment areas so vital to the survival of man and beast alike – are a priceless heritage for the future.

Kenyatta also added a codicil, but his was a bit more direct:

At present we are unable, unaided, to provide the specialist staff and money which is necessary. We therefore invite other nations, and lovers of nature throughout the world, to assist us in honouring this pledge.

I had not realised that Richard Leakey was singing from so old a songbook.

The International Conservation Movement took this mandate (it was issued in 1963) as its mission statement. But the fact is that for the next thirty years wild animals dropped like flies in all the countries which had published these pious manifestos in spite of an ever-more entrenched conservation movement.

Ten years later, when the poaching of elephants was so intense it could not be kept from the international press, Kenyatta actually became patron of the newly founded World Wildlife Fund East Africa and accepted a cheque for 175,000KS from Prince Bernhard of the Netherlands who described Nairobi as 'a mecca for the conservation of wildlife'. More accurately, it had become one of the main sidings for the wildlife gravy train.

Nyerere's gentle brand of African socialism quietly bankrupted Tanzania, and the Americans were content to watch it happen. The Masai, as usual, did not help. With American support, Kenyatta, who had taken to wearing gold-braided uniforms, remained the ringmaster in the East African circus. The Americans and the World Bank were content for him to blunder on until he died in 1978 and Vice President Daniel Arap Moi took over.

With hindsight it has always seemed to me that Kenya's burgeoning conservation establishment learned their eco-speak and their laws of survival in the Jomo Kenyatta era – and arguably they picked them up from their bosses abroad. More simply, they learned how to look the other way. Going against the big man with the staring eyes and the fly-whisk simply got you booted out of this new Africa for the Africans, and how did that help the wildlife?

It is a justification that has always made me queasy because all it really protected was a huge number of jobs in the International Conservation Movement. It did little for the animals. At least 40,000 elephants would die in the Kenyatta decade and all the International Conservation Movement did was count the carcasses. As I intend to prove this statement in an upcoming chapter I will not go into them here, but almost anything would have been better than this.

I arrived in Tanzania with my little film crew armed only with a vague foreboding of the magnitude of the looming storm. Myles Turner had just been made the warden in charge of anti-poaching for the whole of the Serengeti ecosystem, an appointment which showed the writing that was on the wall. Myles should have been chief warden but that job was obviously going to an African when they could find one. (It went quite soon thereafter to Solomon Ole Saibul, as we know.) Myles agreed that we could come on patrol and film his anti-poaching operations but he insisted that I first went on to the Arusha to meet another warden, Eric Balson, whom Myles said had 'stuff' no one else had.

'What sort of stuff?'

'Chapter and verse. Just the sort of stuff you're after. But you need to go and see Eric now,' Myles said. 'He's working on a job for the president personally but I reckon when he submits his report there'll be a whitewash and Eric will get his marching orders.' This, for the record, is exactly what happened, but not before Eric had handed me some 300 photocopies of documents which I still have to this day and a key draft chapter for a book he had written which so far as I know has never been published.

'Be careful,' Myles warned as we set off for the coast. 'Eric's been getting death threats and he's taken to carrying a lot of heavy ordnance. I've told him you're coming and where you'll be staying. Wait for him to contact you.' This was my first real encounter with the cloak-and-dagger world of the New Africa. I took it very seriously and we sat around in a mediocre out-of-season hotel for several nail-biting days until a cheerful voice phoned and deflated the James Bond atmosphere which I had been quite enjoying.

'Eric Balson here! Sorry, I only just got Myles's chittie. Been on safari up country. Like to come over to the house for a sundowner?' Eric's 'safari up country', I was to learn later, had involved him blacking up and posing as a rhino-horn poacher to a Jeep-load of Arab buyers and their heavily armed bodyguards. This he was doing on average about once a week, acting on the information he had culled from dozens of forged ivory and rhino import permits.

On the surface, Eric's house seemed as innocent as this cheery man had sounded on the telephone. But on closer inspection one noted that it occupied a hillside site with what a military expert would have described as an open field of fire. Here and there, working or just sitting under the flamboyant trees and in shaded areas of tall bamboo, were several gardeners, but surely many more than a garden of this size needed. Moreover, their gardening tools seemed to consist solely of lethal-looking *pangas*. There were two men in huge military overcoats and sandals made of old car tyres, each of whom carried a knobkerrie, one or two stout sticks and a long spear.

'Those are my askaris [house guards],' Eric said. 'Masai. Only sort of work they'll do for a *mzungu*. That's fine by me, they're very good at it.'

'And the gardeners?'

'I can't afford gardeners,' Eric grinned. 'Not since the British government started fiddling our pay and pensions. Those are my safari boys. They make my tea.' They were his field force.

'Have you had death threats? Myles said . . .'

'Their tea isn't quite that bad,' Eric laughed. 'I've had a couple of people take pot-shots at me, but that's because they took me for police. My fault really.'

I later discovered (from the draft chapter Eric gave me) that he had already applied to the regional police commissioner for protection and two armed officers came to his house every night. A number of death threats had been made on his phone – so he had the post office remove it. Away from home he carried two handguns, a .38 pistol and a .38 automatic.

Over the next week, Eric gradually revealed the deadly job he had
been doing. President Nyerere, whom Eric shared my liking for, had
transferred him from his game wardenship to undertake a secret
investigation, confidential to the presidential office, into the reports
of serious poaching, illegal cross-border trade in high-value game
goods, and corruption in the Game Department and in government.
Balson believed that Nyerere genuinely wanted to put a stop to all
this, and Balson was proceeding on his dangerous way confident
that his report would be for the president's eyes alone.

Eric needed witness statements and other hard evidence if he was
to prove that the many accusations against people in high places
(one such was a Game Department official whose brother was the
vice president) would stand up in court. Eric would vanish into his
office for days on end, meticulously looking for anomalies in records
of game deals from his own department in Tanzania and from
friends and colleagues in Kenya, Uganda and even Zaire (as it was
then).

At night the Eric Balson everyone knew and liked vanished like a
character from a John Buchan novel, and from the shadows there
emerged a mysterious trader without a name and of no particular
race but with a famously fat wallet. Eric set up his own secret
network of middlemen (some of the 'gardeners' were also employed
on this work) who went out into the countryside, bragging that they
could get unlimited cash for game products, particularly prized
skins, ivory and rhino horn. Other agents recruited by Eric posed as
the middlemen for a 'guy from Kenya' who had so many tusks and
ivory he was eager to get rid of them at bargain rates. Finally there
was a small shed in Eric's garden where it was known you could
come at night and he would pay you for information about anything
to do with game products, no matter how trivial.

'That was the most tiring bit,' Eric admitted. 'I was once offered a
mangy old lion skin that must have been fifty years old and was
probably poached by *my* grandfather. People used to accuse their
neighbours of some menial crime as revenge for something of no
interest to me whatsoever.' But occasionally, and increasingly
regularly as the word got around, he started to lure the big fish,
men, and occasionally women, who would meet him in either very
remote places at night or very public places like bars or restaurants.

Like all secret agents Eric also had to be very careful about what he passed on to the police for fear it could be traced back to him. He compromised by only occasionally parting with any of the funds which had been set aside for the operation. Usually he only paid for porterage, saying he would pay for the goods when he could inspect them. Thus the situations he found himself in were increasingly fraught with tension and every time he went on a mission he wondered whether it would be his last, especially when the word spread that he was up to something for the president. This became increasingly worrying when he began to find evidence that corruption was very widespread, reaching out to every branch of government, the police and especially his own Game Department. Then the death threats started.

Eric told me the details of only a few of these missions and some of them would certainly have put James Bond to shame. A common feature of these contacts was that Tanzanian poacher-dealers were most interested in meeting '*mzungus* from Kenya'. Eric agreed that he would meet a dealer who went under the name of Saida at a remote spot in the forests outside Arusha. Eric recorded:

I had in the meantime been given a CID corporal, Dominic, to act as my assistant and bodyguard who was a crack shot. After two weeks of bargaining as a Kenyan buyer I succeeded in persuading this poacher to agree to show me the trophies and his hide-out in the forest and he sent a man to bring me to him.

I fully expected to be ambushed so Dominic and I kept our weapons at the ready. The mist had already started to settle on the small valleys and we were walking in thick overcoats and hats. Our path took us through banana plantations and my face was cold from the continuous drip of water from the banana plants as we ducked under the overhanging leaves. It must have been a good hour before we left the plantations and entered the forest where it grew dark.

After about a mile the path ended, blocked by a huge fallen tree. On hands and knees we followed our guide down the main stem of this giant tree, slippery and damp with moss, until we came to a hide under its base. Inside there was a smoky fire which stung my eyes. The smell was foul.

I asked this big wheel how many men he had working for him and he told me he operated five teams who did nothing but trap leopards.

'I have about 300 goats which are used only for trapping,' he explained. 'My men operate right in the bush and during the day they tend the grazing goats and look for places to set up the traps.'

Places he mentioned were Manyara National Park, the Kitete, Olmoti and Monduli mountains, and the Ngorongoro Crater highlands and Oldeani forests right down into the conservation area at Endulen. The leopards were trapped in a device shaped like an upside-down V, with the door hanging above, triggered by a trip wire. Apparently they caught more hyenas in the traps than they did leopards and these were just speared. The leopards came to a horrible end.

'When my men find a leopard in the trap they light a small fire and heat up a sharp spear,' this guy told us. 'One man goes in front of the leopard to attract its attention whilst another goes and grabs hold of its tail. Then the hot spear is pushed right up the arse into its stomach and it soon dies. That way you don't mark the skin – "*Marifa, mzuri sana* (very good method)",' he chuckled.

The poacher took Eric into the back of his lair and showed him fourteen leopard skins and twelve rhino horns. After much haggling Eric agreed to pay 800KS for a leopard and 40KS per pound for the rhino horn. Handing over 200KS for porterage, he told the poacher he never carried large sums of money with him but they would meet the following evening to complete the deal. These notes had had their serial numbers taken by the police. The poacher never arrived for this meeting.

On another occasion Eric travelled with two ivory dealers to inspect some tusks they were offering, complete with legal import/export permits, to a remote river delta where an Arab dhow was waiting. Eric was shown a hold full of tusks half hidden under a huge mound of mango poles. He was told the poles had been used to conceal the tusks from Mombasa customs officers who usually could not be bothered to pay the cost of unloading the dhows, knowing that most of them were engaged only in the mango pole trade. He was told that, for a fee, he could ship ivory and rhino horn out of Tanzania by this same method – provided of course that he could produce Tanzanian import/export permits to accompany them.

Reading these accounts from Eric Balson's notes thirty-five years after they were written, I have been struck by something about them which did not occur to me at the time. I, like the rest of the conservation industry and wardens in the field such as Turner and Balson, was really horrified by the extent of this brutal wildlife trade and the methods that were being used to kill animals. But the reality is that this trade had been going on for thousands of years – dhow-type ships have been coming down the east coast since the time of Solomon and there are stories in the Bible of leopard skins being shipped from East Africa to Egypt. This trader in skins was *proud* of his skill in producing unmarked product. We were the oddities, *mzungus* who had only been here a few decades and for some reason were now trying to stop a man from earning his living.

The reason the documentary that resulted from my trip, *The Animal War*, was such a success was that it broke this news and these brutal methods, complete with pictures no one had seen before, to a television audience. I have to be careful in my condemnation of conservation because to a considerable degree television invented it and fed it to the masses.

Eric produced piles of proof against senior officials of the Game Department of Tanzania, officers of the CID, the police, a list of ten dealers who were also poachers, three game assistants in the Arusha Game Division, one senior game assistant, the permits officer, a driver and three clerks, four game scouts and two game assistants in Moshi. And this was just his interim list. In his final report Eric took his accusations right to the top. He named the big wheel as a certain Saidi Kawawa. The Vice President of Tanzania at that time was Saidi's full brother, the Rt Hon. Rashidi Kawawa, President Nyerere's deputy and the man who *de facto* ran the administration of Tanzania.

Again I would like to point out, having had three decades to reflect on it, that there is another way of looking at the whole affair. It occurs to me in retrospect that what is being described was in fact a well-organised, well-conducted wildlife business that spanned the whole country, administered and managed by some of the most skilled and experienced men in the land. It was wrong because it broke laws. But these were laws imposed by colonialists. Everything else to do with the colonialists was being thrown out of the window, why not practices that were ruining an ancient industry which had always been of great value to indigenous people? And what was the crime? Wildlife was not like cattle which belonged to certain people. How could you steal what God had given all the *watu*?

In truth the men who sought to administer the laws in an era of change, men like David Sheldrick, Myles Turner and Eric Balson, were, to the *uhuru* generation, members of the *mzungu* old guard still stubbornly fighting a rearguard action against Africa's New Deal. To see it otherwise involves considerable hypocrisy. Wildlife was cleared from early Europe, and within living memory from America by just such means and morality. Where is the bison today, or its European equivalent the wisent? The land they roamed is now covered by the wheat farms and car plants that fund the North–South divide. Hunting of wild animals is encouraged. The killing of stags and pheasants in the Scottish highlands is a lucrative industry, as is the controlled slaughter of game in the American west. But in destitute Kenya, home as I have said of the biggest conservation establishment on the planet, the hunting of wild animals is still banned under laws laid down in the 1970s as a result of concerted pressure by the international conservation movement.

In Tanzania Eric Balson not only demonstrated that there was a vast underground economy devoted to the trade in wildlife, but as he extended his enquiries he came to realise that this economy encompassed the whole of Central, East and North Africa. Tanzania and Kenya were operating what amounted to a partnership. Eric's office work was now focused on documents, in particular permit books. Hundreds of discrepancies turned up in the copies he inspected of apparently legal Tanzanian import licences for game trophies. He asked a friend in the Kenya Game Department to carry out a similar examination of the copies of permits for ivory, rhino, big cat and zebra skins there.

On one of his missions he was offered ivory weighing over 1,000kg which had legal export permits from Zaire to Belgium via

Uganda. Eric managed to make a note of the date and the number of this permit and arranged to have its origin checked. The Zaire authorities agreed to help him because the permit appeared to have been issued after Zaire banned all ivory exports. The original permit, it emerged, was one of a large batch 'lost in a fire'.

I will not bore you with the details of the hundreds of documents and hours of work Eric put in but eventually he was able to show how the scam worked.

Stage One: Get the Goods. Ivory, skins (preferably big cat skins but also zebra and the valuable antelopes like sable and kudu) and rhino horn would be gathered illegally in any one of the East African countries or Zaire (although Zaire was more of an entrepôt than a producer).

Stage Two: Legalise the Spoils. Stolen or lost permits from Zaire, Kenya, Uganda, Tanzania and (later) the Sudan were taken into another country and matched to this ivory, thereby legalising it for shipment. For example, a tusk poached in Kenya would be driven over the border into Tanzania where a 'lost' permit would be waiting for it. It would then be taken back into Kenya and sold there as 'legal' Tanzanian ivory. The Kenyans never cross-checked with Tanzania and vice versa (and these were countries where checking would not have been too difficult). When the trade was at its height from the mid-1970s onwards, the permits travelled to the ivory instead of the other way round.

Stage Three: Ship it Quick. Out of Tanganyika destined mostly for Hong Kong streamed boatloads of this fenced illegal ivory, all covered by legal permits from other countries in East Africa. Tanzanian (or Ugandan) ivory laundered by stolen or lost Kenyan export permits mostly left by air.

Eric further proved that government officials had to be turning a blind eye to all the missing permits, that Game Department staff were complicit in the illegal hunting and that several senior politicians, or their families, in both Tanzania and Kenya had been found with doubtful game spoils and were either running or were partners in the export businesses.

I should stress that these are conclusions drawn from the several hours of interviews I did with Eric Balson, all of which were professionally recorded and were manually transcribed for me. I still have those transcripts, along with a copy of the report Eric was intending to submit to the president. He wrote:

> This is a gigantic problem we are currently faced with. It is quite obvious to us all here that the poaching problem and the illegal trade in trophies is getting right out of hand; and is on an alarming increase. Poaching in Tanzania has increased by more than 100% within the past few years and is reaching the stage where, if not checked immediately, will certainly affect the whole economy.

Eric says his report was delivered to the president's office via the chief game warden in January 1970.

The 1970s was the end of the age of innocence for the African elephant, but looking back on what was actually happening it still seems hardly credible. Catastrophic elephant poaching in Kenya and Tanzania did not really attract serious public attention until the 1980s but as we have seen, wardens like Balson were calling for emergency action well over a decade before that. Moreover, he had laid the blame firmly on senior heads of government, the army, government departments including those responsible for game, parks, customs and excise, and more than a dozen poacher-dealers. It would surprise me if the International Conservation Movement did not know this was happening.

Eric Balson also suspected that a cover-up was going on throughout East Africa, as is revealed by a single hand-typed letter marked private and confidential which I recently found buried in his files. 'Dear Eric, Excuse my using your first name when we have never met but I have heard so much of you from your friends in both Kenya and Tanzania that I feel I know you.' The letter goes on to ask Eric to contact 'Senior Superintendent Gontier' in Nairobi and promises 'the purpose of this contact would be to foster our mutual aims of Game Preservation which know no territorial boundaries'. The letter is sent 'c/o Mrs. R. Woodley' (Bill's second wife) from Nyeri in Kenya and is signed simply 'Yours sincerely, Rodney Elliot'.

Elliot had just begun working with one of the few Kenyan Africans who appeared genuinely concerned at the damage being done to the country's national game herds, the Attorney General, Charles Njonjo.

Elliot had first contacted Njonjo in 1971 (the same year he wrote to Eric) after investigating strange goings-on at the Kenya Game Department's Nanyuki station, of which the most bizarre was the issue of permits to a private ranch, Ol Pejeta, for twenty-two elephants' ears (the finest leather comes from the ears). But Elliot knew that elephant permits were never allowed on private lands and indeed the Ol Pejeta manager, Rod Herd, confirmed that no elephants had been shot there.

I have not the room here to go into the can of worms Elliot opened with this enquiry; suffice it to say that he proved Game Department staff were shooting elephants, zebra, lion, antelope for meat, and leopard for dealers, all of whom came from Nairobi. A couple of years later Rodney Elliot left the Game Department and went to work for the American millionaire owner of Solio ranch, Court Parfet, who was using its vast acreages to try to save the Kenyan black rhino.

I went to Solio to see Court Parfet as a possible *Nature Watch* subject, but when he thought about the publicity he decided that it would attract unwanted attention to his rhino. At that time we heard a story that there was *mzungu* running Solio who had poachers killed, minced and placed in a sack outside the ranch gates for the lions to enjoy. That *mzungu*, I assume, must have been Rodney Elliot. And, apocryphal as I assume the story to be, it certainly worked. When the black rhino was virtually wiped out all across Kenya, more than sixty were revealed to be thriving on Solio and these animals were used to rebuild a small national herd.

Court Parfet then made the government an offer. He would lend them Elliot to clean up the newly formed Wildlife Conservation and Management Department (WCMD), exactly as Eric Balson had been asked to do in Tanzania. Elliot set down a number of draconian conditions before accepting the task, not least that all his recommendations had to be accepted and that he could pull out if he did not feel he was making progress.

Elliot, like Balson, went back to the CID files and found hundreds of stolen or lost permit books which had been used to legitimise trophies. He found records of four men arrested with four elephant tusks who were later released when a Mau Mau 'field marshal' (she was actually a woman) turned up with a 'Mau Mau Collector's Permit' and identified the men as her 'agents'. Elliot revealed a scam in which more than 6,000kg of (presumed) rhino horn or chopped-up tusks was sent by mail in 10kg parcels from a public post office in Nairobi to an address in West Germany. On another occasion Elliot actually caught officials of the WCMD packing parcels of tusks for export. With Charles Njonjo's help he had all the ivory placed in the custody of the CID but was then hauled over the coals by the CID director for 'exceeding his authority'. In his first year in the job he placed 61 per cent of the staff of the WCMD under investigation.

However, in 1979 Rodney Elliot decided that there was no fixing the WCMD and he told the commissioner of police that he was quitting. The reaction was relief. 'No other person in conservation in Kenya,' Ian Parker wrote, 'ever went to the lengths that Rodney Elliot did to redress the mess that overtook the erstwhile Game Department and WCMD or had taken the risks that he took in doing so.'

The same can be said of Eric Balson in Tanzania. Immediately after his report was delivered Eric was fired from the Game Department, or rather his contract was not renewed and he went to live in South Africa. His report was never heard of again. Eric's demise is a classic case of the fate every professional conservationist has feared since independence and it has, in my opinion, rendered their presence ineffectual and largely pointless for the last several decades. Heroes Balson and Elliot may have been, but were they in fact swimming against a new African tide? Who was out of step here, the 61 per cent of WCMD charged by Rodney Elliot with breaking the laws of the land, or Elliot himself who would not address the fact that in this new Africa *de facto* and *de jure* really were different?

It was a question I still had to ask Myles Turner, so back we climbed into our Land Rovers and headed north again. 'Myles will show you how it's actually being done.' Eric said. 'But watch out,

1. The end of a good day's work for the legendary hunter Frederick Courtney Selous: a nap under a tree surrounded by dead and wounded elephants.

2. By the time of Pliny the use of elephants was so common that they had their own name, *Lucae boves*, or Lucane Oxen. Here they pull a plough in the old Belgian Congo.

3. Bearded, kilted Scots hunter, R. Gordon Cumming surrounded by panicked elephants he was busy slaughtering.

4. Crossing a river the R. Gordon Cumming way by impaling a hippopotamus in the flank and hanging on for grim death.

5. Legendary explorer David Livingstone did much of it on an ox. Here he rides his favourite Sinbad.

6. The most sophisticated Great White Hunter of them all, the Right Hon. Denis Finch Hatton with a pair of 'good' tusks.

7. Poacher-hunter, David Sheldrick with a massive pair of black rhinoceros horn. In Tsavo East where David was Chief Warden, rhino once 'boiled out of very bush'.

8. Rarest hunting prize of all, a four-tusked elephant.

9. The London Ivory salesroom of 1880 sold 65,000 elephant tusks which then passed to ivory factories like this in one Amsterdam.

10. Ivory porters, many enslaved, carried hundreds of thousands of elephant tusks out of the African hinterland.

11. Since time immemorial Arabs have controlled the ivory trade and its portage.

12. Professional hunters in the early days tried to immobilize their prey to save on bullets.

13. Myles Turner who found and lost his 'Animal War' in Tanzania, in one of the many poachers hides which sprang up all over the Serengeti National Park.

14. Natives, hard-put to bring down an elephant with spears, made little or no impact on elephant populations.

15. The Matabele leader, Lobengula, had his own private elephant hunting preserve and fined hunters like Selous when he thought they killed excessively.

16, 17, 18, 19. President Theodore Roosevelt did more for American wildlife for any man then or since – but loved Big Game hunting! Here in 1909 with Selous – everyone's idea of the Great White Hunter *(bottom right)* – they with their Press Corps *(bottom left)* mounted a park bench on the front of the train through Tsavo and shot anything they fancied. Fortunately for the wildlife, Roosevelt was a poor shot with bad eyesight and Selous was well past his hunting prime.

he's just about at the end of his tether too and he's a rough, tough bugger when he's this angry.'

Although I did not fully appreciate it then, we were returning to the killing fields or, more accurately, to watch the Serengeti dying. I was travelling up the road I had first traversed as a boy of nine and it seemed that I had come full circle to record a requiem for the African elephant. In a sense this was true. From this time on life would never be the same for the African elephant. Neither we nor Myles fully appreciated the scale of what was happening.

I have thought long and hard about whether the holocaust resulted from hard decisions or slow attrition. It seems more likely that the killing of elephants started as an opportunistic crime wave which, when the fat cats found out how easily they could get away with it, went on to become a massacre of bush-fire proportions. Myles Turner and I were there right at the start of it.

From 1970 onwards conservation as practised previously was also consumed by this fire. The survival of the conservation establishment became as important as the conservation of the wildlife. Indeed job protection was given as high a priority as wildlife protection. By the time Richard Leakey came along twenty years later to put out the glowing embers of this fire the big game – elephants and rhino certainly – were gone. But in that time the number of people employed in conservation or environmental jobs, mostly in Nairobi, must have risen tenfold.

The killing fields of Tanzania were a strange, awesome and dangerous place. As we waited in the pre-dawn stillness with Myles and his raggedy band (mostly 'turned' poachers), the sun would suddenly flame over a landscape which had changed in only one way since the dawn of recorded time. My memories of this place are the imprinted images of a boy seeing it for the first time, and I remember the animals as a dark frieze silhouetted against this sudden awakening of the light. In 1947 it had been an unbroken frieze from horizon to horizon. Now the frieze had distinct gaps in it. There were almost no elephants standing out in the plain. 'They're there', Myles confirmed. 'The wily ones. But they've learned to hide in the trees or in the thick bush.'

We had been doing this for nearly two weeks: driving off before dawn down tracks I could not see in a convoy of three small Land Rovers in the hope of catching poachers who would be loading their spoils into fast trucks ready for a dash back across the border into Kenya. After the first of these outings I gladly handed the driving over to one of Myles's grinning brigands who obviously had eyes like a cat.

Their trucks were incredibly battered. Their clothes were rags, often just a pair of shorts and *takis* (canvas running shoes), but their rifles were tended with love and wrapped around with small scraps of camouflage material. Myles dressed exactly like the men of his field force, except he kept his park warden's shirt lying beside him on the seat against the time when he had to make an arrest.

In the whole time we were with him he arrested one gang of poachers who were in the process of reducing their elephant to what looked like a long thin line of bloody washing, bright red and dripping, but so cunningly strung behind camouflaging bushes as to be all but invisible. One of Myles's trackers literally smelt the blood trail leading to the butchery camp and Myles grew very gloomy when we noted a set of truck tracks running alongside the blood trail. 'They won't have the ivory,' Myles commented tersely and he stopped to use his radio, calling his 'air wing', a battered Cessna, with instructions to undertake a patrol between our position and the Kenya border. Later that day, driving home down one of the few *murram* roads that crosses the Serengeti, we came across a smart modern Toyota waiting beside a crossroads. There were two Indians dressed in safari suits in the cab and two Masai in red cloths in the back. They waved merrily to us but Myles just roared on past, blanketing them in his dust while he muttered something about, 'Bastards are probably coming home from fencing my ivory.'

In those days he held every black or coloured man he found on his beloved plains to be a potential poacher. This was of course part of his problem and the reason why, a few years later, I found him living a happier life (even though he didn't much appreciate it), looking after animals for a private company in the Masai Mara area of Kenya and writing an adventurous book, *My Serengeti Days*. He knew his anti-poaching activities were behind him, but at least he was able to spend his last years among the animals he so dearly loved.

We arrested the butchers, who were not carrying guns, but as Myles had forecast there was no sign of the ivory and he told me he wouldn't be pushing for a severe sentence as the meat we had seen being prepared as *biltong* would all be sold to local communities. I have seen pictures since of Waliangula preparing elephant meat in exactly this way and it may be that these men were remnants of the old elephant hunter tribe.

The patrol had taken up sixteen hours of a very hot day, and by the time we got home Myles was exhausted and his bitterness showed. On our safari we had picked up about 300 steel-wire snares but Myles knew snares were not the real problem. He observed gloomily:

I'm being outgunned. Just a couple of years ago the worst you ever saw in the Serengeti was a couple of blokes with old .303s and a clapped-out Bedford truck, or boys with bows and arrows. We could handle that. Now they've got modern Toyotas and high-velocity automatic hunting rifles. They can outrun and outshoot me. What's more all the wardens here and elsewhere have been getting reports that the whole of the bloody Ogaden is on the move. There's been a war going up there as long as anyone can remember and the place is awash with weapons.

He was talking of the Somali *shifta* who in the years ahead would, with almost complete impunity, cut great swathes through the East African elephants to rival, indeed exceed, the worst excesses of the bad old days of big game hunting. 'We're really fighting a war here', he said, 'and at this rate we're going to lose it.'

The Animal War served me very well. The first full-length documentary I had produced, written and directed for the ITV Network, it was controversial enough to attract much attention in the press. Questions were asked in Parliament and it won several awards. Bob Heller offered me a job as an ATV staff director (in those days ITV was controlled by a powerful trade union and until Mrs Thatcher came along and destroyed the union this was literally a job for life). I made, on average, three hour-long documentaries a year for the next ten years, travelling all over the world and meeting people like Wilfred Thesiger, Edward Kennedy, Sir Oswald Mosley and Sir Peter Scott, but I did not make another natural history film until I started *Nature Watch* with Julian Pettifer in the early 1980s. We made sixty-eight programmes and the series never dropped out of the ITV top twenty for the next decade until I bought my house in Cape Town and quit my career in television.

For all of those ten years I made a point of going to East Africa at least once a year to do a *Nature Watch* programme on elephants in the hope that someone had found a way to stop the rot. They hadn't; indeed they couldn't.

We featured Iain Douglas-Hamilton in three of these shows, including one which did make a momentary ripple on the static surface of the conservation pond. In it Iain walked through a graveyard of elephant bones in Manyara where he had done the work for his great treatise, *Among the Elephants*. Close to tears, he commented: 'These were my friends!'

We filmed two shows with Daphne Sheldrick when Tsavo had become so poached out that the Somali gunmen had decided the place was not worth the ammunition. Daphne had brought her hand-raised elephant Eleanor back to the park in the hope of attracting funding for a reintroduction programme. A few years later we came back with Oria Douglas-Hamilton to film the first reintroductions, a beguiling set of little elephants which have so charmed the emotional conservationist brigade that Daphne now has funds flowing in from all over Europe and America. She has stuck to her guns and to Tsavo through thick and thin and will rightly go down in history as the grand champion of the African elephant. Tsavo's larger problems sadly are not going to be solved even by the redoubtable Mrs Sheldrick.

Finally there came one last flicker of hope. President Daniel Arap Moi was, in his dotage, blamed for the virtual extermination of his nation's elephant and rhino. Certainly he presided over most of the holocaust decade. Nudged by the World Bank into a move he quickly came to regret, in 1989 Moi appointed Richard Leakey to run a new conservation initiative (Kenya Wildlife Services) and restore the national reputation. Leakey focused on Tsavo, had the SAS train a smart new field force and armed them to the teeth under an African warden, Stephen Gichengi, whom I found quite inspirational.

What happened to Stephen and what became known as the Tsavo War I will leave to Richard to tell. Suffice it to say that Moi lost his nerve, Richard was terribly injured in a much-debated air crash, losing both his legs, and the crusade, in less well-known hands, faded and is now dead.

But I have got ahead of myself. All the above – from Myles Turner's travails in Serengeti to the raft of forged game permits Eric Balson found in Arusha, to the Somali *shifta*, to Daphne Sheldrick's agony as she slowly watched her beloved Tsavo being denuded of elephants – are the product of a piece of writing on the wall that should have been read not as the beginning of the end but more as the end of the beginning. This new beginning began way back in 1964 with a confidential memo to the Chief Game Warden of Kenya, Ian Grimwood, which purported to come from the office of the new president himself, the Mzee Jomo Kenyatta.

TEN

Bloody Ivory

In 1964, shortly after independence, Kenya's Chief Game Warden Ian Grimwood received secret orders from the president's office. Assumed to have been issued by Jomo Kenyatta himself, these instructions said that a number of Mau Mau fighters should be permitted to sell the game trophies they had hunted (illegally of course) and buried in the forest. The order was literally a poacher's charter and Grimwood was aware that it licensed the people most used to living outside the law to take any big game they liked. For example, the order listed big cat skins and rhino horns which could not possibly have survived being buried since the Emergency. The terms of the order authorised listed Mau Mau fighters to 'find' ivory and sell it. Grimwood, trying to put a wedge in a door he might never be able to close, insisted that trophies so 'found' must be brought in and sold to the government at 12KS per kilo. Later Mau Mau field marshal, Muthoni Kirima, went to Kenyatta and had these payments virtually doubled to 22KS. Mr Grimwood resigned.

If one looks at this development in another way, however, from what might be called the 'African perspective', one comes up with an entirely different attitude towards it. It seems to me that this was the moment when an African leader strapped for cash but needing to pay the field marshals who had brought him to power decided to exploit commercially his abundant wildlife. I have no idea, as some have suggested, whether Kenyatta decided also to abandon wildlife as a long-term commercial asset and chose instead to clear the country for agriculture and industrial development. His statements of the time (for which he was awarded the Golden Ark) appeared to recognise the importance of wildlife, but his actions, certainly the actions of his family, made it sound like lip-service.

It was also arguable that Kenya still had elephants and rhino to spare. I remember Daphne Sheldrick describing for *Nature Watch* the huge numbers of black rhino in Tsavo when she was there with David. 'They came boiling out of every bush!' From the 1960s onwards the use of light aircraft increased and most wardens learned to fly. Aerial counting revealed the presence of many more elephants than anyone had suspected. A survey in 1961 of Tsavo East and West came up with 6,000 animals, twice as many as the wardens had expected, but in the years ahead subsequent counts took the figure to over 40,000. At the same time there was a serious drought.

A Tsavo Research Unit was set up headed by Dr Dick Laws who recommended a large reduction programme. David Sheldrick opposed it and he, Laws and Ian Parker, who would probably have been hired to shoot the elephants, fell out in a big way. David was not originally opposed to some reduction of elephant numbers as the Tsavo bush, especially in times of drought, was being badly hammered by them. But he objected strongly to the cull of thousands that was proposed. Daphne told me:

> Dr Laws maintained that the elephant population of the park was made up of ten discrete groups and he wanted to 'sample' 300 animals from each group – a total of 3,000 elephants! Dick Laws threw in his hand at a meeting when he said 'Either Sheldrick goes or I do', and the trustees said they couldn't spare David and it would therefore have to be him! David had actually resigned, but was persuaded to withdraw his resignation. Dr Laws took himself off, wounded to the quick!
>
> The truth is David was also suspicious of Dr Laws's motives, particularly as Dr Laws insisted that only Ian Parker and his company were competent to do the culling exercise – they had worked together in Uganda where Ian culled some 3,000 elephants in Murchison Falls. David insisted that if culling was necessary, for whatever reason, the park's personnel would have to handle it and that he was just as competent at shooting elephants as Ian Parker. He wanted to remove the commercial aspect from the exercise.

Daphne also reported that her husband believed that if a cull was embarked on, it would become 'policy', and in Black Africa it was unrealistic to believe that this would not lead to abuse in view of the corruption prevailing among officials under Kenyatta.

'[David] believed that man's role in a national park should be non consumptive,' she went on. 'The primary role of the national parks service was to administer natural areas in such a way as to maintain an area's ecosystem in as nearly a pristine condition as possible.' The real reason, she said, that poaching eventually ran out of control in Tsavo was David's removal.

It left the field wide open, the Field Force disillusioned and inclined to jump on the bandwagon too. Lack of control, lack of leadership and corruption in high places: it was simple as that. It was claimed that poaching died down after 1978. Wrong! It was rife still but it suited the authorities to put it out that it had died down, the authorities being the major dealers in ivory.

Daphne explained to me that by then David had started to believe in a theory of elephant land occupation which he and a former warden turned wildlife cameraman who lived in Tsavo, Simon Trevor, had named the 'Long Cycle'. Simon had set up fixed-camera positions (rough tripods concreted into strategic points round the park) and had started to photograph the way elephants were altering the landscape and how these changes affected their numbers. Essentially what the Long Cycle theory proposed was that elephant numbers naturally rose and fell according to how much vegetation there was for them to eat. If there were too many elephants (as there arguably were in the 1960s) they would destroy their food trees and 'die back'.

David and Simon were able to show that while elephants might pull down every tree in sight, they rarely destroy the tree and never its saplings. Even at their most destructive they do some good, hence Daphne's euphemistic description 'gardeners of Tsavo' (or sometimes, of 'Eden'!). All that vegetation must, after all, come out the other end as rich manure. Trees bent and broken down to ground level by elephants provided much-needed food for smaller grazers and browsers that had used up all the food plants they could reach. Moreover, these small herbivores would flourish while the forests were regrowing ready for the next lot of elephants. Daphne has shown me photographs of Tsavo when it was reduced to a desert in the 1960s and others of the same view thirty years on. The vegetation had indubitably regrown.

The Sheldrick–Trevor Long Cycle theory could well be right. It will take 300 to 400 years to prove one way or another, and personally I have my doubts: the theory leaves a vital factor out of the equation – people. The Long Cycle depends on pristine conditions and Tsavo is not going to remain pristine and people-free for anything like 300 years. It represents a vast area of potential cattle grazing. If Kenya's population keeps growing at its present exponential rate, cattle not wildlife will be its destiny.

It was not even totally pristine back in the 1970s. Lurking just over the horizon, powered by human corruption fuelled by the infamous Mau Mau finders-keepers permits, was an elephant holocaust worse than anything anyone had even dreamed of. It was not initially entirely man-made. Drought returned to Tsavo in 1971 and the elephants went to work on the few forests left from 1960. Some conservationists renewed their calls for elephant numbers to be reduced but David, armed with his Long Cycle theory, was determined to let nature take its course. The drought also affected the indigenous communities around the edges of Tsavo and they, mostly Kamba, took to poaching small game, largely by snaring.

When elephants and rhino began to die in significant numbers, bands of collectors now roaming the countryside with permits descended on Tsavo en masse. The park gained a reputation as an eldorado for collectors of elephant and rhino material, at first for tusks and horn which could simply be picked up as their owners died of thirst and starvation, and later for easy hunting because most of the animals were in a debilitated condition. The shift from 'found' to poached income came about after 1972 when the rains finally broke. David Sheldrick arrested his first Somali poachers in Tsavo in 1973, although it should be said that in all of his tenure no Somali was ever found within the park with a gun. He also estimated that there could be as many as 500 local gangs entering the park every day. David had just fifty rangers, himself and his deputy to patrol a place the size of Israel and he recognised that the arrival of the Somalis from the far north presaged the end. David deployed his tiny Field Force with military efficiency and the records from 1975 show that he arrested 212 men, recovering more than 1,000 tusks and almost 150 rhino horn. Half as many again were arrested in the first half of 1976, indicating that the flood had not been stopped. Indeed it was strengthening.

'David had been formidable when the colonial government ruled', writes Ian Parker, 'but did not know how to operate with the African system which replaced it. He, like so many of us, felt that if he spoke his mind and voiced his criticisms, he would simply lose his job. And in that he was probably right.' Parker himself was also to learn that lesson the hard way.

Daphne prefers to let the figures speak for themselves. 'David left 20,000 elephants in Tsavo. One year later the population had dropped to 8,000, another year later to 5,000 and today remains at [around] 4,000!'

The last white man (until Richard Leakey's brief tenure) to oversee the affairs of wildlife in Kenya was Mervyn Cowie. He was replaced by Perez Olindo as Director of National Parks when the Game Department came under the new Permanent Secretary of the Ministry of Tourism and Wildlife, Alois Achieng. In 1976 the National Parks Department was merged with the Game Department into the Wildlife Conservation and Management Department (WCMD). The parks' board of trustees, which had been established to give national parks a little independence, was abolished and from then onwards the government pulled the strings.

David Sheldrick was by now a very famous wildlife warrior not averse to calling the attention of the international press and the powerful conservation lobbies to the holocaust overtaking Tsavo. The government decided he had to be removed and in 1976 he and Daphne were transferred from their beloved Tsavo to a desk job. Daphne said it broke his heart and I am sure it did, but his death a year later, aged fifty-seven, was from congenital heart disease, which had also killed his father in his fifties. One way or another David Sheldrick gave his all to Tsavo and his wife has never let the world forget. She formed the David Sheldrick Memorial Trust within a few months, with Tsavo as its priority, and has made that sacred ground her mindset for half a century.

Bill Woodley was called back to Tsavo to take over from David, which rather negates the suggestion that there was no place for *mzungus* in the new Wildlife Conservation and Management Department. The truth is Bill was a native-born Kenyan (David had remained a British citizen) who knew how to work the system (as do his sons, Bongo, Ben and Danny), and in any case the WCMD had no one else half capable of taking on Tsavo. David Sheldrick had written in 1976: 'There is now a singular dearth of young officers in National Parks who are sufficiently interested or dedicated to take an active part in anti-poaching work. Most of them are not prepared to "rough-it" in the bush and share the same dangers and hardships as the rangers.'

Even so, Bill's anti-poaching activities in Tsavo West ended after four years when ill health grounded him from further flying. Throughout that time he turned a largely blind eye to corruption permeating the WCMD, including his own Tsavo park wardens, and simply got on with his job as best he could. Restrictions from on high made his task almost impossible. For example, he was banned from his old part of the park, Tsavo East, even though he often flew that way and in his first year located some fifty elephant and rhino carcasses from the air. On another occasion, asked to investigate a fire, he found forty freshly killed elephants so close to the road he concluded that they had probably been shot from vehicles.

On the ground his men were having an uncomfortable time and their morale was terrible. A force of rangers was attacked by a Somali gang and fled in terror back to their base led by their warden. Eight rangers from Tsavo were accused by Bill Woodley of killing an elephant but none was prosecuted and they all kept their jobs. The Somali raiders grew ever more brazen and in 1982 hit a settlement near a largish town, Mtito Andei. Bill picked up their tracks and located the Somalis who took to their heels as soon as they heard his plane. Flying alone, Bill fired on the group with a small sporting rifle and dropped hand grenades on them, scoring one hit. Two bullets from their automatic rifles passed through his wings. There were twenty rangers pursuing on the ground but all they caught was an exhausted Somali teenager. Bill called for an ambush to be laid across a road out of the park. Nine Somalis were watched crossing the road but there was no ambush – the assistant warden leading the Field

Force decided it was too dangerous to engage the gang. The postscript to this story was even more extraordinary. The gang escaped from Tsavo but sought shelter with a group of Orma herders who pretended to be friendly. The Orma speared five of the Somalis and captured the other four, with their rifles. The rather macabre irony is that this, the most effective hit in the first Tsavo war, was the work of spear-wielding herders, not wardens.

During the four years Bill Woodley was in action, six Somalis were shot and over a hundred arrested; 150 tusks, 15 rifles and almost 1,000 rounds of ammunition were recovered. The conviction rate was paltry. Bill retired in 1991 after forty-three years' service in national parks. I went up to Mount Kenya shortly after Bill's death in 1995 to see his son, Bongo, about a film for the BBC (we were going to call it *The Wild Woodleys*) and we fell to discussing his father's activities and his success rates. Bongo shook his head wryly: 'Dad tried as hard as anyone could, especially a guy who'd had cancer, but it was a drop in the bucket.'

All this, it has to be said, was the state of affairs as seen through *mzungu* eyes. There is a completely different African perspective, which ran rather along these lines. The anti-poaching wars were initiated and led by white wardens of the old colonial school. Rural Africans, especially those living around parks, were delighted with the extra meat and a share of the ivory and rhino-horn income that appeared part of the legacy of *uhuru*. Most of it was coming their way via the Collector permits with which the *Mzee* had rewarded his freedom-fighters.

This African perspective will, of course, have to remain imagined rather than verified, but there is no denying that an all-encompassing African network of adept, skilled officials holding the very top jobs in the government, the army, the parks and game departments, customs and excise, the railways and the airlines was fully operational by 1978. Admittedly this game business was less than entirely efficient because it had to operate covertly. Kenyans knew that to renounce all the colonial game laws, to de-register the colonial parks and to announce a government-sponsored wildlife exploitation programme would turn off the huge sums of hard foreign currency being generated by the burgeoning conservation establishment. International aid would also suffer because the World

Bank and the International Monetary Fund represented western interests which mostly found the killing of wild animals repugnant. Then there was the tourist industry which was also bringing in much-needed hard currency but was increasingly driven by wildlife tourism – foreign people from rich countries who wanted to watch wild live animals. How do you give the *wainuchi* and *wabenzi* what they want (I am convinced that by the 1980s the network of game exploitation was so widespread and endemic that the government could not have stopped it even had it wanted to) and also keep the rich wandering white westerners happy? The answer was to keep game exploitation a secret insofar as that was possible.

Again I cannot see how the International Conservation Movement could not work this out when it seemed so obvious to the rest of us. But if they did (and I will present evidence in my next chapter indicating that they did), then what we have here is a conspiracy of silence during which at least 10,000–20,000 of their charges (counting elephant alone) were dying annually.

Eric Balson's report, for example, has never seen the light of day, but in it he listed (as examples of the extent of the corruption) an ex-Mayor of Nyere (charged with the possession of six elephant tusks), a Regional Commissioner (theft and unlawful possession of four elephant tusks), a Wanza businessman and a Senior game warden (unlawful possession of government tropies worth 225,075/-), Four Parks Department drivers (transporting illegal ivory), a Game Assistant and a farmer (illegal shooting of an elephant), and numerous dealers trafficking illegally and sometimes quite openly in the skins of leopards, hippo teeth, elephant tusks and rhino horn.

'Thank you for your Christmas card,' wrote the Attorney General of Kenya, Charles Njonjo, to Eric Balson in 1972. 'It's just so regrettable that there are so many officers of the Game Department involved in this racket – you mention seventeen in Tanzania and it is my guess that there must be approximately the same number in Kenya.'

Mzee Jomo Kenyatta, dripping gold in his uniform as Commander in Chief of the Army, celebrated the eight years of Independence with a speech that tried to shift the blame back to foreigners.

'Many of those engaged in wild-life rackets are non-citizens, and my government will not hesitate in future to include deportation among the measures taken against them.'

To the average rural African it must have appeared that the white man, no longer in power, was trying to resist change that had been sanctioned by the president in the interests of the people. With the Mau Mau field marshals licensed to collect 'found' ivory, to these rural Africans it must also have seemed that the president had removed the restrictions which applied to parks, which in a sense he had. Ivory could be taken and legally sold to his middlemen, who grew in number throughout the 1970s. And it wasn't just cash goods like ivory and rhino horn that were available. Game parks were veritable food stores, especially during very hard times like the drought of 1971. Indeed bush meat kept a lot of Kamba alive during that period. And then there were the cattle herders who coveted the vast acres of grazing that the white men had given to wild animals. Surely they could not still want them if the big beasts had been shot or chased out (as virtually happened in Tsavo)?

When I filmed *Man-eaters of Tsavo: The True Story* almost three decades later, we interviewed the then chief warden, David Weston, and he startled everyone by confirming that there were still far more wild animals, including elephants and rhinos, living outside Kenya's parks than in them. In fact David was concerned that the elephants in particular (you know what they say about elephants) would never go back to places like Tsavo because they had not forgotten the bad times they once had there. He may be right. In some parts of Africa elephants have avoided intensive poaching by abandoning whole countries. Many of those left alive in Zimbabwe have walked into the safety of Botswana where, sadly, they are eating vegetation badly needed by indigenous herds. Talk of big culls is in the air again.

Jomo Kenyatta made his famous speech about deporting 'non-citizens' in 1971. Two years later the acting head of the Fauna Research Unit, a biologist called Peter Jarman, prepared a confidential report for the chief game warden which, while erring on the side of caution, showed that in five years, some 42,000 elephants from a national population of about 160,000 beasts had died, a drop of 26 per cent. These figures of course covered the drought years and many of these elephants must have died because of the prevailing weather conditions – but not more than a quarter of the national herd. These figures forecast extinction.

The report also drew attention to another excess that, like the 'notorious collectors' letters' (Jarman's description), was impacting on the herds. Legal licences to hunt elephants could be issued by the Game Department and up to independence there had been about 250 of these a year. In the following years the issue of legal licences jumped exponentially: 440 in 1970, almost 600 in 1971, over 800 in 1972 – and 1,358 in the first half of 1973 alone. (Statistics from another source show the figure rose to 2,407 in 1974.) Peter Jarman's work permit was not renewed at the next round and he left Kenya shortly thereafter.

This sad little story also explains in a roundabout way what happened to legal hunting in Kenya, and I am one of a growing number of people who think that had a hunting infrastructure been maintained in East Africa, the shambles which today passes as wildlife policy could have been avoided. Let us take another look at those figures for Game Department hunting licences.

In 1974 enough of the old wildlife warriors were still in influential jobs. Some of them, like the handsome David Sheldrick and the romantic recluse George Adamson, had become media stars and were not prepared to keep the state secret, or as they viewed it the state scandal, to themselves any longer. They started to go public on the subject of the poaching 'epidemic' and soon attracted international headlines.

For once in its life the Kenyatta government operated sensitively and cunningly. The Mzee himself went public in defence of wildlife, admittedly steering his speech to the financial benefits rather than the moral arguments. 'Tourism in Kenya is principally based on the natural resource of wildlife,' he said. 'It is expected that half a million tourists will visit Kenya this year.' And having quietly established that he could still permit the chosen few to hunt as many elephants as he liked (via chief game warden's permits), his government temporarily, and very publicly, stopped issuing normal permits to the hunting professionals. It was something of a media triumph.

In 2005 I went to see Tony Dyer, the last president of the East African Professional Hunters' Association, who now lives in retirement on his large Borana ranch in the north of the country.

Tony told me that the actual effect of this ban was not to encourage tourism but to lose the country almost US$2 million from more than 200 cancelled bookings. The professional hunters quickly made these economic consequences known and the temporary ban was lifted, but the government had noted the good publicity (of which Kenya was seriously short then and now) and a year later permanently stopped the sale of licences to professional hunters. In 1977, to international applause, it banned all hunting of wildlife. *Non*-professional hunting, of course, went on apace. Thus one of the few organisations (in Kenya, the only one) with a vested interest in the close monitoring of illegal hunting and the maintenance of a large, healthy national wildlife herd was neutered, and soon thereafter the association disbanded.

For the International Conservation Movement, which apparently had not spotted the government's sleight of hand with the chief game warden's licences (and was certainly not admitting that 1974 heralded the beginning rather than the end of the worst elephant massacre the world has ever known), the hunting ban was a great coup. Only the international ban on the sale of African ivory voted in by CITES in 1990 (well after Kenya had lost to 'poaching' almost every elephant and rhino it owned) came anywhere near it in terms of publicity.

Tony Dyer had one last stab at putting a spanner in these works, although at the time he did not know that the machine he was trying to influence included the International Conservation Movement as well as the black entrepreneurs who were effectively building a brand new covert Kenyan game business.

Dyer and a Kenyan businessman – hotelier Jack Block – had a very confidential meeting at Block's Norfolk Hotel in Nairobi to discuss what, if anything, might be done about the poaching epidemic they all knew was happening. Tony, when I met him in 2005, told me quite openly that he was hoping he could 'influence' the government to take stock of the situation, review the extent of illegal activities and wildlife corruption, and perhaps recognise that his association had a positive role to play.

The man they chose to write their clandestine report was a complex character. He had trained as a game warden, fought against the Mau Mau, set up the first African game management programme, quit the Game Department when it failed, and become an ivory entrepreneur and a controversial lobbyist for the ivory trade, and he was consulted by the International Conservation Movement on half a dozen major elephant studies. He had shot for profit and in cold blood thousands of African elephants. Daphne Sheldrick hated and loved him by turns and affectionately called him 'Old Pip' (which I suspect stands for Pipsqueak). Dr Iain Douglas-Hamilton felt equally ambivalent about the man; he employed him to do the donkey work on a number of his eminent projects and, I suspect, came to regret it. He wrote a number of erudite books, some of which I have drawn on gratefully for this account, all of which have been reduced in stature by his great fondness for conspiracy theory.

None of that is particularly important. What is important to where we are going next is that he is in my considered opinion the greatest living expert on the affairs of the African elephant, a title he has earned because he has dared to go behind the scenes into the shady, deadly world of the international ivory trade, a place where all other experts, several his intellectual superiors, have lacked the courage to tread.

Nor am I being coy about his name. It took me two years to find it out and another year using the resources of ATV's well-staffed documentary research department to find out whether he in fact completed the Dyer–Block commission. He did. A copy of it has rested in my safe for the last decade. I suspect (given the number of elephant experts like Dr Iain Douglas-Hamilton and Dr John Hanks who have asked to see it) that it may be the only extant copy.

It is called EBUR.

ELEVEN

EBUR

EBUR was written in great secrecy by Ian Parker in 1974. He attempted to camouflage its existence by implying that there were two reports, referring to them as the 'white' and the 'black' reports. The white report is in a fact a document written a year earlier at the request of Jack Block (no mention is made of Tony Dyer in either report) entitled 'A Background to the Ivory Trade'; it carries Ian Parker's name as author and that of his company, Wildlife Services Ltd. The black report is simply called EBUR, with no names of either sponsor or author.

I began to hear tales of this talismanic document towards the end of the 1980s when the holocaust in Kenya was headlines in every newspaper and television news broadcast. Everybody seemed to know of it but no one would ever admit to having seen it. Daphne Sheldrick took me to see Ian Parker, but nothing came of that meeting.

Then on 9 May 1983 a single-sheet blue airmail letter arrived in my office:

Dear Robin,

Greetings. From many quarters I have been informed that you are trying to obtain a copy of the Ivory Report. [No mention of 'EBUR'.] I do not particularly like what I hear! When you came to my house your interest was to obtain material as background for a book. However at least two of the approaches you have made to parties in Britain your interest has escalated to a TV programme. Why no mention of this to me at the time?

At this time virtually every television documentary was accompanied by a book (all mine were), as Ian would have known, and in any case I had not then decided whether the material might be used in a book or a documentary (or for that matter anywhere at all) because obviously I had not seen it. In the event I did use it in a book.

What intrigued me most were the replies we were receiving from those 'parties in Britain'. All the organisations I had presumed would have lobbied for the elephant cause on the strength of EBUR were denying ever having seen it. Typical was the short note from Chris Huxley, Statistical and Information Co-ordinator for the most important monitoring group of all, CITES (the Convention on International Trade in Endangered Species) based in Gland, Switzerland. The World Wildlife Fund was also based in Gland at that time.

Dear Robin,

As I told you when I was Head of the Wildlife Trade Monitoring, that unit does [did] not have a copy of 'EBUR'. Your question about Ian Parker is rather vague, but is perhaps answered by saying that he was representing the Association of European Ivory Traders at the third and fourth meetings of the Conference to the Parties to Cites (1981, New Delhi and 1983, Gaberone).

The letter from Daniel Stiles, spokesperson for UNEP (the United Nations Environment Programme in Nairobi), was even more dramatic, indeed slightly threatening.

The Ebor [wrong spelling] report by Ian Parker is still a sensitive issue here in Kenya. The only place where you might get hold of a copy is from Ian Parker himself and I doubt that he would supply one. He wants to remain in Kenya.

Ian Parker's letter of 9 May 1983 said he 'refused me a copy [of Ebur] on ethical grounds. The work was undertaken as a private consultancy. No one but my clients have a right to the document. [Not true, he had released it to at least three other sources.] That they have not seen fit to have it released is entirely their prerogative as is their right to remain incognito.' This was not true either. As I was later to discover, Jack Block had already released it widely. Ian helped him make the delivery so neither was 'incognito' by then.

Ian wrote a furiously abusive letter to John Burton of the Flora and Fauna Peservation Society on 23 June:

> Thanks to Mr. Brown more people have asked me about this document in the past month than in the previous eight years. Responsible investigation? Bullshit! All that he has done has been to fire both barrels into the 'brown' hoping that one of his pellets will score a hit. It may, but the rest of the flock will have heard both bangs!

True. I was beginning to score 'hits' and the 'rest of the flock' (whoever they were) were beginning to show signs of nervousness. John Burton actually sent Ian's original letter on to me. And the following month I received the letter we had been waiting for from the World Wildlife Fund in Switzerland. It was signed by Arne Schiotz, Director of Conservation.

> Chris Huxley has sent me a copy of your letter asking for information on the fate of the EBUR report [note: he got the spelling of EBUR right] on the ivory trade in Kenya. I know of this report and have discussed it with the Kenya businessman mentioned. We may have a copy here in Gland, but I have never seen it, and as our Director General, Mr. de Haes is away until mid-October we cannot give you a more specific reply. As this report was obviously confidential, I doubt whether we can make it accessible and, anyway it is my impression from what I know of the information it is now greatly outdated, several of the main players being dead or away from power, and that furthermore the contents of the report were most efficiently leaked to the press, both within and outside Kenya.

This letter I frankly never understood. He 'knew' of the report, had 'discussed it' with Jack Block, knew how to spell it (no doubt from the name on the cover) but had 'never seen it'? Neither had Director General de Haes? This was almost a decade after EBUR had been written and was exactly what *Nature Watch* was designed to investigate. We began to prepare the material for a network television exposé. To this day I do not know where my copy of

EBUR came from. It was simply dropped through my letterbox at about this time. But in the same week I also received by post from Switzerland a copy of an internal fax signed by Prince Bernhard. It said that he had been contacted by Ian Parker with a complaint that he had not been paid. Bernhard said, 'Pay the man.'

This was one of the most mysterious twists of the whole saga. It proved that the World Wildlife Fund had received the report (Peter Scott later confirmed that), but it rather contradicted the facts I had meantime received from Ian Parker. Yet another letter had arrived from him on 4 August, still very rude and angry but packed with new information. This time he told me:

- Jack Block did not pay for the report – 'You erred greatly in telling others . . . that he had paid for it. That was untrue for he didn't.' In 2005 I discussed the EBUR affair with Tony Dyer and he admitted that he paid money to Ian but he was not aware he was paying the whole bill. And what was Prince Bernhard paying for?

- Ian and Jack had distributed EBUR to journalists as well as to the embassies – 'a small number in the UK and the US. At the time, believe me, EBUR did constitute a scoop. Yet none of these gentlemen let it drop that the document existed.' This of course puzzled me at the time, but I know now that Ian used these copies as insurance by giving them to journalists who were his friends. He was able to tell the Kenya Special Branch when he was later taken in for questioning that the journos would release their copies if anything happened to him. The ruse worked and the journalists stayed mum.

- I was completely barking up the wrong tree – 'I mean can you really envisage the conservation bodies with their hankering after the sensational, really sitting on cast iron evidence that deals of silence were made with Heads of State over what was, to them, the biggest sensation in their field at the time?' All I can say about this, based on the correspondence which followed, was that he was teasing me.

This letter closed with: 'I will end this correspondence over a storm in a teacup. It grows tedious.' But I could see he was hooked. Ian may have lied to me, abused me and questioned my qualifications and my motives, but he knew what had happened to his beloved EBUR and he wanted to set the record straight, even if it meant he had to deal with an upstart TV journalist.

The correspondence went on for almost seven months, from May to December 1983, and it goes without saying that I never paid Ian, who was used to being paid, a penny for his information. We became the weirdest of penpals. He stopped pretending that my work was not bearing results:

> It is completely true I wrote a report under the title of EBUR. However, I'll be honest with you, there was more than one report. I will mention two of them to you here – the White Report and the Black Report. That some of the writing under EBUR arrived by unauthorised means in IUCN and WWF headquarters is perfectly true. Indeed the only copy of one such document in my possession was actually 'taken back' off a desk top in Switzerland. And I could quite imagine a reluctance among those who acquired it to talk about it for to do so would inevitably lead to questions over the manner of its acquisition. However, as you have the resources to piece it all together, no doubt the truth will out in due course! And I believe you that you will put the bits of the puzzle together 'one way or another'. However, whether this will be believable is another matter altogether.

This was verging on the friendly, but he was right, would anyone believe it? My research budget was running out and I had serious doubts about credibility. 'So Sherlock,' the letter closed, 'it is up to you to unravel the tangle created! From my point of view I have the making of a humorous story and I look forward to the great revelations in due course. Who knows, your researches may lead to an award. Keep on truckin', Robin.'

The last letter from Ian came just before Christmas 1983. He drew my attention to two articles which had mentioned EBUR, one by Jon Tinker, the other by the London *Times*'s Brian Jackman, both quoting an interview with Jack Block. Both pieces had missed their target, Ian claimed, because they had been based on the EBUR white report – written 'nearly a year before any ulcer-forming material ever arrived on JB's desk'. He further claimed that Jack Block had not commissioned EBUR for WWF. This is probably technically true (Tony Dyer commissioned it for the Professional Hunters' Association), but I don't think Ian knew much about its circulation within the fund anyway. Dr John Hanks, who was then in charge of elephant policies at WWF, says he never saw it.

As his last letter to me continued, Ian's hurt and his anger all came spilling out. This was, after all, a man who had put his life and career at considerable risk, literally a voice in a dangerous wilderness, to try to stop the elephant holocaust. He was extremely angry with WWF and IUCN:

> About them they have a galaxy of camp-followers and consogroupies. . . . All claim, with coyness and appropriate 'it's-too-confidential-old boy', to be in the know. They will drop titbits of scuttlebutt – very often like fortune-tellers, using what you have let drop yourself – that make you think that they <u>do know</u>.
>
> If you wanted a real novel and highly-controversial scoop, you are on the fringes of it now. The whole edifice of conservation teeters and, if you don't want to be the one media man who is in with cameras when it comes crashing, then someone else will! You are approaching the chance of a life-time my boy, the chance of a life-time! As the subject of a set of TV documentaries (in which the ivory scene is but a minor, though potent, vignette) the whole set-up is a winner.

So what on earth did black EBUR say? It is a very substantial document comprising some forty pages of Ian's 'report', a similar number of pages of ivory statistics and graphs, and then thirty-nine actual cases in which real individuals are named and shamed. The report starts conservatively with six pages of astute analysis of the ivory trade, slightly biased in favour of what Ian terms 'legal' ivory trading (his new business). There are also hints that the ivory trade statistics have been doctored. Hong Kong, Ian reveals, consistently imported more ivory from East Africa than these countries, particularly Kenya, claimed to be exporting. The loss to East Africa in the period he was reviewing (1959 to 1973) could have been as much as $52 million.

But it is not until page 28 that he gives the first whiff of the 'ulcer-making' material he referred to in one of his letters to me.

Illegal ivory trading concerns all strata of Kenya society. The supposed guardians of the trade – the Game Department – appear to have become a pivotal institution in the business it is supposed to suppress. Subordinate staff and wardens in the field actually indulge in poaching elephants. The Department's purchases of heavy rifle ammunition in 1973 exceeded those in all previous years, even though there was no unusual increase in game control to explain it.

And once he had sipped from this poison chalice, there was no stopping him, which is perhaps ironic, because it is this unremitting *angst* that has thus far prevented the EBUR report from being published in its original form. A great deal of it is incontrovertibly libellous. I can therefore give you but a taste of what the original contains and, incidentally, have always kept my copy of EBUR housed separately from my family.

Here therefore is EBUR in microcosm, using an italicised summary of those parts that the law will not allow me to publish.

Departmental ivory has been ear-marked for private sales to people such as the two *ministers in the tourist department* (unnamed) as well as *a close relative of the President (named) and her trading corporation.*

The highest game official in the land (named) is widely acknowledged within the ivory trade to be active in it himself and most helpful to those who pay for his services. Senior police officials are involved in the trade and prosecutions for ivory offences are frequently withdrawn *nolle prosequi* on orders from *the highest law official in the land*. Such sentences as are pronounced are often ridiculously low. The *law officer* himself is said to offer cover for ivory trading – at a price.

This disregard for law would be a minor issue if it concerned ivory alone: but it does not. Corruption extends to all walks of national life.

Overall is the brooding figure of a *senior elected official (named)* – clearly implicated with personal instructions that certain people should be given a permit to export ivory. Within 11 years, *he* is said to have become among the world's richest men – and one of the greatest landowners.

Ian then lets his angst get the better of him and lapses into vituperation with racist overtones, denigrating what is otherwise a remarkably objective document.

In this situation of general corruption, there is little hope that the ivory 'racket' can be tackled or contained on its own. Even though it has grown to unprecedented proportions under African 'management' it is only a small aspect of the national malaise. To aproach the problem from the ivory angle alone is analogous to treating the patient's in-growing toe-nails before considering his generalised affliction of leprosy.

(It was reading lines like this that did finally convince me that Ian really did think that the EBUR report was only going to be read by the two white men who had commissioned it.)

His next chapter is given over to the 'long-term' implications of all this (which I found somewhat ironic if you think that the 'implications' for him personally were surely likely to be short term).

The evidence was, Ian stormed on, that Kenya's leaders were systematically plundering national resources.

'China and Somalia', he quoted as examples, 'have vested interests in Kenya and both have extensive knowledge of the *senior elected offical's (named)* involvement in ivory. Both could use this to their advantage in discreet blackmail. And as such, laying themselves wide-open to international blackmail.'

Then there was the damage it could do to Kenya in relation to international aid. Corrupt countries had their charitable monies cut off, he warned, and agencies that donated to such countries would be discredited. Ian reminded his readers that Prince Bernhard had presented President Jomo Kenyatta with conservation's top award, the Golden Ark: 'If it was publicised that he was aware of Kenyatta's involvement in illegal ivory when the award was made, both he and his fund's (WWF:RB) ability to raise further revenue from charity would be severely compromised.'

Then we are given instructions on how EBUR might be used as part of a concerted attack 'with the full broadside of evidence on corruption'. 'To fire the ivory shot would pain the *senior elected official*, damage his credence overseas a little (but not in Africa) and guarantee a vindictive response to the white man in general, for it's really only they who fear for elephants.' What was needed, he said, was 'drastic political reorganisation'!

Let us pause and consider what Ian was risking. There was a law in Kenya at the time under which you could be imprisoned for such talk. But this was much worse than that. Ian was talking treason – bringing down the Government – or getting very close to it.

By page 43 of EBUR there is no holding Ian. If he is going to commit political suicide, he is obviously determined to do it in style: 'If we want the rule of law, as perceived by westerners (and to which Africans in public pay lip-service) to prevail, then westerners must involve themselves in African affairs. If we want elephants to survive in Africa we will have to take strong action to ensure it happens.'

I frankly do not think that Ian Parker was actually suggesting the reintroduction of Colonialism or British military intervention, but he was coming perilously close to it. What I do know for sure from all the time I spent working in Kenya during these years is that if Jomo Kenyatta, whom Ian appeared to have so firmly in his sights, had ever got his hands on EBUR (and there are indications that he did), Ian's days as a free citizen were numbered.

Not satisfied with all that had gone before, Ian went on to conclude his EBUR report with thirty-nine 'cases' of wildlife corruption and crooked behaviour for which he claimed to have proof and was quite prepared to name and shame the guilty parties. Sadly the law will not allow me to follow in his footsteps. Suffice it to say that he named and shamed (claiming hard evidence in his own files) the cream of Kenya's political elite, game managers, businessmen, lawyers and nine members of the Kenyatta family! I will not bore you with all thirty-nine case-histories, but here is a taste of some of the more bloody cuts.

Ivory was being traded illicitedly and exported illegally to Hong Kong by the hundreds of tons. Officials including an ex-official of the World Bank had made Nairobi the hub of an ivory-dealing network using the authority of people 'higher than the game department'. Parker claimed he had been asked to buy five tons of illegal ivory from a cartel that included a very senior police official. The ivory was not legal, but all the documents needed to sanitise it would be provided. Ex-Mau Mau generals assured him ivory had been declared *mutanda yetu* (their fruit) by the highest authority in the land and that the bans on trading in ivory had infuriated them. A woman close to the president had used contraband currency to buy twenty-one houses in an expensive part of London.

How Ian Parker is still alive and well, writing material almost as controversial as this, and still living in Nairobi I hardly know. In a sense this book has been made possible by his decision to put new material on the public record in a small recent publication of his own, *What I Tell You Three Times is True* (Librario Publishing Ltd).

Ian lives on, in my opinion, because of what happened (or rather didn't happen) in the immediate aftermath of the distribution of EBUR. The following story of the abrupt demise of Kenyan politician J.M. Kariuki, an active opponent of Kenyatta, illustrates the kind of place Nairobi was and the kind of dangers Ian knew he was facing.

According to Ian, he had an agitated call from Jack Block, some time after the delivery of EBUR, at a time when the town was extremely jumpy after a series of bombings. Jack claimed 'J.M.' (Kariuki) had approached him after a lunch at the New Stanley hotel, clapped him on the shoulder and whispered that he was entirely behind the 'Ivory Report'. Jack Block said he had no idea how J.M. knew about EBUR or what they should do about it. Was this also the report J.M. had referred to in Parliament a day or so previously? J.M. had apparently threatened, the following Monday, to lay before the house a report that he said would document corruption by the highest in the land.

Neither Ian nor Jack ever found out if this was to be the EBUR report, because two days later J.M. Kariuki was taken from the Hilton Hotel in Nairobi and never seen again. He was shot dead and left in the bush behind the Ngong Hills.

EBUR was it seems drawing Ian Parker and Jack Block ever closer to a truly dangerous confrontation with the Kenyatta government and its notorious police, and eventually it came. (Tony Dyer, the other sponsor of EBUR, apparently had no further involvement in the affair but was obviously keen for me to know the details of what happened as he gave me his personal copy, signed by Ian Parker, of *What I Tell You Three Times is True* to work from.)

In this book Ian claims that Jack Block had wanted to give copies of EBUR to the American Ambassador and the British High Commissioner in Nairobi. Ian claims this was against their confidentiality agreement, although he recognised that Jack would send a copy to WWF, but he went along with it, and he claims they delivered the copies together, first to the Americans then to the British High Commissioner, Tony Duff.

Ian then flew out of Nairobi on business and only later heard from his wife, Chris, of a call from Jack, 'who was in a panic'. Jack had claimed both copies of EBUR had been returned to Jack and that the High Commissioner and the Ambassador apparently intended to deny they had ever seen it, or indeed that it existed! Jack asked Chris to rush round to his office and remove other copies of EBUR, but when she got there all she found was a handwritten note on his official notepaper:

Memo from J. Block. (The original of this note is reproduced in Ian's book)

My dear Chris. I have just read Ian's report and also had a discussion with U.S Ambassador. We both agree it is too hot a potato to be in any ones hands. Please do not distribute any copies until I can talk to you. In the meantime I have locked all copies in my safe. Do not give any to Dyer, your own copy will go with Sir Peter Scott (Chairman of WWF) to London. I have withdrawn Sir P.S.'s copy and as an interim report given him Ian's original report to me. Y. Jack.

This also clears up another mystery for me. I made a biographical film of Sir Peter Scott's life, *Interest the Boy in Nature: A Life of Sir Peter Scott* (Central TV), some years later and asked Peter, who always struck me as an exceptionally honest character, whether he had seen EBUR. He said he had known of it but never actually read it, which is supported by Jack Block's rather garbled letter to Chris Parker.

Chris (writes Ian) very bravely removed the remaining copy of EBUR from Jack Block's office. There followed a couple of months of uneasy quiet, then, in January 1975, while Ian was again out of the country, Kenya's Director of Intelligence and officials of Special Branch came knocking at Block's door.

Jack, Ian alleges, tried to fob these officers off with a copy of Ian's 1973 'White' report and they left. Half an hour later they were back, however, demanding the 'real' report.

Here the plot thickens for me considerably. If Jack Block thought the Special Branch would be satisfied with a copy of the White report, it means he assumed they had never seen the Black one, and Ian Parker's account of the affair supports that view. If they *did* know of the Black report, it seems to me there are only two places where they could have got that information, namely the only two other recipients – the American or the British embassies. Ian Parker believes it was the latter.

Jack, according to Ian, then started to behave badly. He told the policemen that they could get a copy of black EBUR from Chris Parker, and soon thereafter two white members of the Special Branch, Ian Barratt and John Arkle, were knocking at *her* door.

'I found that disappointing of Jack,' writes Ian in a masterly piece of understatement. He also says Block never paid for his part of EBUR. 'I assume he felt that paying would be proof of his role in the genesis which, given his many responsibilities, was too big a risk to take.' (This must also have accounted for the chain of telexes about payment, one of which was secretly copied to me, from Prince Bernhard.)

At about this time Ian and Jack 'agreed EBUR should be forgotten'.

But now it had come back with a vengeance.

Chris Parker told the Special Branch that they would have to wait until Ian returned, as she did not know where the report was. Ian claims that it was at this time that he took out his 'insurance' by sending copies of EBUR to Martin Meredith of *The Times*, Dial Torgensen of the *Los Angeles Times*, and James Pringle of *Newsweek*. All three, Ian claims, agreed not to publish the contents unless he got into trouble with the Kenyan authorities.

Then he phoned the Special Branch officers and invited them to tea!

Ian Parker says in his book that the Special Branch men, Arkle and Barratt, told him that Jomo Kenyatta was 'climbing the ceiling' and wanted to see EBUR personally. (This would indicate that Kenyatta had heard of EBUR but had not actually seen it.) Ian says he told them he did not have a copy on the premises, and that anyway it was a confidential document and his client's property. The Special Branch men reminded Ian that they knew Block was his client and Block had told them to come to Ian.

Arkle and Barratt left but returned in the middle of the night. The President, they said, was furious, wanted the report immediately, and if Ian did not hand it over, Special Branch would 'get rough'. He was reminded that, if they failed, others would come and 'pull the place apart'.

Ian told them how he had 'insured' against just such a situation. If there was any harassment, then the report with all its contents would be 'splashed across the headlines'. They went away, but he was ordered to report in the morning to the Director of Intelligence at Special Branch headquarters.

In defence of Ian in terms of what happened next I have to say I would have been down on my knees and licking boots if I had found myself in a similar predicament. The Special Branch at this time was notorious and its cells in Nairobi had much the same reputation as Moscow Lubianka prison. It would, for example, emerge that the two men who had taken J.M. Kariuki from the Hilton on his last trip to the Ngong hills had been policemen. Ian understandably dived for any cover he could. He told the Director of Intelligence:

> I said that I was sure that the report's sponsors had no interest in publicising the document. Its value to the regimes [Kenyatta's] opponents was recognised, but as we rated them as worse prospects than the party in power we saw no point in acting against the incumbent government's interests.

Never short of nerve, and after a number of such meetings, Ian handed over a doctored copy of EBUR – and asked for a meeting with Jomo Kenyatta to discuss it. Not surprisingly, 'no meeting with Kenyatta ever took place'. So Ian escaped, I think, by the skin of his teeth and I now fully understand why he went nearly apoplectic when, some eight years in the future, I wrote to him and said I wanted to dig up EBUR as I believed it to be a smoking bomb not a sleeping dog.

Down the years the EBUR report has gained significance because people genuinely interested in the preservation of Africa's unique wildlife, rather than the protection of jobs in conservation, have asked: was there not a moment when some course of action could have been taken to stop the people who were perpetrating the killing?

I do believe that, had EBUR been courageously followed through by western governments and the very influential world conservation organisations of the time, it could have made a difference. It was specifically designed for that purpose, its factual content was in the main accurate, and it was planted in the right places – the embassies of Britain and the United States and, through Jack Block's conservation affiliates, the World Wildlife Fund. It was also timely. In the years that followed elephants and black rhino died like flies. We cannot exclude the possibility that, once the Kenyattas recognised that the so-called caring West was not going to rock their boat, the final extermination of the elephant as we knew it was inevitable.

My criticism of Ian's report is that it appears to be covertly racist and that Ian's angst at the ability of Africans *per se* to run governments and/or game departments leaks from it like a river of despair. His calls for direct western intervention, and his sarcastic references to African 'management' typified by that ever-famous piece of snarling nastiness – 'To approach the problem from the ivory angle alone is analogous to treating the patient's in-growing toe-nails before considering his generalised affliction of leprosy' – doomed EBUR in political and conservation circles from the start and provided career conservationists with an opportunity to side-step it. If only Ian had stuck to what he knew, elephants.

Dr Iain Douglas-Hamilton, who has always remained a credible elephant scientist, seemed to me to typify the stance decided upon by the conservation establishment. Very involved with much of the statistical information in the white report, he wrote to me at the time of the investigation:

A very much belated reply to your letter [about EBUR] which I cannot supply you with a copy as I gave an undertaking to Parker not to release it. In fact the material in the four chapters are contained in a more up to date report on the ivory trade, which I commissioned him to do, and this is publicly available. I believe that the TRAFFIC group at Cambridge have a copy. [If they did, they sat on it too.] The fifth chapter consists of rather out of date and unsubstantiated allegations of corruption amongst members of officialdom and ruling late elite, some of whom are in the highest positions today. For that reason it cannot become general material.

Ian Parker had been Iain Douglas-Hamilton's assistant in the writing, in 1979, of a prestigious report for the International Union for the Conservation of Nature, surveying the whole trade in African ivory, but things had started to go sour between them even then. Accusing Ian Parker of going beyond his terms of reference, Iain Douglas-Hamilton added this disclaimer to the introduction to the African Elephant Ivory Trade Study (a comment, bear in mind, made after EBUR was distributed):

It is evident that at times Parker has more sympathy for the ivory trade than for conservationists, whom he tends to lump under one blanket and he may consequently lay himself open to a charge of bias. It is provocative, will undoubtedly be controversial in parts [and] the facts presented should put both conservationists and ivory traders on their mettle and cause both to re-examine their ground.

Jolly Daphne Sheldrick (who you'll remember scorns 'boffins' like Iain Douglas-Hamilton) was much more straight with me. She wrote:

I hope Iain Douglas-Hamilton will be persuaded to release the Ivory report you need. There is no love lost whatsoever between him and Parker so I am sure he will in the end . . . but I trust you will remove anything that will land me in court and naturally, direct references to the Kenyatta involvement which might upset the Kenya government and end up with me on the next plane!

Daphne had been in the game a long time and she understood exactly why everybody was running scared over EBUR.

Others like John Burton, then Executive Secretary of the influential Fauna and Flora Preservation Society – whose vice presidents included two former Chief Game Wardens of Kenya, Ian Grimwood and Mervyn Cowie, and whose patron was the queen – preferred not to know. John wrote to say he did not have a copy of EBUR, 'to his knowledge' there had never been a copy in the UK, and that he may have read it but 'quite honestly I have read so many it is difficult to recall anything with certainty'. He concluded with a telling remark: 'As far as I am aware, making it public will not serve any conservation purpose.'

Lord Fenner Brockway, long-term supporter of African *uhuru* and the Kenyattas, heard of the contents of EBUR, and he reacted with shock and horror in a letter to *The Times* from the House of Lords: 'I find it difficult to believe that Kenyatta himself has been aware of – still less participated in – the exploitation of man and nature. Nevertheless, the evidence against Kenya's elite appears to be damning.' He alone called for action, proposing that the Kenyans appoint a commission to investigate the allegations 'and the whole system of aggrandisement which lies behind them, and to advise how it be ended'. But even this grand straw blew away in the wind of evasion and indifference which prevailed elsewhere.

Since Ian Parker wrote EBUR, other Africa-based conservationists have treated him with caution, although he has been employed on several subsequent studies. Some, like Dr John Hanks, his late partner in the Galana game project and former senior elephant scientist at WWF, developed an extreme loathing for Ian, but we will understand in a moment where that came from.

Parker wrote bitterly of what was otherwise an almost complete rejection of EBUR:

Others must have been aware of what was happening and none more so than the British and American diplomats stationed in Kenya. The cold war still dominated political agendas. If the price of keeping Kenya within the western camp was a blind eye to corruption, then the exigencies of the moment must prevail.

But however you look at it, whether through the eyes of top diplomats protecting what they saw as the best interests of their own governments, or of top conservationists and nature scientists worried about their jobs, we were left with an elephant disaster to which no one was admitting.

EBUR and Ian Parker were harbingers of this disaster and he should be commended for blowing the whistle early enough for these powerful interests to have promoted effective preventative action against the fragile Kenyatta regime. In 1963, for example, Ian showed that Hong Kong was importing less than $1 million worth of African ivory annually. By 1973, in an appendix to EBUR, he revealed that this had risen to more than $18 million.

In the years following EBUR, IUCN's authoritative *African Elephant and Rhino Group Newsletter* would record that the Kenyan national elephant population fell by more than half between 1970 and 1977. Moreover, it then kept falling until Richard Leakey in the late 1990s launched a last-ditch effort to prevent elephant extinction.

The grand irony of course is that the passage of time has shown Ian Parker to have been right. We know now that it is impossible to isolate and tackle a single aspect of corruption – the wildlife trade – when governance *per se* is infested with corruption. That was particularly true in Kenya, where the illegal wildlife trade enjoyed a 'royal' charter and game trophies, particularly ivory, were quid pro quos to war heroes. By the time an ageing President Moi came to read the figures, which showed that wildlife-based tourism was his largest and most reliable source of foreign income, the goose that laid this golden egg was virtually dead.

Vindication for Ian Parker came finally in 2005 from an unlikely but authoritative source. Thirty years after Parker called for western intervention (and was for his troubles regarded as a pariah by many of his colleagues), the British High Commissioner in Nairobi finally broke cover on the subject of corruption in Kenya. In a speech at a dinner party Sir Edward Clay bemoaned what he described as the 'massive looting' of public funds by senior officials of the Kibaki administration. The UK envoy told his stunned audience that he had handed the Kenyan authorities a dossier of twenty dubious contracts and allegedly crooked procurement ventures only six months after complaining that corrupt Kenyan ministers were 'eating like gluttons' and 'vomiting on the shoes of foreign donors'.

Thirty years ago, Ian Parker's exposé of wildlife corruption was couched in no stronger terms than these and in those days the fledgling Kenyan democracy was much more open to foreign diplomatic influence. Possibly, just possibly, Kenya might have been a different place today had we listened to him. There would certainly have been a lot more elephants.

TWELVE

Animal Lovers

When the Kenyan government realised *nobody* had the desire or the political will to act against them, the killing really started in earnest.

Ian Parker had been silenced by threats from the dreaded Special Branch, Jack Block had not survived a fishing trip he took to South America, Tony Dyer had kept his low profile and eventually closed down the East African Professional Hunters' Association, Britain and America were denying any knowledge of EBUR (although it seems one of them had revealed its contents to the Kenyatta regime), and the World Wildlife Fund was in a similar state of denial. Put more simply, the most powerful institutions on the world stage of conservation and politics judged that the only way to maintain their positions or their alliances was to keep mum about the EBUR report. That, anyway, is the way the Kenyan elite seem to have read the deep silence which followed the dissemination of EBUR.

Margaret Kenyatta's company, United Africa Corporation, according to airline weighbills inspected by Ian Parker for American broadcaster NBC, exported to China more than 6,000kg of ivory (about 500 tusks) which did not feature anywhere in Kenyan customs records. Investigative reporters like the *New Scientist*'s Jon Tinker had heard rumours of what was going on and visited Kenya undercover because (as Ian Parker must have known) you could be sent to prison for what was called rumour-mongering. He met the assistant Minister of Tourism and Wildlife, Clement Lubembe, asked about the Kenyatta exports, and was told that, in spite of the government's having recently banned the private export of ivory from Kenya, Margaret Kenyatta had legal licences pre-dating the ban. She just hadn't taken them up.

A Kenyan newspaper, the *Weekly Review*, published the official government reply to Tinker's story, which was essentially that there had been a 'period of grace' to allow dealers to dispose properly of their stocks of ivory. It just hadn't been announced to the public. This was too much even for a pro-government journal like the *Weekly Review* and its next edition asked: 'When is an ivory ban not a ban? The fact that for months the Government kept silent about the extension of the deadline is the main cause for the concern conservationists have shown in this matter.'

The fact that everyone was now regarding the government's explanation as a farce was reflected in that bible of farce, the English satirical journal *Private Eye*, famous for mixing facts with half truths. Kenya and its elephant saga became 'fair game' for the magazine.

EBUR, while dead politically, refused to lie down.

The BBC's Julian Mounter took up the investigation I had started with *The Animal War* and, in June 1977, broadcast the story in the prestigious series *The World about Us*.

By then a team led by Iain Douglas-Hamilton had completed an aerial survey of Kenya's elephants, and the figures he revealed were grisly. The national herd of approximately 100,000 elephants was being reduced by between 10,000 and 20,000 a year. A similar aerial count by Dr Keith Eltringham in Uganda revealed that its elephant population of about 14,000 was down to 2,000!

'The elephant has survived in Africa for more than 40 million years,' Mounter commented. 'It is now questionable whether it will survive the next fifty.'

Mounter found a workshop in Nairobi containing about 100 tusks allegedly bought from the Government, but his search of the official ivory register could find no record of the deal. He interviewed their current owner, who said there were at least ten or twelve dealers from whom ivory could be purchased working openly in Nairobi. This, remember, was three years after the Government ban on private ivory dealing.

Mathew Ogutu, Minister of Tourism and Wildlife, appeared on the show to confirm that the ban was still in place but explained that the government could still deal in ivory and had limited old stock that was being sold directly to curio shop dealers.

We could go on like this all day. Kenyans, some very senior, obviously held their own laws in contempt. When EBUR buzzed through the system like an angry mosquito, Kenyatta irritably waved his famous fly-whisk and the Special Branch moved in to swat it down. When its authors had been sufficiently intimidated and the whole affair swept well under the carpet, everyone went back to business as normal.

It has always struck me that there could be another story lurking behind the one Julian Mounter told, one of confusion verging on ararchy. Iain Douglas-Hamilton made the following quote to *The World about Us* on the overall elephant problem as it was then:

> I think there is probably a more serious threat to elephants now than since the turn of the century when the game laws were first brought in. It is a very complex situation. Overall there is probably a drastic decline, but within the parks you tend to get an over-concentration of refugee elephants and because one often hears of over-population within the parks, it tends to mask the overall decline. But I think that there is a very serious threat and that the elephant may disappear from many of the ecosystems where it normally appears for no good reason at all.

This comment follows Mounter's introduction, in which, quoting Douglas-Hamilton, we were being told that Kenya's remaining population of about 100,000 elephants was being reduced at the rate of between 10,000 and 20,000 a year.

Put these two statements together and what you get is that most of the trouble is *outside* the parks – which means that loss of habitat to human settlement is as big a problem as poaching.

What occurs to me with hindsight is that, as Kenya went into the 1980s, opportunistic poaching by indigenous Africans, later stimulated and in a sense legitimised by the Mau Mau collectors who we know were allowed to operate with gangs (and who in the main were very simple souls), started to get out of hand.

What appeared to an *organised* evil empire of poaching (because it included so many figures in authority) may not have been very organised at all.

The exploitation of wildlife, particularly elephants, became Kenya's 'black' economy in which (but not necessarily together) some ministers, heads of police, army units on patrol in game rich areas, wardens who thought no one was looking, permit officers on the make and the common people who resented that so much land had been set aside by *mzungus* for dangerous wild animals joined in what was literally a free-for-all. ('Free-for-all', remember, was one of the many ways Kenya's peasant population chose to interpret *UHURU*.)

By the time President Moi came along Kenya corruption was so opportunistic, endemic and essentially *disorganised* that no political leader facing re-election every few years dared do more than pay lip-service to tackling it.

More simply, a kind of market-led chaos ruled the day.

This perspective certainly makes sense of the many speeches promising action on poaching and corruption that Moi and Kenyatta in his latter days made almost every month but largely failed to follow up.

Eventually, President Moi, under pressure from Iain Douglas-Hamilton, staged a publicity bonfire, burning a large stack of valuable ivory as a symbolic gesture when CITES (the Convention on International Trade in Endangered Species) got the votes it needed to ban the interational trade in ivory. By then, however, terminal damage had been done to Moi's reputation, and gestures could not hide the fact that Kenya's elephant and black rhino population had fallen catastrophically.

Only a chaotic situation in the wildlife hierarchy coupled with fierce condemnation from foreign governments and media could have persuaded President Moi in the late 1990s to pick squeaky-clean Richard Leakey (a *white* self-taught primatologist who by his own admission knew little about wildlife) to attempt a last-ditch stand against the poaching holocaust.

The initiative that everyone remembers is the CITES ban I have just mentioned, which was marked by Moi's big bonfire. But this came a decade and a half after Kenya's elephant stocks had reached crisis point. There were probably too few elephants left to make long-range poacher hunts of the type launched from Somalia worth the costs of the ordnance. Richard Leakey tried to close the stable door long after the horses had bolted.

A number of influential elephant experts regard the CITES ban as misguided, claiming that the one conservation lesson Africa has to learn is that wild animals can thrive across the continent only if they pay their way. It is certainly the case that the ban was introduced to prevent an East African worse-case scenario and one that was of Kenya's own making: the total extinction of elephants and rhino in that country. Other countries, indeed all of the south – Botswana, Zimbabwe and South Africa – had an excess of elephants, which were culled annually to protect elephant and human habitats. These countries claimed that they needed the revenue from this ivory to support their parks structures; this was true, certainly in Zimbabwe, where without it the parks are now struggling.

My view is that the CITES ban was useful at the time. It gave Kenya a breathing space and it wiped out most of the fringe dealers, opportunists who were dealing in ivory. But it should not be allowed to continue indefinitely. Elephants do have to pay their way, no matter how repugnant a thought the culling, or killing, of the natural excess of elephants may be to animal lovers. The harsh truth is that, in the long run, if East Africa cannot protect its elephants, they will vanish from all but private properties.

The International Conservation Movement should be devoting itself to the task of re-educating its membership to this reality, but I doubt that it can. Indeed, the trend today seems to be in the opposite direction, towards animal rights activism. This could mean European nature charities will have a real conflict of interest in Africa. It is ridiculous to try to sell wild animal rights, especially land rights, to, say, the town-sized camps in the Congo's gorilla forests, or the Samburu pastoralists in the Horn of Africa, who as I write are watching their herds die in the terrible drought probably being brought about by climate change.

I was sucked into this murky world of conservation's soft under-belly through a strange funnel that at first I did not take very seriously, but as events grew ever more bizarre I felt as though my partner, Heather, and I were becoming characters in a James Bond novel.

My weekly series on Central, *Nature Watch*, was now attracting a huge audience and many of our viewers (all of whom were undeniably animal lovers) were sending us small contributions to the conservation causes we featured. To handle these funds properly

we registered the Nature Watch Trust and I immediately began to
have much more sympathy for the WWF. A skilled, accounts-
conscious bureaucracy is utterly essential if worthy conservation
causes are to be identified from among the innumerable, often
bizarre demands you receive for this sort of money.

As well as *Nature Watch*, I was filming about three wildlife stories
a year which required more time than our half-hour series format,
one of which was the tragic story of rhino in Zimbabwe. We called
it 'Black Rhino: The Last Stand'. Heather became personally
interested in this story. At the time, 1987, black rhino in the
Zambesi valley numbered some 400. This was the largest national
'herd' left alive on the continent. Virtually all Kenya's rhinos, other
than a few dozen on private ranches like Solio, had gone, and the
Zimbabwe rhino were patently heading down the same extinction
route.

A number of private Zimbabwe-based groups had come up with
a plan under which a significant number of highly threatened rhino
would be transferred to private ranches in the midlands where they
could be guarded by farmers well away from the Zambian poacher
gangs. These translocated animals would be a 'reserve herd', a
national gene pool. The scheme was perfectly viable as the
Zimbabweans, under a warden called Clem Coetzee, were expert at
translocating rhino, the land was ready and waiting, and funds for
the operation had been raised in Britain by several small rhino-
rescue charities including the Nature Watch Trust. Heather hired
the British Museum of Natural History near where we lived in
South Kensington, staged the Ritzy Ball (Rhino in Trouble in
Zimbabwe) and raised some £20,000 in one night. She also went
out to the Zimbabwe midlands and 'bought' the first young animal
for the reserve herd, a female called Rosalind, whom she used to
visit and feed, rather riskily, with oranges.

To cut a long, sad story short, the project never came to pass
because the Zimbabwe government refused to let the animals be
moved on the fatuous grounds that it would change the 'natural
balance' of the valley. The rhino continued to die. Heather tried to
find another outlet for her money, offering to help pay for a London
Zoo vet to go to the Zambesi valley to dehorn the rhino, assuming
poachers would then lose interest in them. But by the time the vet

arrived he could not find enough rhino to justify the cost of the project and a decade thereafter, there were none at all left.

Some months after the failure of the project I was working in my study in London when the phone rang. It was rather late at night and a voice that sounded as though it was coming down a long-distance line asked to talk to Heather. I told the caller (no name was ever given) that she had gone to bed but could I help or give her a message. I was told that the call was on behalf of Colonel David Stirling and the caller wanted to talk to Heather about money she had raised for black rhino. I was immediately on my guard because we had already had one threatening call on this subject from the Zimbabwe Game Department, which said we had raised money for 'their rhino' and it should be sent out forthwith if we wanted to avoid 'tax' problems.

I told this new voice that we had made the decision not to hand over cash (which very often was never seen or heard of again) but would consider essential supplies. He replied that the money was needed for 'night sights to hunt down poachers'. I immediately hung up. Night sights – low-light telescopic rifle sights – can just as easily be used to shoot rhino as poachers and this was one scheme we were not having anything to do with, even though I knew of David Stirling as a good friend of Wilfred Thesiger. (I had been at the Royal Geographical Society party the night David gave Wilfred a spear for his eightieth birthday and I must admit this sounded just like the sort of adventure these two would have got up to when they worked together in the Long Range Desert Group.)

Heather eventually spent most of the Ritzy Ball money on two-way radios for the Zimbabwe ranger force, taking them to Zimbabwe and handing them over in person. We knew at least that they were in good hands, even if they didn't stay in those hands for very long.

What we did not know is that we had been right at the heart of an operation which, in my view, exemplified the confused state of many large conservation charities like the WWF by the end of the bloody 1980s. This story emanates again from the records of Ian Parker and involves another man who we have met before, Dr John Hanks.

John by this time was a very eminent elephant expert at WWF HQ in Switzerland. Ian Parker was earning a good living as a conservation consultant and he had openly and unashamedly started to trade in ivory. Admittedly this was causing pariah status with people like John Hanks and Iain Douglas-Hamilton but it also made him the world expert on the ivory trade who was regularly contracted to represent the ivory traders at conferences like those staged by CITES.

Ian claims in his book that he was contacted by Zimbabwe's leading elephant scientist, Dr Rowan Martin, to find out what he knew of a Colonel Ian Crooke who was reported, with the founder of the British SAS regiment, Colonel David Stirling, to be planning a covert anti-poaching operation in Southern Africa from a base in South Africa. Ian Parker suggests in his book that this operation was being supported by John Hanks.

David Stirling's name had been mentioned when we were contacted about supplying 'night sights' for anti-poaching.

The story Ian Parker tells about the operation (which became known to the media as *Operation Lock* and was given full public exposure in an article in the London *Daily Mail* in 1989) reads like a 'who-dunnit.' There were, according to Ian, secret meetings in various foreign countries involving senior scientists of international conservation groups and former British war heroes, a 'shoot-to-kill' commando-style squad evolving in the desert wastes of Namibia trained by ex-British SAS officers and hard men from the South African Defence Force's *Koevert* Battalion. It was, said Ian, 'a force of British-officered right wing muscle under a conservation screen.'

All of this might (indeed probably would) have passed into history as 'scuttlebutt' (Ian's word) from the murky years prior to South Africa's transition from Apartheid. But Nelson Mandela had obviously been worried by the suggestion that there was South African Defence Force involvement in *Operation Lock* and that WWF, represented by John Hanks, was more involved than was wise.

In October 1994 Mr Justice M.E. Kumleben, a South African Judge of Appeal, was ordered to conduct an enquiry into the alleged smuggling of, and illegal trade in, ivory and rhino horn in South Africa. Dr John Hanks was called to give evidence to the enquiry. Judge Kumleben did not find some of his explanations 'convincing' but concluded on the evidence available to the Commission that *Operation Lock* was not a WWF 'venture' but that WWF was not totally divorced from it.

John Hanks is a friend of mine and we talk quite often in Cape Town. He has told me that what the media labelled WWF 'funds' offered to *Operation Lock* were funds offered by a third party not WWF and his only role was that of 'middle man.' John Hanks is, as I go Press, writing a book about these events so it's really a matter of 'watch this space.' I seriously doubt, however, that the big guns of international conservation will emerge unscathed from this exposé. (In January 2008, the news reached me from Africa that John Hanks has been appointed to the Board of Trustee of the WWF and been awarded their WWF-SA Lonmin Platinum Medal for outstanding achievement in Conservation. As a close friend of ours aptly observed: 'It is well deserved after all he put up with from them.' I could not agree more.)

So, as the century came to within a decade of its end there was a general air of doom and gloom in the conservation industry and in Africa a sense of growing disarray. On *Nature Watch* we were closing virtually every programme, particularly those on elephant and rhino, with a forecast of extinction *'by the turn of the century.'*

In early 1990 my mysterious 'Deep Throat' at WWF International in Switzerland suddenly surfaced with a photocopy of a hand-written memo on WWF International headed paper from Peter Kramer, WWF-I. to J. Barber of WWF-UK (*c.c.* J. Hanks) I realised immediately that here was evidence of the disarray I had been talking about.

The memo was accompanied by an article from the then still prestigious *Zimbabwe Wildlife* magazine which condemned President Moi of Kenya's famous bonfire with which the president and particularly the Douglas-Hamiltons, had celebrated the CITES ban on the international sale of ivory. Zimbabwe, of course, then and now, was vehemently opposed to a blanket ban, claiming good management techniques had resulted in a commercially-exploitable excess of elephants.

Peter Kramer drew the attention of the others to this article which carried the headline (with a note of sarcasm which reflected the Zimbabwe attitude) 'Monument to the Burning of Ivory', an obvious reference to the Moi publicity bonfire. But Mr Kramer then went on:

It may be useful to show publications like the attached from 'Zimbabwe Wildlife' to those who may want to put our logo on that monument. There is a real danger *that we will be cemented into an alliance with the animal lovers fore-ever*. (Author's emphasis)

What does this comment mean? If the World Wide Fund is not an alliance of animal lovers, what is it?

It means, I think, that in a changing world WWF was no longer sure of the way ahead. It had begun to suspect that the species it knew as 'animal lover' was a many-headed beast and there were dangers ahead for an organisation in transition which became 'cemented' into the wrong alliances.

Elsewhere in this book I have used the term 'bunny-hugger' and we will soon be meeting 'animal activists'. (The former is a lover of wild animals who finds all or any form of 'wildlife resources management' particularly culling an anathema, the latter animal lovers prepared to promote their views with action, sometimes illegal extreme action.)

Had Mr Kramer's memo read for example 'there is a real danger that we will be cemented into an alliance with *bunny-huggers* (likewise *animal activists*) fore-ever' today's conservationists would have immediately understood what he was getting at. But twenty years ago, for me anyway, it spoke of an organisation which had lost its way.

African conservationists were having much the same debate.

Elephants, it was widely agreed, were in deep trouble across the whole of middle Africa (conservation policies were based on that general assumption). However, there was no way conservationists could propose a survival plan because no one had the faintest idea how many elephants there actually were. A case in point was the vast Congo Basin where elephants had been worked by the Belgian colonial regime. Conservationist feared that if poaching was going on in remote areas there to the same extent as in parts of East Africa, at least half the continent's elephants would have vanished before anyone from the West had ever seen them.

In those days we did not even know exactly how many elephants were needed in a group to sustain normal reproduction. What was known was that poachers were selecting mature bulls because of the weight of their ivory and this had to be having an impact on the birth rate. There were also worrying reports from Mozambique and Uganda of bands of disturbed teenage elephants, mostly orphans who had received no adult training in the social graces, storming in and out of parks and terrorising smallholders.

The African Elephant Ivory Trade Study – the first-ever attempt to count and report on the state of elephants thoughout Africa – was completed by Dr Iain Douglas-Hamilton in August 1979. He hired Ian Parker, by then a paid lobbyist for the ivory trade, to report on the ivory entrepôts and Ian ended up writing the bulk of the finished report. The two then had a falling-out based, as Douglas-Hamilton wrote in his introduction, on the fact that 'Parker has more sympathy for the ivory trade than conservationists'. In truth it was more than that. Ian Parker thought that Iain Douglas-Hamilton's parts of the report, in particular his elephant counts, were dubious and therefore that the entire tone of the document which warned of an impending elephant disaster – Africa as a vast elephant graveyard – was flawed.

I filmed with Iain and his wife Oria soon after they returned from their very adventurous flights in a light aircraft round most of Africa. Iain and Oria have always been the darlings of African elephant conservation but in these dangerous days they, like every other white conservationist in East Africa, were having to watch their backs. Oria, as is her wont, remained very outspoken, while Iain remained resolute: worked away at his science convinced he would be proven right in the long run.

The trade study tried to be specific about how many elephants there were in Africa and it came up with remarkably exact numbers, even though it was labelled 'provisional'. There were, said Iain, 1,339,180 elephants in Africa on 7,272,600 square kilometres of range. This number, compared to the previous decade, represented a dramatic fall. Based on extended guestimates (the report is well over 100 pages long), Iain concluded that the surge in the ivory trade had led to excessive killing of elephants. East African declines, he said, were matched elsewhere in the continent. In the long term an even greater threat was competition with man for habitat. 'The best way of conserving elephants is to build up or reinforce existing or proposed national parks', said Iain, ever the traditional conservationist. 'United international action is also needed to control the trade in ivory through the wider application of the Convention in International Trade in Endangered Species (CITES), and the stricter application of existing law.' And, as we now know, he got his way. A decade later everyone in Africa and the rest of the world was asked to stop trading any ivory and most signed up to this CITES-monitored deal.

Ian Parker thought it was all bunkum. He questioned both the figures and the conclusion and was particularly scathing of a proposal for an African Elephant Action Plan which was based on these statistics. Most of all Ian derided a plan which admitted it did not know the status of three-quarters of the elephants in Africa. Either give up the whole plan until better statistics were available, he suggested, or accept that the 27 per cent of elephants whose status was known reasonably authoritatively was a large enough sample and probably represented the overall position. If this was accepted, the indication was that 70 per cent of Africa's elephants were safe, 23 per cent were vulnerable and 7 per cent endangered – hardly a projection of calamity. Small wonder that Iain Douglas-Hamilton then accused Ian Parker of having more sympathy for the ivory trade than for conservationists. This was unfair. Parker just did not believe in Iain's kind of conservation.

It is pointless anyway to go too deeply into the details of these elephant counts. They were obviously guestimates and Iain had done the best he could on his three-month field study of 'francophone' West and Central Africa 'to augment our better known anglophone [East African] sources'. His conservationist view prevailed. WWF raised more than $1 million from its faithful members for elephant conservation using a plan which, I agree, wasn't worth the paper it took up and was in any event rewritten in 1982 at an IUCN meeting of elephant experts held at Wankie (Hwange) in Zimbabwe.

Africa was divided into four regions: western, central, eastern and southern. The consensus from this meeting was that the western region was the most seriously affected; elephants there were drowning in a sea of people. The central region around the Congo Basin remained largely unknown but probably contained more elephants than any other. The eastern region was well known and not altogether bad; and in the south, with the exception of Mozambique and Angola (which had long-running wars), conditions for elephants were good. This meeting concluded that there were closer to two million elephants in Africa than one million and the species was not in immediate danger of extinction. A list of conservation priorities was prepared. Had we finally formulated a plan which would propose a sensible, practical way forward for Africa's remaining elephants? No, the conclusions of this meeting were never followed up.

Iain Douglas-Hamilton went on beating the conservation drum until it ended with President Moi's big bonfire. Ian Parker, on the other hand, was dancing to another tune. He claimed that the real crisis was the loss of elephant habitat to human settlement. Iain Douglas-Hamilton agreed but had projected the issue as a long-term one. Parker said it was a problem of the here and now.

With Dr Esmond Bradley Martin, Parker wrote influential articles in *Oryx* (journal of the British Fauna and Flora Preservation Society) which asked whether the current elephant die-off was for the most part unavoidable because it was the product of an increase in human numbers. They concluded that statistics (mostly customs records) showed that the ivory from fewer than 40,000 elephants – 'a very small proportion of the estimated standing crop of elephants' – was being traded each year. Many of these tusks were the product of natural mortality, and a percentage of animals – as many as 10,000 a year throughout Africa – were 'legally' killed.

> In summary the number of elephant deaths accounted for in the ivory trade is so much less than has hitherto been suggested that we need an explanation. We do not claim that the situation *vis-à-vis* elephant conservation is satisfactory – nor that it is unsatisfactory – but our findings give grounds for less pessimism over one aspect – the ivory trade.

Sadly, few listened to this because by the 1980s Ian Parker was openly trading in ivory and making it clear that he believed in the historic importance to Africa of a well-organised, above-board ivory industry. Indeed, he was trying to set one up. He failed in all these endeavours but he has left me with a deep-rooted gut feeling that much of what he said was right. More to the point, this long and bitter argument convinced me finally that the majority of the conservation establishment, certainly those north of the Zambesi, and their animal-lover following simply will not countenance any form of elephant conservation that is not based on wildlife segregation and policing. Western public opinion, together with poaching and habitat loss, is becoming the covert third factor in the politics of ivory.

Money talks in Africa probably more loudly than in any other continent on earth simply because the indigenous people have so little of it. What that money is saying is that it prefers the status quo. Conservation today is still ruled by the affluent West: the WWF, the African Wildlife Foundation, Conservation International, the CITES Directorate, the Fauna and Flora Preservation Society, Ele-Friends, and so on. Then there is UNEP and the World Bank, both of which have conservation objectives in their rules. Google lists 146,000 articles if you do an Internet search for 'elephant poaching' and probably two-thirds of these will mention some conservation organisation or other. Although their glory days are past and their influence much reduced, these organisations still draw in millions of dollars a year and, of course, if you include the World Bank as a 'conservation' organisation (an accolade I doubt that it would deny) this income exceeds the GNP of a large number of UN members, many of them in Africa.

Africa knows to its cost that the largely western lobby is expert at winning friends and influencing people and that you ignore it, or defy it, at your peril. These people have been convinced by the pundits of conservation that trading ivory is evil and will materially contribute to the demise of the African elephant. They open or close their purse-strings accordingly. But 70 per cent of Africa rejects the view outright, in my view on good grounds.

Two groups in particular have proved particularly vulnerable to the western argument – the young who come to conservation as their first taste of adult politics having been raised politically correctly on animal causes from the time they learn to read, and the old but young-at-heart who have the time and the spare funds to think green and go eco-touring. Ask either of these groups whether they would approve of the shooting of some 50,000 African elephants a year to maintain healthy elephant habitats and to supply a legal trade and you would get a resounding 'No!' I say this with some authority because I once spent Nature Watch Trust money on just such a poll. Put more simply, the club which supports the International Conservation Movement would defect in droves if you were to insist that conservation in Africa has no future unless elephants pay for themselves, which means they be 'managed', or 'culled' or treated as a 'viable resource', or any of the other clichés.

Now consider the other side of the same coin. African leaders are not stupid. Indeed, their survival instincts need to be more developed than those of their contemporaries in the West. They know where the conservation money comes from. A little lip-service never hurt anyone and might even save the odd elephant, so African governments echo the conservation paradigms and the western organisations happily broadcast them. Moreover, bad news about elephants pulls in the money while good news, which needs the money to sustain it, pulls far less.

Human expansion at rates of 3 per cent and above coupled with climate change will, of course, ensure that the bad news for elephants and habitat gets progressively worse, and the 'illegal ivory trade' is a good way of camouflaging the real causes of the attrition. And yet almost all conservation organisations maintain the lowest of profiles on the subject of African population growth.

The fact of the matter is that the International Conservation Movement has never dared to change its tune materially on this subject. They have thought about it a number of times. The change of name from World Wildlife Fund to World Wide Fund for Nature was an attempt to alter subtly the emphasis of the organisation from caring for wildlife to caring for nature in general: from animal lovers to biodiversity, if you like.

Some of WWF's most recent policy bulletins, for example, could have been lifted direct from Iain Douglas-Hamilton's African Elephant Ivory Trade Study of 1979. You will recall that a quarter of a century ago he wrote: 'While the African elephant as a species is not endangered it is threatened locally and regionally by the ivory trade. In the long term a greater threat is competition with man for habitat.' Compare that with this excerpt from a WWF bulletin of 2006:

Elephants continue to roam the African land, but remain under threat from poaching and habitat loss. Although poaching of elephants for their ivory has declined since the 1989 'ivory ban', it remains a widespread problem in west and central Africa. Large quantities of African ivory are still finding their way in to illegal markets in Africa and beyond in places such as Asia. A more long-term threat to the species, however, is the reduction of habitat available to elephants in the face of expanding human populations.

As far as I can see, this still lists the dangers to elephants *exactly* according to the priorities Iain Douglas-Hamilton set all those years ago. Most significantly, Ian Parker's warning from the same period that reducing conflict between human and elephant populations was of immediate importance is no higher up the WWF's priority list than it was twenty-five years ago. It is still a 'long-term' threat. Is WWF really saying that nothing has changed for elephants in a quarter of a century?

What is the truth? Africa south of the Zambesi has an excess of elephants that are either going to eat themselves out of house and home or will have to be disposed of in huge numbers. There is not a single national park in South Africa capable of carrying the numbers projected for ten years hence. (More of this in my closing chapter.) Many of the other assertions in the WWF report are also untrue. That the trade in ivory has fallen significantly since the CITES ban is a dubious claim. Two factors have skewed the figures, the first of which is that large quantities of ivory have gone into storage, much of it secretly in places like Zimbabwe.

In the north – the Congo Basin, Sudan, Ethiopia, etc – the trade is back in the hands of the people who have run it since time immemorial, the Arabs. It has never been in their nature to reveal their trade secrets to enemy infidels, be they Sir Richard Baker or George W. Bush. This ivory trade, as a reaction to CITES, has simply gone underground, which is what usually happens with prohibition. Hong Kong and China now routinely report larger official imports of ivory than these North African countries (and others like Burundi which has no elephants) say they exported.

So elephant numbers have continued to fall in spite of the CITES ban on the sale of ivory and its supposed constraint on poaching. By 1990 the all-African total of elephants was down from the 'official' 1.3 million in 1979 to 600,000. Most West African countries are down to 100 elephants or fewer, and the whole vast region has at best a few thousand. Most of this loss can be blamed on habitat competition with humans. Habitat competition is indubitably the most important current threat to the African elephant.

Still nobody has the vaguest idea of how many elephants there are in the vast Congo Basin. With each passing year the country vanishes ever deeper into the heart of darkness and relies ever more on its bush-meat resources. A panic attack was suffered by field workers of the Zoological Society of London in October 2005 when a particularly nasty Congolese militia called the Mai Mai were reported to be munching through the local hippopotamus population. The word was that these cannibals (I had luckily avoided by a mere three days one of the first Mai Mai gangs who had kidnapped and reportedly eaten six Scandinavian eco-tourists in Uganda) had set up a thriving Congo-wide hippo-meat trade from their base in the gorilla forests of the Virungus National Park.

In a fortnight 400 hippos had been butchered and the conservationists warned that if this hit-rate was kept up, the park's entire population would be gone by Christmas. That, in reality, would be in line with the general prognosis for the Virungus National Park which I have visited on several occasions, always to report a bad-news story. The 2-million-acre Virungus, once regarded as the most species-rich park in Africa, is the park with the worst human conflict problems. In 1988 there were 22,000 hippos there. Today, as I write, the figure is possibly no more than 500. It is the same story with elephants: well over 4,000 in the 1960s, today an optimist would be hard put to find 300. Game guards, whose government pay is 55p a month, are not doing much better. A hundred or so have died as they tried to stem the poaching. Theirs is a thankless job anyway. Most of the people they attempt to 'stem' are refugees from one of the region's frequent genocidal wars who need bush-meat to stay alive.

Other countries fringing the Great Lakes basin are in much the same state. My worse-case scenario is that there could now be fewer than half a million elephants left in the entire African continent, but I admit that it is no more than an informed guess. Certainly, the Congo Basin is a place in need of a rescue plan now, not in the long term.

My friend Will Travers of the Born Free Foundation has recently published figures compiled from statistics for the years up to 2002. For supporters of CITES (as Will still is), they make grim reading

- More than 16 tonnes of illegal ivory were seized in customs operations around the world in 2002 alone.
- Kenya's elephant poaching was up from 57 elephants in 2001 to 71 in 2002. (The national herd was by now tiny.)
- 6,200kg of ivory, including 41,000 semi-worked ivory 'hankos' (or Japanese name-seals), were intercepted in Singapore, having been shipped from South Africa.
- Save the Elephants (STE) counted 51,000 ivory items on sale in 354 outlets in seven cities in four countries.
- Over 500 elephants were confirmed poached in Zimbabwe in the first seven months of 2002.
- STE reports that, between 1996 and September 2002, 45 tonnes of ivory destined for China were seized by authorities.
- The official CITES ivory trade monitoring protocol, ETIS (Elephant Trade Information System), reports (4 October 2002) that across much of Africa the situation facing elephants has deteriorated since 1998.

These statistics prove that the ivory trade is alive, well and apparently thriving.

The truth of this came home with a vengeance when one of England's oldest and most traditional firms, holder of a royal warrant (which means it supplies the British royal family), George F. Trumpers Ltd of Mayfair and Piccadilly was in October 2005 fined £10,000 for trading in ivory – shaving brushes, hair brushes, glove stretchers and an elephant tusk.

'The illegal trade in endangered species is one of the major threats facing wildlife today,' trumpeted Andy Fisher head of the Metropolitan Police's Wildlife Crime Unit. 'It also damages local communities in other countries and helps to fund criminal networks.' This is typical of what I now regard as the arcane, dubious, and knee-jerk reaction of an indoctrinated establishment to topics like this. There is much more evidence that the *absence* of a structured, legal ivory market 'damages local communities in other countries' indeed 'helps fund criminal networks.'

Raul Matamoros from the International Fund for Animal Welfare, also climbed aboard this bandwagon.

'It is unacceptable,' Mr Matamaros opined, 'That despite an international ivory trade ban, an estimated 10,000 elephants are still dying each year for their tusks. Consumer demand drives this bloody trade and we urge people to remember that every piece of ivory represents a dead elephant.'

Again this is typical conservation bombast. By my count 10,000 elephants dying a year from the 1,000,000–1,300,000 plus elephants in Africa is well below a *natural* mortality rate. That is not to say that elephants are not still being poached nor that an illegal trade network still exists. But I would argue that poaching and the illegal ivory trade are also sustained by present draconian laws which restrict sensible and sustainable trade in ivory where good management has resulted in an excess of elephants.

'Every piece of ivory represents a dead elephant' is an obvious, emotive and Western-biased perspective nor does it recognise the essential fact that Africans have the right to do as they will with their elephant resources.

I doubt moreover that the ivory ban has had much real impact on Kenya's elephants or on poaching. WWF reported recently that 'despite the stipulated decreases in ivory trade volumes to pre-1950s levels, reports show that the restrictions under CITES have not aided the plight of the African elephant.' Part of this is, I suspect, comes down to the fact that East African countries are no longer a worthwhile place to invest ammunition and ordnance when you have easy alternatives like the Congo Basin. Even so poaching has gone on and up in Kenya by about 20 per cent annually. Last year Richard Leakey warned me of new levels of poaching back in the park which had been the focus of his attentions and so much investment of money and manpower, Tsavo.

So what has really happened to CITES and the much-lauded international ban on the sale of ivory? Was President Moi's bonfire really just a waste of good ivory? It is certainly arguable (though not proven) that it gave desperate countries like Kenya, time to organise a last-ditch stand against poaching but how useful it has been elsewhere is dubious.

Put another way: If CITES is not keeping the African elephant alive in countries where they are most threatened (Kenya, Uganda, the Sudan and the Congo Basin) what is the point of it? In countries where elephants are not threatened, indeed overcrowded, my tour of Africa in 2005 revealed widespread doubts about the scope of CITES, where it was generally regarded as little more than a high-profile propaganda exercise for the International Conservation Movement. There are many who would argue that its continuance has disguised the need for more effective elephant management schemes.

Admittedly, what exists of CITES today is a tattered remnant of the original. Most ordinary people would, I think, believe that there is still an international ban on the trade in ivory. Not so; it lasted for a little over seven years. In 1997 the CITES signatories, under the threat of the south quitting, voted to allow Botswana, Namibia and Zimbabwe to down-list their elephant populations to Appendix II which allows limited trade. The CITES conference sanctioned a one-time sale of their existing raw ivory stocks. The door was now open.

The next CITES meeting in 2000 allowed South Africa to join this elite group and its elephant population went to Appendix II. East Africa claimed that there was still heavy poaching in parts of Africa and in Asia. Its opponents countered by pointing out that this meant the ivory market had not died and poaching was being encouraged by the blanket CITES ban.

There was another CITES meeting in Santiago, Chile, in November 2002 at which Botswana, Namibia, South Africa and Zimbabwe submitted proposals to allow sales of their existing stocks of ivory as well as a future trade in ivory under an annual quota. Meanwhile, Zambia requested that its elephant population be down-listed from Appendix I to Appendix II, allowing it to sell ivory stocks.

By now everyone knew that Botswana, Namibia and South Africa all had healthy, well-policed and protected elephant ranges. If they didn't cull, they told the conference in no uncertain terms, the natural increase in elephant numbers would reduce available food, cause conflict with indigenous people and destroy habitats crucial to many other more threatened species. South Africa even had a modern meat-packing plant built at Kruger where culled elephants were efficiently processed. It produced ivory, skins and canned elephant meat. Leftovers were fed to a crocodile farm. Literally nothing was wasted.

Zimbabwe and Zambia (especially Zimbabwe) also had large numbers of elephants left, even though their governments were shaky and their game departments run down and underfunded. CITES's champions wagged their fingers and said that this band-wagoning was exactly why the door should never have been opened. Kenya and India proposed that all African elephant populations be returned to Appendix I. When the proposals finally came to a vote, Namibia, Botswana and South Africa were given the green light for a one-off sale of roughly 66 tonnes of stockpiled ivory. The meeting rejected similar applications from Zambia and Zimbabwe where covert, government-supported hunting and poaching were shown to be rife.

So the CITES ivory ban has, in effect, split Africa down the middle and is currently producing paradoxes and much resentment. It is protecting countries like Kenya which have already sacrificed their once-mighty national herd of elephants to commercial gain, but is sanctioning Zimbabwe where there is still a large national elephant herd (some of which are admittedly browsing Botswana where they feel safer but cannot be accommodated).

In Kenya the Game Department and parks administrations have collapsed (Richard Leakey's word) because they have little left to police nor the money to pay for game officers. As I have mentioned, when I met Bongo Woodley, Chief Warden of the Mountains National Park last year, he had just returned from Afghanistan where he had been using his piloting experience to subsidise privately a minuscule Game Department salary from security work. The situation in Zimbabwe is also one of crisis and a collapsed Game Department. Zimbabwe, quite literally, has no alternative but to trade ivory 'illegally'. As a former national I have watched with great sadness the decline of the once self-sufficient Zimbabwe, but I simply cannot credit that the International Conservation Movement still believes that rules like CITES can ever be applied to countries where the population is starving to death.

So just who or what is the CITES ban protecting? The only answer I can see to this question is that it is protecting the illegal ivory trade – and quite a lot of jobs in the International Conservation Movement, of course. CITES is obliging the ivory trade to operate under prohibition rules, which, as everyone knows, pushes the price of ivory (or booze) sky high. The great CITES junkets to places like Santiago, attended by the full-time CITES Secretariat, conference delegates and hundreds of conservation NGOs, are also costing millions. Surely we have to abandon all this in favour of something that works? There always has been and always will be a trade in ivory. Indeed, ivory is better recognised as an African currency than as a product. It is a trade that most African countries want and need and one which they are entitled to have if their elephants can be properly and professionally managed as a resource. Ironically, what we now call the 'illegal' ivory trade is quite good at doing that management.

Yet I doubt that it is ever going to work out that simply. This is not just a debate about ending an unworkable ban: it touches on the wider and infinitely more difficult topic of the International Conservation Movement's future. A new Africa-friendly elephant management plan hinges on an unavoidable and seminal tenet – some elephants have to die for it to work. Nor should you think that I or the other advocates of such a difficult solution particularly want it. The fact is, Africa has run out of *protectable* elephant habitat.

Most animal lovers will not, of course, countenance this: they see it as being in conflict with the purpose of conservation and will fight it by snapping their purses shut. That is not a sound even the South Africans like. I have spent the last three years posing this dilemma to some of the most hallowed names in elephant conservation and their answer with the exception of Dr John Hanks is unequivocal: CITES may be a flawed plan but it is the best we've got.

It is a debate going nowhere. In October 2004 the CITES circus gathered again for the thirteenth of its expensive junkets, this time in Bangkok, and again the African elephant was the subject of hot debate. The delegates agreed yet another 'action plan' for cracking down on unregulated domestic markets in elephant ivory. African elephant range states promised to strengthen their legislation and their enforcement efforts, launch public awareness campaigns and report on progress by March 2005. If precedents prevail nothing will come of any of this. CITES meetings have turned into an exercise in public posturing to keep conservation groups happy. But the wheeler-dealing still goes on apace. Namibia, Botswana and South Africa were told they could go ahead with a 'one-off' sale of their existing ivory stocks (there had already been one 'one-off' sale in 1997), with Namibia also receiving permission to sell ivory carvings (known as *ekipas*) as tourist souvenirs. These were judged to be culturally important to Namibians.

Only Kenya and India still insisted that all elephants be kept on Appendix 1, which would uphold the ivory ban. Ironically this has made the country which systematically and bloodily slaughtered three-quarters of its elephants in a remarkably short time the darling of many of the International Conservation Movement's most powerful groups. The huge and very affluent Humane Society of America, for example, called on all its members to campaign against the proposals of Botswana, Namibia, South Africa, Zimbabwe and Zambia and to support the minority proposal by Kenya and India. The Humane Society posted this message on its website. For me it is proof positive that the two sides are irreconcilable and an indication of how simplistic the presentation of the case has become:

Both African and Asian elephants remain at serious risk from ivory poaching. There is already a significant and growing illegal trade in ivory in many Asian nations, and large amounts of ivory are being imported illegally by tourists into the European Union and the United States. Legalizing the trade in ivory will make it far more difficult to stop the trade in ivory from poached elephants. An expanded ivory trade will also provide further incentives for poaching, as it is impossible to distinguish between ivory that has been legally or illegally obtained.

When the Parties agreed in 1997 to allow the transfer to Appendix II of the elephant populations of Botswana, Namibia, and Zimbabwe – and a subsequent one-time auction of raw ivory to buyers from Japan – they viewed it as an experiment to see if a controlled legal ivory trade was possible. The understanding was that CITES's Monitoring of the Illegal Killing of Elephants (MIKE) program would provide the Parties with information that would allow them to assess whether the downlisting had caused a surge in elephant poaching. Since most nations haven't implemented MIKE, the program has been unable to produce any information about the effect of downlisting. Most African nations with elephant populations don't submit any official data regarding poaching, ivory seizures, and stockpiles.

Furthermore, there have been no official reports on the 'benefits' of the ivory auctions, whose proceeds were to help elephant conservation. That was one of the principal justifications for the 1997 downlisting and the ivory trade proposals.

This is almost the best description I have heard of a market which is impossible to control. Surely the logical extension of the above is to abandon failed controls and try something new? But the only 'new' idea left on the table is to manage elephants as a sustainable resource.

And while the International Conservation Movement sits on its hands the ivory river flows powerfully on, albeit underground. You can change its course a little but you cannot stop it flowing. If you dam it, as is the case with South African, Botswanan and Namibian ivory, eventually it spills over. Down the years we have tried to build several such ivory dams in Zanzibar, Burundi, the Sudan, Nairobi and even in South Africa. The flow has vanished for a while and then bubbled up somewhere else. Now the stream is going back down its age-old course to the Arab countries. Indeed, the ivory river has always run very like the Nile, with its source in the countries of central Africa and its destination the deltas of North Africa.

Dr Esmond Bradley Martin, still assiduously mapping the flow of the river, reported in 2005 that in addition to feeding demand for tourist souvenirs in Khartoum, significant quantities of tusks were being exported to Egypt. The ivory trade in Khartoum and Omdurman was connected with the large, illegal Chinese ivory market. Chinese buyers accounted for about three-quarters of all the ivory items purchased. South Koreans, Saudi Arabians and buyers from several other Arab states had also been identified as major entrepôts. Several thousand expatriate Chinese in Sudan working in the petroleum, construction and mining sectors frequent the souvenir shops looking for ivory items to purchase. Organised Chinese ivory trade networks were also said to be purchasing tusks in Khartoum and the Central African Republic for illegal export to the Far East. Since the 1990s, China has been the world's largest importing nation of illegal ivory tusks, environmentalist groups agree, with many tusks coming from the Central African region.

Investigations undertaken by Dr Martin established that the Sudanese military – and a smaller number of private traders – were selling tusks wholesale to the owners of craft workshops and souvenir outlets in Khartoum and Omdurman for between US$44 and US$148 per kilogram. A survey of fifty souvenir shops in Khartoum, Omdurman and Khartoum North carried out by Dr Martin in February 2005 revealed more than 11,000 ivory items on sale. Individual shops carried between two and 1,021 ivory objects. Animal figurines, pendants, rings, bangles, human figurines, earrings and chopsticks were among objects on sale. Prices were low, he observed, illustrating the widespread availability of ivory and cheap labour. A ring cost the purchaser a mere US$2, a 4cm pendant US$3, and a pair of chopsticks US$13, Martin said.

Dr Martin's investigations also revealed that an increasing number of elephant tusks were moving from Sudan into Egypt, where there is also a flourishing trade in ivory. He found some 100 craftsmen in Egypt processing Central African ivory brought in through Sudan. In the markets in Cairo, Luxor and Aswan he found over 20,000 ivory objects.

If this ivory river truly does never stop but simply changes direction, it means that the ivory debate has also lost its way. Africa's elephants, a vital national resource could instead be driving hard currency eco-tourism, commercial hunting, the souvenir trade, wilderness holidays and all the associated money-pumps which service these industries. All this is being wasted for want of a pragmatic set of policies on wildlife management. The main stumbling block to achieving practical solutions is disorientated western conservation planning. Do you wonder why so much of Africa is so dismissive and angry?

I know there are people at the heart of the International Conservation Movement (I am one of them) who recognised long ago the desperate need for a policy which would allow elephants to pay their own way – but have never proposed it other than in private memoranda. Is this not what WWF International's Peter Kramer was worrying about when he wrote to Janet Barber and John Hanks in 1990: 'There is a real danger that we will be cemented into an alliance with the animal lovers fore-ever.' (see page 190) I believe this was, and is, a note of much greater importance and relevance than the rather cynical first impression it creates.

John Hanks (to whom the note was copied) told me in 2006 that to be an effective worker or an NGO for conservation in Africa you have to watch what you say: 'No matter how right you might be, if you speak out against any government in today's Africa you will simply be kicked out and a huge amount of non-controversial work by a lot of very committed people would be wasted.'

What I had not realised is that some twenty years ago a huge schism, detectable if you read between the lines of the Kramer–Barber–Hanks memo, appears to have split the International Conservation Movement. Essentially what I think was being revealed here is that three of the top people in the World Wildlife Fund (in those days WWF was much the most influential conservation group) were doubtful of the CITES international ivory ban.

The 'alliance with the animal lovers' these top brass were determined not to get 'cemented' into was the CITES ivory ban. It is the nuance in the term 'animal lover' which, as I suggested earlier, gives the game away. Kramer was warning his colleagues off emotional individuals who would never contemplate a pragmatic approach to wild animal husbandry which involved elephants dying. Most members of the American Humane Society would, I suspect, proudly fall into this category. What Kramer was really saying was that there was a powerful lobby (including in his own organisation) who could stick WWF with an unworkable elephant policy 'fore-ever'. (I have used Kramer's misspelling of this phrase throughout to confirm the authenticity of my source material.)

Is that not exactly what has happened? WWF's stance on the regular culling of elephants as part of a game management plan has always, from that day to this, been muted and ambivalent. I suggested a few paragraphs ago that the elephant debate was deadlocked. Is this the nature of the deadlock? Has the future of the African elephant become the pawn of a western-dominated conservation axis controlled by an 'alliance of animal lovers fore-ever'?

I do not believe that Africa will stand for this. If necessary, and it is happening now in the southern, elephant-rich states, Africa will take back the initiative with a new set of plans essentially based on a single absolute imperative – elephants must pay their way for a future in the new Africa. Indeed, they must occasionally die for it.

THIRTEEN

The Great Elephant Indaba

When this book was conceived I had severe doubts about the path modern conservation had chosen to follow to secure the future of the African elephant. I had certainly not realised, however, that it had effectively ceased to be a force for change and was now essentially engaged in servicing the agencies and responsibilities with which it had been associated for the last half century. Admittedly, this was not entirely the International Conservation Movement's fault: a subjective, sentimental and at times quite militant following had obliged it to tread warily on matters African.

This truth really struck home when I sat down to consider what a more Africa-friendly, modern and realistic policy based on my own long contacts with the continent might look like. It came out much more radical than I had thought it would, largely as a result of the main areas of controversy being much more polarised than I had ever anticipated. I did, however, feel that I had managed to narrow the problems down to their main headings and that I could at least address answers to these points.

- Why keep national parks whose wildlife stocks have been severely depleted when such parks are so disliked by indigenous people with a claim on the land.
- Park rules, indeed park demarcations, are far too rigid. Can they be made more people-friendly?
- Other plans exist for preserving the wildlife Africans want, such as Zimbabwe's Campfire Programme whereby wildlife is both eaten by native peoples and sold for hunting. Why not introduce such schemes continent-wide?
- Africans may decide that they don't want anything more than a representative selection of wildlife if wildlife interests stand in the way of agricultural and industrial development. The rest of

the world cleared its own land for this purpose. Why not accept this fate for Africa?

- Africa believes wildlife must pay its way. South Africa has demonstrated that it is possible to live by these rules. Indeed, wildlife flourishes when combined with modern tourism. What's wrong with the South African system?
- The regular killing, or culling, of the excess of elephants produced by good management seems inevitable. Can we educate the supporters of wildlife charities to accept that not only can it be done humanely but it is also essential if biodiversity is to be maintained?
- The ivory trade is a good not a bad thing. Ivory is an African currency and a valuable and naturally produced resource from which rural people have a right to benefit. Should not the expert entrepreneurs, the traditional ivory dealers, be allowed back to control and regulate the trade?
- Elephant hunting under controlled conditions (as was practised for example by the East African Professional Hunters' Association) is a good not a bad thing. What is wrong with earning much-needed hard currency, creating employment for indigenous Africans, and setting up a permanent, experienced and free 'field force' with a vested interest in monitoring and preserving game stocks?
- The International Conservation Movement has no moral right whatsoever to tell Africa what to do with its elephants. This course of action produces an opposite reaction to that which is intended.

I can say for certain that if some if not all of the concepts listed above were in operation the African elephant would be looking into a more secure future than the limbo most of them occupy at present. At the same time it is a fact that some if not all of these concepts are a complete anathema to the International Conservation Movement. Is there any way of bridging this gap? Are African realities so different from the Western mindset as to be irreconcilable? I don't think so, but first of all I want to tackle an area of dispute that makes all of the above rather irrelevant and that must be solved before anything else can be tried.

Is African wildlife a national or a world heritage?

This may seem a simple (or even a simplistic) question but it isn't because it masks the seminal question of who should be paying for the conservation of wild animal in Africa. It is also pivotal because as each year goes by wildlife-rich parts of Africa (with the arguable exception of South Africa) grow poorer while Western conservation groups grow more numerous and richer.

The temptation is for Western conservation to take on more and more of the bill and is there anything wrong with this?

Look at Central Africa and what do you see? Vast swathes of the Sudan, Congo, Rwanda, Ethiopia, Kenya, Tanzania, Zambia and Zimbabwe all with largely destitute populations, run-down Game administrations, despotic or corrupt governance, poaching still going on apace in places were there are enough animals worth the risk, rifles and bullets; most people still as poor as church mice.

Now consider the same view through the eyes of UNEP, WWF, Conservation International and the hundreds of other organisations whose entire *raison d'etre* is the spending of money on wild animals.

So why do I raise questions – post alarms – as to how this money is spent? Because the subject represents a giant, yawning elephant-trap for all these Western groups, one that for some reason many of them are either too blind or too arrogant to see.

All that many African states have left these days is their national pride, and while I am with Richard Leakey in believing that African wildlife is both a national and an international responsibility (I do not want to live in a world without elephants), the final decision on how elephants should be preserved should and will be made by Africans.

Remember, all that money has been raised because most people don't want to live in a world without elephants. But are we prepared to change our policy from that beloved old Western principle of *'he who pays the piper calls the tune'* to one of *'pay the piper and whatever tune he plays is up to him'*. I doubt it!

The difficulty Western folk have with this principle reminds me of an incident I witnessed in the Ngorongoro Crater when filming there with the Chief Warden of Tanzania National Parks, Solomon Saibull. We were on the crater floor when he saw a mini-bus draw up at a manyatta, and all the children, many of whom were painted black and white, were all called out to be photographed. Solomon Saibull immediately drove our vehicle alongside the other one, putting us between the tourists and a young Masai *moran* who was hurtling back from minding his cattle, a spear raised ready to kill somebody.

Solomon managed to calm the warrior down, and both cars drove off to a sensible distance. Solomon then ordered the tourists down again (they were Americans) and took their names and addresses. He lined them up and told them that the following week he had been invited to America to address the prestigious Sierra Club and receive an award for his work in the Crater.

'Then,' he said, 'I'm going to come over to your houses in Dallas, wait until you're out to work, haul young children out without asking you, line them up in your yard and insist they smile at me. If I can find a few who are in religious purdah (the Masai children painted black and white) all the better.'

The response from the tourists (who were in Ngorongoro because they were animal lovers and no doubt gave money to animal charities) was: 'But we gave our tour leader a load of dollars for those photographs!' I should add that Solomon later had the tour leader banned from the Crater.

The point of this story is that Western conservationalists should not think that because they have the money they can then dictate the entire repertoire of African conservation. It is the same petard upon which colonialism hoisted itself and soon after, died. Western conservation could suffer the same fate if it is not careful.

This taint of the colonial era and its attitudes pervades almost every issue concerned with African wildlife. For evidence of that let us go back to my list:

- Why keep national parks whose wildlife stocks have been severely depleted when such parks are so disliked by indigenous people with a claim on the land.

It was Dr David Weston, who followed Richard Leakey as Head of the Kenya Wildlife Services, who in 2002 confirmed for me (when I interviewed him for the BBC's *Maneaters of Tsavo*) the peculiar population statistics that now applied to some national parks – for example, there were now lots more elephants living outside the boundaries of Tsavo because elephants appeared to have learnt that the park was dangerous. In the Tsavo eco-system therefore we have a huge park largely emptied of elephants while in the heavily populated lands surrounding the park (the Tuli Hills in particular) big blundering beasts trample crops and people with impunity. That is the view of a lot of rural Africans anyway, and it was being voiced sufficiently strongly for David Weston to be building an expensive elephant fence between Tuli and the park.

It can also be taken as read that most rural Africans feel too much of their country was reserved for wildlife in colonial times and today is kept for the use of (foreign) tourists. I found some acceptance of the value of eco-tourism but it fades fast when populations and cattle build up round the parks. The peoples of the Tsavo area live with their cattle, for example, in circular *manyattas* entirely denuded of vegetation that from the air look like bomb craters. Tsavo is now entirely circled by these *manyatta* craters. This is a feature of most of Africa's wildlife parks and national reserves, even the well-protected ones in South Africa where *manyattas* are often replaced by elegant tourist lodges.

Part of the problem with the African attitude to national parks is that it is also internally polarised. In rural areas wildlife is often seen not as a valuable, uniquely African heritage but as a destructive nuisance, positive control of which is frustrated by foreign conservationists. Yet Clive Walker, when he was head of South Africa's Elephant and Rhino Foundation, realised that young urban Africans actually have less personal experience of African big game than European kids. They do not have the money to travel and stay in the comparatively expensive accommodation so they very rarely visit a national park. Also, they watch a lot less television than their European counterparts.

Clive set up a children's camp for kids from Soweto on his private game ranch in the bush north of Johannesburg and recalls the state of pure terror and utter wonder he witnessed when these innocents were shown their first live white rhino. African attitudes to conservation are the key to the formulation and success of future policies, yet we have no real idea exactly what those attitudes are other than that they are very different in urban and rural areas.

Do we need so many parks and why are the strictures on people living in parks so draconian? There is no single answer to this question. In South Africa where national parks and private game sanctuaries run in a lucrative partnership and an increasingly well-educated and affluent black population is visiting them (at subsidised rates) you can see a developing national wildlife awareness. South African National Parks pay at least as much attention to hearts-and-minds work with rural people as they do to wildlife promotion (and get help to fund this from some conservation groups). If things go on as they are now, I see no reason why South Africa should not expand land prioritised for wildlife. Eco-tourism is a rich, burgeoning business bringing in large amounts of hard currency. But it does require that the tourists have something to watch, and in those countries where the game has virtually gone and the demand on the land is growing, then the parks should probably be slimmed down to commercially viable facilities.

It will prove impossible to hold the neo-colonial conservation lines in Kenya, Uganda, Tanzania, Congo, the Sudan and probably Zimbabwe and Zambia. Even to try to hold the lines could of itself be damaging in the longer term. New lines will need to be much more acceptable to Africans; they could involve scrapping state control and state exploitation of wildlife and wildlife lands and putting the whole up for sale as a business (to privatise it). But I doubt that this would be politically achievable in Somalia, southern Sudan and parts of the Congo. It may well be beyond the organisational strengths of Zimbabwe and Zambia.

We need to take a long hard look at the dozens of African game parks and reserves largely set up during colonial times and review both their numbers and their structures? Every park should be a viable tourist facility cum inviolate 'gene sanctuary' doing its best to pay for itself. Few of them are.

We know that wild animals will tolerate many different levels of human intrusions. The Mara and Addo are both examples of intense intrusion and tourist interaction that would have been considered unacceptable when these sanctuaries were promulgated. I can envisage a new doughnut-like structure for a game park that would constitute a series of interactive rings. These doughnut parks would be large, but as they would meet all the needs of tourism, conservation and various forms and levels of game contact (including hunting), there would not need to be so many of them.

Human intrusions would be largely confined to a very large outer ring providing full services for wildlife tourism: lodges to suit every budget, safari drives, intensive game viewing, even expensive, licensed hunting in very restricted pockets, all heavily policed by a well-paid ranger force and backed up by a roving veterinary service.

Within this a ring of minimal animal disturbance would be confined to walking safaris, photography and the work of scientists and of conservationists engaged in hands-on conserving. My friend Dr Carl Jones, who has written the foreword to this book, is a world expert on ensuring that threatened species stay alive, and I could see him active here. Rhinos, for example, on the verge of extinction twenty years ago, can be bred very successfully in areas of virtually invisible containment and will thrive if the poachers are kept away. A park of this structure, with each inner ring made much more difficult to penetrate, would be much easier to police.

Finally there would be the innermost pristine 'core', a true sanctuary where I would allow no human intrusion whatsoever. Wild animals could come and go between these rings as *they* wished (or could be lured to various parts of the tourist areas with promises of food and water as is done today in Kruger and was pioneered years ago by David Sheldrick when he built Tsavo's Aruba Dam). This inner sanctuary, a pure gene sanctuary, could easily be monitored remotely by satellite.

The single great advantage of this kind of restructuring is that these new parks would be built and run by private enterprise as self-financing and income-generating businesses. (As a one-time television producer I imagine that the television rights to a place like this could rival in value those of a major football team.) Large doughnut parks would allow many old depleted parks to be taken out of the system and the land returned to the people.

We come now to the crunch question: do Africans actually want wildlife or would they rather have the right to develop their land for agriculture and industry? There is no doubt that affluence affects how people think about conservation, and I am sure that there is a level of poverty common to much of Africa, where a conservation ethic is not even vaguely affordable. I asked this question of virtually every African I met in 2005 and mostly got a peculiar 'yes–no' answer. Yes, a lot of Africans now have enough education to know that conservation is the favoured answer of the politically correct, but no, you cannot give land exclusively to wild animals if people have no land and are starving.

The dangerous truth is that poor urban Africans – who may now represent the bulk of the population in the countries we have been talking about and many of whom are the inhabitants of the vast sprawls that grow like mushrooms round the edges of African cities – do not give even a passing thought to the wildlife issue. Why should they? Other than as a television image, elephants might as well live on Mars. If you were to suggest holding up urban development in the form of new homes or job improvement from new industries in favour of land rights for wild animals, you would get not a laugh but a riot. If the International Conservation Movement wants to save African wildlife, these are the people and the issues it must address. There *is* a case for conserving a manageable cross-section of African wildlife and no case at all for letting any of the large species go extinct, but that case will be made to Africa's urban poor only if they can be convinced that land set aside for wildlife is earning money to improve their lives. This means the conservation 'business' must make more money than would come from industry, and produce more jobs than would come from dirt farming.

The really tough bullet the International Conservation Movement has to bite is that some of the controversial suggestions I have made – the rationalisation and reduction, say, of wildlife lands – are the easy options by comparison with the case that has to be made to the African urban poor. And remember, each of them now holds a vital card in this argument – the vote. When occasionally I grow deeply pessimistic about the future of the big game of Africa it is a vision of poverty-stricken African poor that inhabits my nightmares.

Now let's turn to the idea that in order to survive Africa's big game must pay its own way. This seems to me to be self-evident. The only person I know who does not believe it is true at least in part is Richard Leakey, and we will give him his own platform in a moment. South Africa is proof positive that it works (at a price) and its private wildlife industry appears to be one of the models the rest of Africa must consider.

There is, however, one problem with the South African model, one that the country has been fudging for some years now. What do you do with the excess of animals good management breeds, particularly elephants which are quite destructive? It is the nature of all beasts that if they frolic in paradise, have enough to eat and are not troubled by the one truly lethal predator in their habitat (us), they will multiply. There were twenty elephants in South Africa's pocket park, Addo, in the 1930s. Today this little jewel, admittedly much expanded, has 400. Kruger National Park, as near my gene pool national sanctuary as you will find in Africa, started out 100 years or so ago with 200 elephants; now it has 7,000. On average, elephants in paradise increase in number by about 9 per cent a year.

What do you do with these elephants? South Africa has tried to avoid conflict with the emotional supporters of the international conservation movement because it still attracts very large sums of green money. So in the recent past it has sold the excess of elephants to private game sanctuaries and wildlife farms, tried messy contraception techniques with potentially adverse long-term consequences, and translocated elephants around the country, sometimes out of the country. There was a worthy initiative started by John Hanks called Peace Parks which hoped to repopulate Mozambique parks emptied during the war with unwanted elephants from Kruger. The Kruger elephants did not like their new country, however, and made a high-mortality march home. (The concept, I am pleased to say, is meeting with some success elsewhere.)

South Africa does have a solution to its excess of elephants ready to be unwrapped if anyone can find the courage to do so. As I have mentioned Kruger has a big modern abattoir specifically designed for this purpose. A few years ago, to the delight of local Africans, tasty tins of elephant meat came jogging down the production line while beautifully tanned elephant skins ideal for up-market briefcases and shoes were drying on the walls. Nothing was wasted and there was lots of work for local people.

The sad irony of this whole initiative is that it was a solution implemented by the old apartheid bosses of South Africa who by then did not give a damn for world opinion, especially politically correct conservation opinions. When Nelson Mandela brought his squeaky-clean Rainbow Nation to the international arena, Kruger's abattoir was quietly tucked under the political table. But it is still there and I was able to unearth some new information clearly indicating that South Africa, now more confident of its elephant policies, is ready to use it again. We will go there too in a moment.

What of my statement that the ivory trade is a good thing? Frankly, does anyone really believe prohibition works? It steers trade underground and once it is outside the law, as Esmond Bradley Martin has so recently confirmed, it is inevitable that criminals will seek to control it and usually succeed in doing so.

Ian Parker reported that in his dealings with Arab traders he came across several who expressed deep offence at the suggestion that they were criminals because they dealt in ivory. Dealers from Egypt who bought tusks in the Sudan were the descendants of families who had been legitimately engaged in this trade for hundreds of years. They and other international traders cooperated very openly with Ian when he proposed that an international system of licensed dealers be set up. This never happened because those who support the ivory ban universally ranged against them.

The West has now outgrown its need for specialised ivory products (only about four billiard balls, for example, could be cut from a single elephant tusk as only the hardest material along the nerve canal was used) or seen them replaced by plastics. We have forgotten just how large the ivory market once was and how attractive an art material ivory remains for the carvers of the Orient. Piano manufacturers were among the largest users of ivory in the nineteenth century and their factories provide us with the best records. There were piano factories in most countries in Europe and large ones in America where in the eight years 1852–60 piano production rose from 9,000 to 22,000 instruments a year. There was even a place called Ivoryton in Connecticut where ivory keyboards were made for famous brands like Steinway, each board containing about 2lb of ivory.

But it is as an art material that there always has been a market for ivory, a market which in China dates back thousands of years. At least in terms of quality, ivory is as aesthetically important now as it was then, and almost as lucrative. The situation is similar in Japan where the carved seals with which documents and paintings are signed are all, by long tradition, made from small blocks of ivory.

Dr Esmond Bradley Martin, whose ivory sales statistics I quoted in the last chapter, once told me a revelatory story about the daggers Arab sheiks like to wear in deference to the one Mohammed wore as a feature of his ceremonial dress. Esmond was at that time trying to get the sheiks to accept that a dagger with a taiga antelope handle was indistinguishable from a dagger with a handle made from the horn of the highly threatened rhino. He placed two such daggers on the table and challenged the sheik to choose between the two. 'Are you mad?' the sheik asked, offended. 'This is a religious matter. I will only have the one with a handle of rhinoceros horn.'

Similar principles of tradition, rigid and irrational but as inflexible as time, apply to Japanese ivory seals even though they could as well be made of plastic. In India wedding bangles, which every bride must have, are made of ivory. Similarly *netsuke* toggles which are used in Japan to hold string belts bearing little ritual bags and boxes have become extremely valuable. None of these ancient trades has been significantly affected by the ban.

It has been estimated that Britain imported year on year some 500 tonnes of ivory in the late nineteenth century, the equivalent of at least 30,000 elephants a year. But while this statistic may shock, it should be remembered that this was a well-conducted, legal trade and at the time it was probably sustainable. High-powered rifles were only just beginning to come into common use and no one was at all inhibited about using or wearing ivory. Dieppe in France was famous for the ivory trinkets produced by *ivoiriers* who numbered French royalty, including Napoleon and Josephine, among their clients.

Legalised ivory export is essential. As I have said previously, elephant ivory has always been an African currency rather than a transitory product. Elephants die; ivory is found. So there will always be a limited amount of African ivory for sale unless extinction, driven by excessive demand stimulated by a prohibition market, finally dries it up. In these circumstances the only way to maintain a stable market is to gain control of the exporting process. As Eric Balson has shown Africa only began to bleed ivory when exporters, driven underground, found other ways of getting the stuff out of the country.

Next, my point that the International Conservation Movement has no moral right whatsoever to tell Africa what to do: it is patronising and produces a reaction that is self-defeating. This is a proposition that seems to me utterly self-evident. What is in fact self-evident is that it is not being practised!

A complete attitude change is needed on both sides. I have already mentioned the need to re-educate Africans with arguments which must be attractive and appealing to them economically, and I have said that it is at least as important to retrain conservation's emotional supporters in the pragmatic African conservation realities. (If only the two groups could change places for a year or two!) But is this realistic? Is there the time and indeed the desire for so huge a programme of re-education?

In 2005 I toured a lot of Africa's elephant country and found to my great surprise that much of what I have been proposing has been started in a small and experimental way by disparate groups of people all bound by a common rule – maintain a low profile. The reason they are all keeping a low profile is that they are working outside state conservation (and outside the stated objectives of the International Conservation Movement). More prosaically, conservation has begun quietly to privatise itself.

As a start there has been a subtle shift in the way people talk about game parks or national parks or even game reserves – the phrase 'wilderness experience' has crept in. As recently as ten years ago it was reserved for ascetic adventurers like Wilfred Thesiger who liked nothing better than to sweat across the Empty Quarter with a couple of Arabs and a camel. But all over Africa today the phrase is newly in fashion and the facilities which have been set up to supply it are providing a measure of much needed relief to Africa's hard-pressed game-tourist industry.

What this industry has discovered is that people are very happy just to chill out and will pay a lot of money for a glimpse of the African sky at night, the smell of the great plains, the song of the cicadas and a general feeling of having got away from it all. Wildlife? Well, the cough of a lion in the night will take care of that. The more luxurious and 'organic' the camp – a bath with proper taps, tall G'n'Ts, and clever fresh food (preferably helicoptered in from Nairobi every day) – the more the rich 'eco-tourists' will pay.

The wilderness experience, from which the clients come away genuinely refreshed, is in fact a discovery (perhaps marketing ploy is a better phrase) of sheer genius because Africa is, of course, over-endowed with sites to take the average western breath away. And who am I to question what is being marketed here? For me, because this is Africa there should be wildlife around, but it does not seem to bother the tourists, especially the rich retired, who are arriving in increasing numbers.

One step up as experiences (and costs) go is the private game ranch or wildlife safari park. This 'experience' (it is not my fault that they all sound like Disney rides) has been brought to a state of near perfection in South Africa and has assured the future of the African elephant there. A game ranch is an old farm, or ranch, with a new solar-electric fence, a luxurious lodge, half a dozen 'safari cars' (Land Rovers packed with seats) driven by young 'game rangers' whose knowledge of wildlife is one step above the Collins pocket guides sold in the tourist shop. Two daily game drives are thrown in for a price of some hundreds of dollars a day, as is a campfire in a concrete pit, and in the evening a tribal dance by the off-duty kitchen staff. The game viewing (to a spoilt old cynic like me) is limited because often the wildlife has been purchased from a nearby national park. It is usually a 'reintroduction' of game which was there once, but not always. Having game is what matters, not necessarily having the right game.

White rhino are preferred to black because they are much less aggressive. The rangers are very knowledgeable about birds and bush-pigs of which everyone has a lot. It is the ambition of all of these places to grow (usually by joining up with the neighbour's ranch) and to end up eventually with the Big Five: elephant, buffalo, rhino, lion and leopard.

You find game ranches and safari lodges in South Africa gathered as thick as Kenyan *manyattas* round the bigger national parks like Kruger because they can use the same animals. Poaching is now all but gone from South African parks, so animals like elephants wander about at will (especially now that Kruger has an excess of them), munching up trees to the delight of tourists. Kruger, of course, has room for the Big Five, so you occasionally get a visit from a truanting lion, leopard or cheetah.

The relationship between national parks and the private sector is now symbiotic. National parks have learnt that to attract tourists you need to improve the quality of the accommodation and at places like Addo Elephant Park, which I visited, there is an extraordinary range of places to stay from humble rondavels to camp sites, luxury tents and air-conditioned family bungalows. Addo is fenced so the many private hotels within a mile or two of the perimeter should not really be advertising game viewing. But they are all 'elephant lodges' or 'safari halts' and they solve their lack of game by driving their clientele straight into the park.

Addo has its own game drive facilities, offering trips round the park in state-of-the-art safari cars. Guides from the local community can be hired at the gate (Addo spends a lot on hearts-and-minds initiatives) and have sharper eyes than the ranger-drivers. Cunningly the Addo drivers have a network of private roads not open to the general public and a lively radio network which allows them to guarantee excellent elephant viewing. Addo planners have calculated that eco-tourism could create four times as many jobs as currently exist in agriculture.

The future looks extremely bright at Addo. In fact there are already plans afoot to expand the park so that it can house 2,000 elephants. Moreover, the infrastructure planning, which includes a programme guaranteeing resettled farmers jobs in the parks or other government rural projects, is being heavily subsidised (some $36 million thus far) by the World Bank's Global Environment Facility, an example at last of the International Conservation Movement investing wisely.

It is hard to believe that this South African model is not the shape of things to come. It has certainly proved that a private 'game' industry, rather like the new 'wilderness experience' I described a moment ago, is not dependent upon the game I grew up with in my youth on the plains of Kenya and Tanzania. I have sat with tourists in a 'safari' car on a game ranch of a few square kilometres and watched with total amazement their excited sense of fear and wonder at the sight of fat white rhino grazing like prize bulls. You could have got out and stroked them! Worse, when I boasted that I had once been chased by a *group* of bad-tempered black rhino, or trapped in a real safari car with Solomon ole Saibul on the wall of the Ngorongoro crater while a hundred elephant, angry at our blocking their path, trumpeted by, I, quite rightly, got pitying looks and comments like: 'But that's not the sort of thing you could bring the children to, is it?'

Today the safari – a term that between these pages has encompassed the deadly slaughter of the fiery Scot R. Gordon Cumming, that legendary hunter-explorer Frederick Courteney Selous, the elegant Denys Finch Hatton, and the biggest killer of them all, Karamojo Bell – has been subsumed into something you can bring the children to. And why not, if it will keep the elephant alive?

We must accept, however, that this is going to be bought at a price – and that price is going to be heavier than western public opinion presently expects. In 2005 South African National Parks (SANParks) sent a report to the minister of environmental affairs and tourism on developing elephant management plans for national parks with recommendations for the process that should be followed. SANParks has been meeting regularly with what it calls multi-stakeholders (parties with a vested interest in the topic); the last get-together held in 2004 was rather grandly labelled 'The Great Elephant Indaba'. An *indaba* is an African talking-shop and attending this one were community representatives from around Addo and Kruger, livestock and animal welfare experts, hunters' interests, zoologists, the Ministry of Tourism and the Environment, government representatives from Botswana and Namibia, a representative of the Zimbabwe resource management programme (Campfire), a philosopher and several conservationists.

The *indaba* was essentially about South Africa resuming the culling of elephants. Views, as you may imagine, varied widely. Conservationists predictably argued that culling is unethical and inhumane and should never be used, resource managers worried about the economic costs of increased elephant numbers on local communities. The professional hunter and the zoologist teamed up to express concern that avoidance of elephant population management might lead to the loss of biodiversity. The *indaba* heard a paper suggesting that 'international' outrage against culling could seriously affect tourism.

One paragraph from the resultant report to the minister struck me particularly. Indeed, part of it was underlined: 'Given the value placed on the maintenance of biodiversity in South Africa's new legislation, and the potential for economic returns for both communities and parks, *it has to be accepted in principle that it is legitimate to apply population management as a precaution.*' Or to put that in plain English, if elephants are destroying the habitat of other animals (biodiversity) and/or the economic viability of the park and the surrounding native communities, it is 'legitimate' to reduce their numbers.

Another line from the report must also be bothering international conservationists. Pointing out that in Namibia, Botswana, Zimbabwe and numerous other African countries localised excesses of elephants pose a threat to community livelihoods which can only be countered by expensive fencing or culling, the report says: '[These pressures] increase animosity between the communities and conservation authorities. In these cases there seems a good case for assigning the burden of proof to those who are against elephant population management rather than those who support its adoption.'

Finally we come to the 'Recommendations for the Minister'. Recommendation 3 jumps straight off the page: 'It is recommended that the Minister of Environmental Affairs and Tourism approves the usage of culling as a means of reducing elephant populations as is provided for under the Protected Areas Act 57 of 2003.' And to strengthen this, 'management tools such as translocation, contraception and migration corridors' should be regarded as 'medium to long term management interventions'.

Should the minister take up these recommendations, which would appear to be the preferred way forward for South African National Parks (although I should stress that nothing has happened yet). There will be some stark consequences if you cull elephants you start producing valuable ivory, ivory you will want to sell for the benefit of national parks and the community. The elephant abattoir will probably start production again. Namibia, Botswana, Zimbabwe and Mozambique will almost certainly follow South Africa's lead.

But has the International Conservation Movement seen all this coming and is there about to be paradigm shift in its policies? In

April 2005 the African Wildlife Consultative Forum (facilitated by the International Union for the Conservation of Nature and others) met at the Victoria Falls. A report (commissioned by WWF) was presented and the discussions will form the basis of a draft southern African regional strategy for the conservation and management of elephants.

Certain broad agreements that came out of this meeting are surprising given that it was essentially an International Conservation Movement forum. Firstly, it was recognised that there is a 'sense of urgency' around the elephant overabundance problem in three main zones in the region, one of which includes South Africa, particularly regarding 'the use of one of the essential tools in the "management toolbox" namely culling'. There was also agreement that 'the full range of tools in the toolbox should be available for range states to use according to their needs . . . the key bottleneck' being 'the reluctance to use culling as a key ancillary tool'. Furthermore it was claimed (although we should remember that this is the South African report of the meeting) that 'Countries are looking for leadership, in the form of one country being bold enough to now break this impasse'. 'There appeared to be complete solidarity', the report says, 'in terms of in-principle support.' If I may translate this into plain English, I am fairly certain that what is being said here is that, with the support of the WWF and the IUCN, South Africa, Zimbabwe, Botswana and Namibia and maybe more countries could start shooting substantial numbers of elephants in the near future.

This I was fairly certain would not sit well with Kenya's conservation elite and I was lucky enough to catch Richard Leakey in Nairobi. Richard is indubitably the greatest wildlife warrior of the modern age and has spent his entire life keeping elephants alive. We have known each other for many years, having shared a publication tour for Michael Joseph, he for *Making of Mankind*, me for *Nature Watch*. He also appeared in my film with Jessica Tandy and Hume Cronyn entitled *An African Love Story*.

I found him a rather changed man who might even be starting to come to terms with attitudes in the south. Normally ebullient, he was on this occasion expressing despair at the state of the Kenya Game Department. He told me quite openly that it was in a state of collapse, the government seemingly unable to pay wages.

I told Richard that I had been in South Africa and had been impressed with the way things were working at parks like Addo. I asked him whether he had changed his mind about a working model for the future of elephants. Had the South Africans started to get it right? I was not surprised to see him shake his head – but it was not with the usual vehemence.

The thing to remember about Richard is that he is an African, albeit a white African. He was born, bred, raised and became famous in Kenya, finally out-starring even his famous parents, Mary and Louis Leakey, with his discoveries of early man. He has been Director of Kenya Museums, using his fame to bring in millions of dollars to support one of the finest anthropological collections in the world, and he rebuilt and revitalised game management in Kenya when, at the invitation of a desperate President Moi, he formed a quango called the Kenya Wildlife Service which literally blew poachers away. But he has always been a conservationist of the old school at heart, and now he proceeded to give me what I know to be his traditional discourse on African wildlife being a world heritage and if the world wants it to survive and multiply then the world must be prepared to pay substantially towards the costs of its conservation.

I know why Richard believes in this. Indeed, I don't disagree with him. The truth is that when Leakey went out into the world with his begging bowl he was so admired and well known the bowl literally overflowed with western largesse. But, as I have said elsewhere, it does not do so for any lesser mortal. It is quite beyond me why anyone should want the job of running Kenya's wildlife services while Leakey's tenure is still in the public mind. As David Weston and others have found out to their cost, you are on a hiding to nowhere. Richard has always declared that his and other Kenya conservationists' prime responsibility is to hold the fort until the world wakes up. But this time he was noticeably less emphatic. For the first time in all the years I have known him Richard seemed unsure of himself and depressed at the state of affairs in Kenya. Admittedly, the country had just been though a referendum where the *watu* had been asked to vote for constitutional changes (symbolised by either an orange or a banana) which had been rejected and Kenya had been without a government for some weeks.

I know that Richard believes that the South Africans have always over-regulated their wildlife, particularly in the old apartheid days, and although I've never spoken to him of the Kruger elephant abattoir I suspect it is complete anathema to him. There are Kenyans I know who hold South African wildlife management in quiet contempt because they believe that the south is in the process of confining its wildlife within facilities which resemble zoos more than wildlife sanctuaries, and I would not be surprised to find Leakey lurking in this company somewhere.

It was to my great surprise therefore that Richard told me that he thought Kenya's government-run Game Departments and their offspring, the National Parks, comprised a system well beyond its sell-by date. I knew this had been on his mind for some time because of the way he had attempted to make Kenya Wildlife Services independent of government. He had only managed quasi-autonomy, but it had been a start. Now, however, he declared that his experience suggested that it was probably not possible to run an efficient game management facility such as a national park, with all its modern adjuncts like luxury tourist facilities, as a division of a government department. The two were incompatible and invariably involved major conflicts of interests.

This sounded to me very like the relationship the South Africans had recognised and were encouraging between the state and private tourism, but in a sense Richard's concept was more radical than that. In his view of things the state could dictate policy but all the actual wildlife business should be contracted out to specialists. This did not necessarily mean private commercial specialists. The job could, in theory, be done equally well by conservation groups funding and training specialist wildlife management organisations. Richard and I did not have long enough together to discuss the concept in any detail, and I certainly don't want to misrepresent what he thinks, so we will leave it there.

Subsequently I was supplied with a draft of a long survey recently completed by a group of experts on the present state of elephants in Kenya. In spite of its obvious desire to be upbeat it made pretty dismal reading. It began with a set of official figures, probably the best ever collated, on what had happened to Kenya's original state herd. In Tsavo for example between 1973 and 1991 the herd dropped from tens of thousands to about 6,000, a population mostly consisting of orphans and adolescents. Poaching had in fact never stopped. Although it had fallen substantially in the new millennium it was now on the increase again, reflecting Richard's concerns; 59 per cent of all carcasses found in 1999 were the result of poaching and by 2002 this had gone up to 69 per cent. Somali gangs returned to the park in 2002 and the report complained of too many guns from Somalia in the hands of local populations: if people started to use them against elephants it would be 'difficult to contain them'.

Human–animal conflict was increasing, the report also noted, adding ominously that in the last two decades the human population in the Taita Hills (a small contiguous area between Tsavo East and Tsavo West) had quadrupled, leading to more elephants being 'controlled'. Elephant numbers had been slow to grow – averaging under 3 per cent per annum – and there were still only 9,284 elephants in the whole huge area of Tsavo.

Moreover there is still in Kenya considerable concern that the International Conservation Movement represented by several hundred animal rights NGO's continues to exert arcane, some say neo-colonial, influence on a weak Kenya Government.

In 2004 the veteran MP, G.G. Karuiki introduced a private members bill which sought to give rural people a much greater say in the way Kenya Wildlife Services (which since Richard Leakey's day has been seen as government department) applied the rules. The bill sought to introduce elected members to the KWS Board of Trustees, to oblige owners of wildlife land to assume some liability for the damage their animals did, and to appoint local elected district councils to advise KWS.

Opponents of the Bill, including powerful animal rights activists like the International Fund for Animal Welfare claimed it was a step towards to the reintroduction of hunting in Kenya and to the liberalisation of the bush-meat trade. But, reflecting the views I have suggested are held at grass-roots level, the Bill was passed by Parliament. When in January 2005 however it went to the President for his assent he refused to give it, causing many to suggest that there were still huge differences between the views of foreign conservation aid donors and the people who shared their lives with wildlife.

When I left Richard's office I abandoned plans I had for a nostalgic visit to Tsavo and sought to find a facility which reflected, albeit at an embryonic stage, some of these ideas. Through a close friend of ours, Caroline Clarke – who is married to a professional biologist-conservationist, Chris Thouless, a former assistant of Iain Douglas-Hamilton – we were taken to the lovely slopes of Mount Kenya and a vast ranch called Lewa Down run by the Craig family. Chris, who now works, as Leakey had done, at the National Museum, had also worked at Lewa. He is a member of a new generation of Kenya conservationists, and I asked him whether he had a model for future elephant management. He said:

> The concept of a model is probably wrong to start with. There are no Africa-wide models. Things work in different ways in different places. What you call the old models are all flawed. Take tourism which is always raised as a plus factor in conservation (because it brings in hard currency income). Tourism doesn't always benefit communities. It can sometimes expose them. It has been a disaster for the Masai.

He agreed with Leakey that national parks were growing old and perhaps redundant. 'But think of the alternatives. We should admire the way they keep struggling on, and I don't think de-gazetting is likely to happen. A commercial operation would be much more difficult to monitor.' Chris was not particularly impressed by the South African 'model' either. 'It's all so *bijou*,' he observed, finding a word for an aspect that had been secretly worrying me. 'I think it would be a pity if the rest of Africa goes the way of South Africa.'

Ironically, we spent our first night in the bush at Roberts Camp under Mount Kenya's shoulder, one of the best 'wilderness experience' camps I have ever seen – yes, the idea is catching on in Kenya as well. And then, completely out of the blue, I found myself invited to lunch with Tony Dyer, who is over eighty but still lives a very active life on his ranch next door to Lewa. Indeed, he had just passed his medical for another 800 hours of private flying! Tony was able to fill in all the pieces I was missing from the EBUR jigsaw, so this trip north was becoming quite auspicious.

Lewa does not look or feel like a game park, probably because it isn't one. You drive in past a sturdy electric gate trailing long wires that elephants don't like and will not usually cross. Then you wend your way through the foothills of Mount Kenya through long grass downs, acacia woodlands, gorges and rivers. There are small groups of elephants grazing peacefully on the downs, rhinos lying quietly out in the open, herds of the quite rare Grevy's zebra (20 per cent of all the Grevys left are at Lewa), big groups of elands, giraffe in abundance, northern oryx with their straight 'unicorn' horns, and all the big and little cats and canids – silver-backed jackals, cheetah and leopard. Lions have been reintroduced but their presence is quite controversial because they do snack on Grevys.

I first came here about twenty years ago (for *Nature Watch*) to see a remarkable woman called Anna Mertz who had persuaded the Craig family to let her spend an enormous amount of her own money trying to save Kenya's black rhino whose situation in those dark days was dire. Looking back there seems little doubt that Anna's little sanctuary, which began to have positive results almost instantly, changed the Craigs from ranchers to a new breed of commercial conservationists.

There are a lot of Kenyans who were quite suspicious of the Craigs (and quite jealous of the fact that British royals now visit regularly) because in the beginning I think they thought that there were rather more commercial than conservation interests on display at Lewa. But that is not the case any more no matter which way you look at modern Lewa, although commercial considerations still remain high on the priority list.

The Craigs had ranched these 17,000 hectares since 1922. Anna Mertz set up her Ngare Sergio Rhino Sanctuary in 1983 and ten years later the sanctuary was extended to cover the entire ranch. In 1995 the Craigs handed over the management to a non-profit-making organisation, the Lewa Wildlife Conservancy. Since then conservancy has gone from strength to strength. In 1997 Lewa UK and Lewa USA were founded and they are veritable money pumps (Lewa Austria, Asia, Switzerland and Canada are also coming on line). The conservancy places great emphasis on modern management and has used the Internet to its advantage. Even those who once regarded the Craigs as 'Kenya cowboys' concede that they are adept at policing the conservancy via helicopters and light aircraft and at maintaining good relations with the government by subsidising a well-trained squad of Kenya Wildlife Service rangers on the property.

Lewa remains essentially a large eco-tourism facility – a game ranch along South African lines – and this income is the key to its survival. But built on this well-managed and viable business there is now a much larger eco-conservation programme which is rapidly becoming a business in itself. The Lewa Conservancy management team also looks after the nearby Ol Pejeta rhino sanctuary of some 90,000 acres, the largest black rhino sanctuary on earth; is offering its expertise to other large estates in the area; is contributing to the 2.2 million km of land in North Kenya now under conservation programmes; and spends $40,000 on school buildings and $184,000 on community projects like water and healthcare. The annual budget for all this is $2.2 million!

Ian Craig, who was as condemning of exclusive government game management as Richard Leakey, told me he thought government had simply 'lost the plot' by trying to take on too much of what had become a multi-faceted, multi-skilled business. Private, conservation-funded organisations able to offer their management skills to other stakeholders were unquestionably the way forward.

If this is not the *business* model for modern conservation then I am not sure what is, and certainly the many elephants we saw were living happy, contented and well-protected lives. They had a future. Significantly, the report I mentioned earlier (whose authors had no relationship with Lewa) specifically drew attention to the fact that wildlife had actually increased in the dryland country around Ol Pejeta and elephants had also started using it as a migration route.

As I left Lewa I realised of course that these were not the big herds I remember from my youthful journey through the Serengeti all those years ago, but it also occurred to me that those herds had gone for ever now and were not coming back. It was time I started getting used to the idea that my Africa and this Africa are two different places. This Africa, moreover, has not quite 'lost the plot' and on these lovely acres there is hope for the elephant yet.

Select Bibliography

Adamson, George, *Bwana Game*, London, 1968

Adamson, Joy, *Born Free*, London, 1960

Alpers, Edward A., *Ivory and Slaves in East Central Africa*, Cambridge, Mass., 1958

Ardrey, R., *African Genesis*, London, 1961

Arrian, *Alexander's Expedition*, London, 1779

Baker, S.W., *The Albert Nyanza, Great Basin on the Nile*, London, 1890

Baldwin, William C., *African Hunting and Adventure*, London, 1864

Barbier, E.B., Burgess, J.C., Swanson, T.M. and Pearce, D.W., *Elephants, Economics and Ivory*, London, 1990

Beachey, R.W., 'The East African Elephant Trade in the Nineteenth Century', *African History* 8, 1967

Beard, Peter, *The End of the Game*, London, 1998

Becker, Peter, *Path of Blood*, London, 1979

Bell, W.D.M., *The Wanderings of an Elephant Hunter*, London, 1923

——, *Karamojo Safari*, London, 1949; repr. London, 1984

——, *Bell of Africa*, London, 1960

Blunt, D.E., *Elephant*, London, 1933

Bosman, P. and Hall-Martin, A., *Elephants of Africa*, Cape Town, 1986

Brown, R., *When the Woods Became the Trees*, London, 1965

——, *Nature Watchers*, London, 1982

——, *Bye Bye Shangri-La*, London, 1989

——, *Bloody Ivory*, London, 1990

——, *Nature Watch*, London, 1994

Bryden, H.A., 'The Decline and Fall of the South African Elephant', *Fortnightly Review* 79, London

Bull, Bartle, *Safari: A Chronicle of Adventure*, London, 1988

Burton, Richard F., *The Lake Regions of Central Africa*, London, 1860

Buxton, Edward North, *Short Stalks*, London, 1898

Cambridge History of Southern Africa, Cambridge, 1976

Cattrick, Allan, *Spoor of Blood*, Cape Town, 1959

Churchill, Randolph, *Men, Mines and Animals in Africa*, London, 1892

Conrad, J., *Heart of Darkness*, London, 1902

Cranford, Lord, *A Colony in the Making*, London, 1912

Cumming, R. Gordon, *A Hunter's Life in South Africa*, 2 vols, London, 1850

——, *Five Years in a Hunter's Life in the Far Interior of South Africa*, London, 1850

——, *The Lion Hunter of South Africa*, London, 1904

De Beer, J., *Alps and Elephants: Hannibal's March*, London, 1955

Dineson, Isak, *Out of Africa*, London, 1937

DiSilvestro, R.L., *The African Elephant*, New York, 1991

Douglas-Hamilton, I. and O., *Among the Elephants*, London, 1975

——, 'The African Elephant Action Plan', 1979

Dugard, Martin, *Into Africa*, London, 2003

Eastman, George, *Chronicles of an African Trip*, New York, 1927

Edward, Prince of Wales, *Sport and Travel in East Africa*, compiled from his diaries by Patrick C. Chalmers, London, 1934

Eltringham, S.K., *Elephants*, Poole, 1982

——, *The Illustrated Encyclopaedia of Elephants*, London, 1991

Farrant, Leda, *Tippu Tip and The East African Elephant Trade*, London, 1975

Finaughty, William, *The Recollections of an Elephant Hunter*, Bulawayo, 1890

Fox, James, *White Mischief*, London, 1982

Gray, Richard, *A History of the Southern Sudan 1839–1889*, London, 1961

Haggard, H. Rider, *King Solomon's Mines*, London, 1885

Hall, Richard, *Lovers on the Nile*, London and New York, 1980

——, *Empires of the Monsoon: A History of the Indian Ocean and its Invaders*, London and New York, 1996

Hanks, John, *A Struggle for Survival: The Elephant Problem*, Cape Town, 1979

Harms, Robert W., *River of Wealth, River of Sorrow: The Central Zaire Basin in the era of the Slave and Ivory Trade 1500–1891*, New Haven, CT, 1981

Harris, Sir William Cornwallis, *The Wild Sports of Southern Africa*, London, 1852

Holder, Charles F., *The Ivory King: A Popular History of the Elephant and Its Allies*, London, 1886

Hunter, J.A., *Hunter*, New York, 1952

Huxley, Elspeth, *White Man's Country*, London, 1956

Ingham, Kenneth, *A History of East Africa*, London, 1965

ITRG reporting for CITES 7th Conference 1989, *The Ivory Trade and the Future of the African Elephant*, Oxford, 1989

Jeal, Tim, *Livingstone*, London, 1973

Johnson, Osa, *I Married Adventure*, Philadelphia, 1940

Johnston, Sir Harry H., *British Central Africa*, London, 1897

Knight, Charles, *The Elephant Principally Viewed in Relation to Man*, London, 1884

Kunkel, Reinhard, *Elephants*, New York, 1982

Laws, R.M., Parker, I.S.C. and Johnstone, R.C.M., *Elephants and their Habitat: The Ecology of Elephants in North Bunyoro, Uganda*, Oxford, 1975

Leakey, Richard, *Origins*, London, 1977

——, *The Making of Mankind*, London, 1981

——, *Human Origin*, London, 1996

——, with Morell, V., *Wildlife Wars: My Battle to Save Kenya's Elephants*, London, 2001

Livingstone, David, *Missionary Travels and Researches in South Africa*, London, 1857

——, *Narrative of an Expedition to the Zambesi and its Tributaries*, London, 1865

——, *Last Journals*, London, 1874

Livy, Titus, *The War with Hannibal*, London, 1920

Lunderberg, A. and Seymour, F., *The Great Roosevelt Africa Hunt*, New York, 1910

Meredith, Martin, *Elephant Destiny: Biography of an Endangered Species in Africa*, New York, 2001

Moore, E.S., *Ivory, Scourge of Africa*, New York, 1994

Moorhead, Alan, *The White Nile*, London, 1960

——, *The Blue Nile*, London, 1962

Moss, Cynthia, *Portraits in the Wild: Animal Behaviour in East Africa*, London, 1989

——, *Elephant Memories*, Chicago, 2000

Neumann, Arthur H., *Elephant Hunting in East Central Africa*, London, 1868

Offermann, P.P.M., 'The Elephant in the Belgian Congo', in R. Ward (ed.), *The Elephant in East Central Africa: a monograph*, London, 1953

Orenstein, Ronald, *Saving the Gentle Giants*, London, 1991

Osborn, Henry F., *Proboscidea: A Monograph on the Discovery, Evolution, Migration and Extinction of the Mastodonts and Elephants of the World*, New York, 1936 and 1942

Oswell, W.E., *William Cotton Oswell, Hunter and Explorer*, London, 1900

Parker, I.S.C., EBUR, Report for Jack Block (WWF) and Tony Dyer (East Africa Professional Hunters' Association), Nairobi, 1974

——, *The Ivory Trade. Report for US Fish and Wildlife Service*, Nairobi, 1979

——, with Amin, M., *Ivory Crisis*, London, 1979

——, *What I Tell You Three Times is True*, Kinloss, 2005

Payne, Katy, *Silent Thunder: The Hidden Voice of Elephants*, London, 1998

Perry, John, 'The Growth and Reproduction of Elephants in Uganda', *The Uganda Journal* 1952

Pliny (the Elder), *Natural History*, 2 vols, London, 1855

Poole, Joyce, *Coming of Age with Elephants*, London, 1996

Roosevelt, Theodore, *African Game Trails*, New York, 1910

Ross, Doran H. (ed.), *Elephant: The Animal and Its Ivory in African Culture*, Los Angeles, 1992

St Aubyn, Fiona, *Ivory: A History and Collectors Guide*, London, 1987

Scullard, H.H., *The Elephant in the Greek and Roman World*, London, 1974

Selous, Frederick Courteney, *A Hunter's Wanderings in Africa*, London, 1881

——, *Travel and Adventure in South-East Africa*, London, 1893

Schillings, C.G., *In Wildest Africa*, New York, 1907

Schreiner, Olive (under the pseudonym Ralph Irons), *Life on an African Farm*, 1882 (second edition under her own name, 1891)

——, *Trooper Peter Halket of Mashonaland*, 1897

Spinage, C., *Elephants*, London, 1994

Stanley, Henry M., *How I found Livingstone: Travels, Adventures and Discoveries in Central Africa*, London, 1872

——, *Through the Dark Continent*, London, 1878

——, *In Darkest Africa: or, The Quest, Rescue and Retreat of Emin, Governor Equatoria*, London, 1890

Stevenson-Hamilton, James, *Wild Life in South Africa*, London, 1947

Sutherland, James, *The Adventures of an Elephant Hunter*, London, 1912

Sykes, Silvia K., *The Natural History of the Indian Elephant*, London, 1971

Thesiger, Wilfred, *Arabian Sands*, London, 1959

——, *The Marsh Arabs*, London, 1964

Thorbahn, Peter F., 'The Pre-Colonial Ivory Trade of East Africa', thesis, University of Manchester, 1979

Thornton, A. and Currey, D., *To Save an Elephant: The Undercover Investigation into the Illegal Ivory Trade*, London, 1991

Tippu Tib, *Maisa ya Hamed bin Mohammed et Murjebi Yaani Tippu Tib*, Nairobi, 1966

Toynbee, J.M.C., *Animals in Roman Life and Art*, London, 1973
Trzebinski, Errol, *The Kenya Pioneers*, London, 1985
——, *Silence will Speak*, London, 1997
Turner, Myles, *My Serengeti Years: The Memoirs of an African Game Warden*, London, 1987
von Blixen-Finecke, Bror, *African Hunter*, New York, 1986
Western, David, *In the Dust of Kilimanjaro*, Washington, 1997
Williams, Heathcote, *Sacred Elephant*, London, 1989
Wilson, D. and Ayerst, P., *White Gold: The Story of African Ivory*, London, 1976

Index